Praise for *The Holy and the Broken*

'As challenging and as contemporary as it is compassionate. In a world broken by war and polarisation, Ittay offers peaceful possibilities and nuanced perspectives' – Rabbi Ralph Genende OAM, author of *Living in an Upside-down World*

'*The Holy and the Broken* breaks new ground. Yet what makes it truly singular is its consistent humanity, and its centring of ordinary Israelis and Palestinians' – John Lyndon, executive director, Alliance for Middle East Peace

'A powerful testament to the possibilities of reconciliation and mutual empathy during conflict, what sets this book apart is its commitment to showcasing the experiences of the diverse individuals involved – especially the integral, yet frequently overlooked, stories of women. By highlighting the gender dynamics at play, Flescher enriches our understanding of the conflict and underscores the importance of supporting a world where more voices are heard and valued' – Sheila Katz, CEO, National Council of Jewish Women

'This account of the writer's devotion to peacebuilding in our war-torn region is a shining testament to what can and should be done by those who can imagine a future peace. It lights a candle in an age of darkness!' – Sari Nusseibeh, author of *Once Upon a Country: A Palestinian Life*

'When you finish it, you will not only know more about what's happening between the Jordan River and the Mediterranean Sea, but you will also know more about yourself' – Maoz Inon, Israeli peacemaker and social entrepreneur

'When I picked this book up, I erroneously believed I already "understood" much about the ongoing, collective trauma of Palestinians and Israelis. But this thoughtful and deeply compassionate book shattered that illusion. By the time I put the book down, I was not the same person' – Miriam Anzovin, creator of Daf Reactions and Jewish Lore Reactions

'Courageous and considered. Ittay nurtures the tender, fragile shoots of peace. The world could do with more people like him' – Paul Kelly, Australian singer-songwriter and guitarist

'A book of rare insight and compassion, *The Holy and the Broken* offers the one thing we thought we'd lost after October 7: a glimmer of hope for meaningful lasting peace between Israelis and Palestinians' – Bram Presser, author of *The Book of Dirt*

'This is a thoughtful and thought-provoking book, heartfelt and honest. You do not need to agree with everything Flescher has to say to find the book moving and challenging' – Michael Gawenda, former editor in chief, *The Age*

Ittay Flescher at Jerusalem's First Train Station, which opened in 1892.

Ittay Flescher is the education director at Kids4Peace Jerusalem, an interfaith youth movement for Israelis and Palestinians, and the Jerusalem correspondent for Australian news site *The Jewish Independent*. As an insightful analyst of Israeli politics, he has been published in *Haaretz*, *Crikey*, ABC Religion and Ethics, *Jerusalem Post*, *Fathom* and many other publications and newspapers.

Before moving to Jerusalem in 2018, Ittay was a high-school educator in Melbourne for 15 years, teaching Australian history, Jewish studies, and religion and society. Married with two children, he is inspired by all the people around him who challenge him to be a better human.

www.ittay.au

ITTAY FLESCHER

The holy and the broken

A cry for Israeli–Palestinian peace
from a land that must be shared

HarperCollinsPublishers

HarperCollins*Publishers*
Australia • Brazil • Canada • France • Germany • Holland • India
Italy • Japan • Mexico • New Zealand • Poland • Spain • Sweden
Switzerland • United Kingdom • United States of America

HarperCollins acknowledges the Traditional Custodians
of the lands upon which we live and work, and pays respect
to Elders past and present.

First published on Gadigal Country in Australia in 2025
by HarperCollins*Publishers* Australia Pty Limited
ABN 36 009 913 517
harpercollins.com.au

A catalogue record for this book is available from the National Library of Australia

ISBN 978 1 4607 6707 8 (paperback)
ISBN 978 1 4607 1824 7 (ebook)
ISBN 978 1 4607 3090 4 (audiobook)

Part of Chapter 7 was originally published in *Haaretz*: Ittay Flescher, 'What can Israelis and
Palestinians learn from Northern Ireland's 25 years of peace?', *Haaretz*, April 10, 2023.
Part of Chapter 13 was originally published in *The Jewish Independent*: Ittay Flescher,
'The problem with "Never Again"', *The Jewish Independent*, May 29, 2024.

Cover design by Tamarra Bonnici, HarperCollins Design Studio
Cover image by John Theodor / shutterstock.com
Photo of the author on page iii by Nava Flescher
Typeset in Adobe Garamond Pro by Kirby Jones

Printed and bound in the United States

This book is dedicated to Mark Raphael Baker
1959–2023

A brilliant scholar, author, academic, grandfather, father
and husband. Mark's writings, ideas and actions inspired
multitudes of Melbourne Jews to practise our faith,
tradition and culture in a manner that honours both
our ancient heritage and the ideal that all humans are
created equally.

His life inspired me to be who I am.
His death inspired me to write this book.
May his memory be a blessing.

CONTENTS

Preface   1

Chapter 1   Fifty years and one day: How October 7   5
            changed everything

Chapter 2   Holocaust, Hashem and Israel: Reflections   35
            on my school education

Chapter 3   Where it all began: Two nations,   62
            one homeland

Chapter 4   The first Palestinian–Zionist dialogue   77

Chapter 5   Indigenous Australians, Jews and Palestinians   85

Chapter 6   Keeping hope alive: Inside Jerusalem's youth   100
            movement for peace

Chapter 7   'Peace is possible': Lessons from Belfast   122

Chapter 8   Daring to dialogue: How supporters of   132
            Palestine and Israel can talk to one another

Chapter 9   Gaza: The quest for reckoning   147

Chapter 10 Peace journalism: All the news we never print   166

Chapter 11 To the boys in the room: Hearing the missing   184
            voices of women

Chapter 12 If it be your will: Faith and peacebuilding   192

Chapter 13 Inside the classroom: Dominant narratives   202
            and untold stories

Chapter 14 So, what's your solution for Israel/Palestine?   210

Chapter 15   Challenging dehumanisation and   214
             suspending disbelief
Chapter 16   Letters to Israeli and Palestinian children   224
Chapter 17   When there is peace   235

Coda   Those who made me   251
Timelines   271
             Important events in Palestine and Israel   272
             Israel–Gaza wars   282
             Agreements, negotiations and peace proposals 289
Acknowledgments   294
Notes   303

PREFACE

Walk past any busker with a guitar on any day of the week in Jerusalem, and I guarantee you that if you wait long enough, you will eventually hear them play Leonard Cohen's 'Hallelujah'. If Jerusalem were a soundtrack instead of a city, I'm almost sure this would be her anthem.

With an opening verse that sets a scene on King David's ancient balcony in Jerusalem, it's well known across the city to Jews and Arabs in its English, Hebrew and Arabic versions. Perhaps this is because the song expresses the very human emotions we all have around love, loss, betrayal, anger and reconciliation in ways that few other lyrics about this city have managed to do.

For that reason, when choosing a title for this book about the humans of Palestine and Israel, and my relationship with them as a Jewish-Australian journalist and peace educator, I knew it had to reference this song.

This book is ultimately about both the holy and the broken. The holy hallelujahs are requests from the heart that somehow find answers to the questions their petitioners seek. The broken hallelujahs are the multitudes of prayers, hopes and dreams that go unanswered yet live on more powerfully than one could ever imagine through our words, deeds and actions.

The Holy and the Broken was primarily written in 2024 during the war between Israel and Hamas in Gaza. I hope it achieves the same goal I set for all the classes I have taught from Melbourne to Jerusalem and beyond, which is to comfort the troubled and trouble the comfortable.

How to read this book

The Holy and the Broken is organised into three parts.

The first section (Chapters 1 to 5) covers my experience of October 7 and the development of my Jewish identity, as well as the history of Israel and Palestine. It delves into how we remember the past and considers the possible outcomes had different choices been made over the past 120 years.

The second section (Chapters 6 to 9) focuses on the importance of moral reckoning and the challenges of peacebuilding during the Israel–Gaza War, with an emphasis on the interfaith youth organisation Kids4Peace Jerusalem.

The final section (Chapters 10 to 17) explores the role of journalists, female peacebuilders, people of faith, schools and grassroots movements in envisioning and creating a movement for social change, one that can potentially disrupt the cycle of violence.

The book concludes with a coda about my parents and Mark Baker, reflecting on what I learned from them in order to make me who I am today.

Finally, there are three timelines that may be a useful resource for those new to this subject matter. They provide overviews of the history of Israel and Palestine, Israel–Gaza wars, and agreements, negotiations and peace proposals.

Feel free to read the book in order or start wherever your interest is strongest – it's your own adventure to choose.

Ittay Flescher, Jerusalem, October 2024

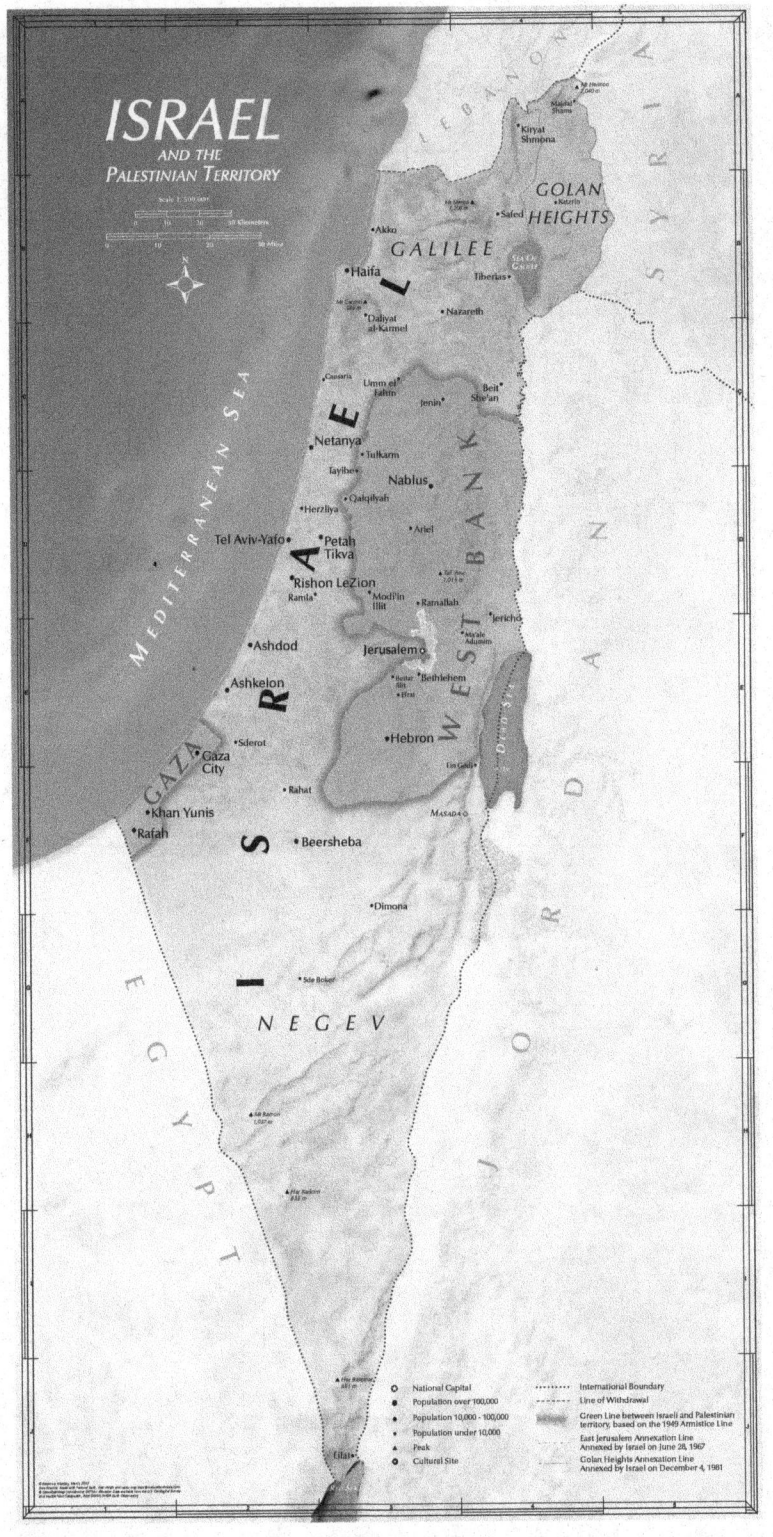

Source: J Street; jstreet.org/the-green-line

CHAPTER 1

Fifty years and one day: How October 7 changed everything

On the afternoon of October 6, Yom Kippur, 1973, my father broke his fast at 2 pm as sirens sounded above the Ramat Gan synagogue north of Tel Aviv where he had come to pray on the holiest day in the Jewish calendar. Within hours he had replaced his white shirt and tallit for army greens and was off to war, the third in his life at only 23 years of age. By the time of the festival of Sukkot a week later, he was in a tank fighting the Egyptians in the Sinai Peninsula.

Fifty years and one day later on October 7, 2023, I began the morning by checking my phone as always at around 6 am. Nothing special was happening. It was exceptionally quiet, with few cars on the road and no sound of early morning rubbish trucks to disturb the peace because it was both a Saturday, Shabbat, and the Jewish festival of Simchat Torah.

During the festival of Simchat Torah, Jews celebrate the completion of the annual cycle of Torah readings in synagogue, only to begin retelling the story anew the moment it ends. The Torah is the Hebrew Bible, consisting of the Five Books of Moses. The festival involves much celebration and dancing with the sacred scroll, a ritual Jews have been practising for centuries.

At around 6:30 am, I saw the first news alerts of rockets in the south, which sadly happens frequently. I wasn't concerned, knowing the Iron Dome was there to protect civilian lives in Israel.

At 8:14 am, I saw the first of what would be seven Jerusalem rocket-attack notifications on the Home Front Command app on my phone. I quickly woke my wife and two children while sirens sounded above our Emek Refaim apartment in the predominantly English-speaking community of south Jerusalem. We made our way down to the basement shelter shared by the residents of our building, but forgot to bring the keys, so we waited in the stairwell for the required ten minutes, laughing at what we presumed was a false alarm. The ten-minute wait after a siren is a precaution against falling shrapnel or debris, and the stairwell is considered an adequate 'plan b' if you cannot access your shelter.

By the third siren that morning, we had the shelter unlocked, tidied and equipped with enough folding chairs for us and all the neighbours. We continued to run up and down the stairwell over the next four hours, no longer laughing now that we realised the severity of what was unfolding in the south.

During the fifth siren, at 9:57 am, a family from upstairs joined us in the shelter. They had been attending Simchat Torah services in their synagogue, and the rabbi had told everyone to head home. Their Orthodox religious observance forbade them from using their phones to check the news, so they asked me to update them. It felt surreal to me. They had spent their morning dancing with the Torah, hearing sirens and running to the synagogue's shelter where they recited psalms in prayer together, then returning upstairs after the ten-minute wait time to continue their celebrations, before repeating the shelter-and-psalms process several more times. All without knowing what was happening down south.

My 11-year-old English-speaking, Aussie-accented son, who usually has no interest in anything other than video games, suddenly had lots of hard questions. He wanted to know who was firing rockets at us and why. He wanted a history lesson on how we got here.

My job as a journalist is to explain Israeli current affairs to audiences worldwide, so naturally my wife said, 'You answer his questions.' I found, however, that as soon as I started talking, I was lost for words.

Where to begin? Should I tell him about the horrific videos I was seeing on Instagram? About the shootings at the outdoor music festival on the Gaza border? About the children taken captive from their living rooms on kibbutzim and about Hamas gunmen roaming the streets of Sderot? Definitely not, I thought. I didn't want to freak him out.

Should I answer his questions about Hamas? About what this organisation seeks to achieve? About why they want to harm us? These I did answer.

But the questions didn't stop coming. How is Gaza different from Jerusalem? How many people live there? What is a siege? Why has it been there for so long? Why are they so angry with us? What's going to happen tomorrow? Will I go to school?

Some questions I could answer; others I could not.

WhatsApp messages rolled in every few minutes. Friends and professional colleagues in Australia, the United States and other parts of Israel were all asking the same question: 'Are you OK?'

I said we were fine, but my mind was occupied with the Yom Kippur War, 50 years earlier in 1973. Maybe it was all those documentaries about that catastrophic October war that had flooded our TV screens over the preceding month. I kept thinking about how history never changes, it only repeats.

In the first few days, I couldn't help but continue to compare this war to the Yom Kippur War. Again, Israel was attacked by surprise. Again, the horror of the violence against civilians on the border was too brutal to describe. Again, the shock. Again, the false perception of invincibility exploding in our faces. Again, the tears of the bereaved parents, the pain of families who didn't know the fate of their loved ones taken hostage, the fear for the wellbeing of every son and daughter, every spouse or sibling called up for reserve duty.

Some felt that the date of the Hamas attack had nothing to do with the anniversary of the Yom Kippur War. The timing might have been in response to Hamas's weakened position within internal Palestinian politics. It might have been opportunistic because of heightened civil discord between Jewish Israelis over the Netanyahu government's proposed judicial overhaul, which brought hundreds of thousands of Israelis to the streets in protest, many stating they would refuse to serve in the IDF reserves. Others suggested the timing might have been chosen in response to increased Jewish prayer on the Temple Mount/Al-Aqsa, or the impending Israel–Saudi normalisation agreement that would have sidelined the Palestinian issue from

Israeli–Arab peace negotiations. In the end, though, none of the reasons mattered to the victims.

The ultimate result of Hamas's barbarity was that over a thousand Israelis who had woken up that Saturday morning to dance with the Torah in a public square or at a music festival now lay lifeless under white prayer shawls awaiting burial in the earth of the Promised Land.

Simchat Torah marks the end of the week-long festival of Sukkot, meaning 'booths'. Jews build temporary outdoor huts to remember the flimsy shelters our forefathers used during their 40-year sojourn in the desert after leaving Egypt, placing their trust in God to provide for them. The period of the Jewish calendar that follows is often referred to in Israel as 'after the chaggim' – meaning 'after the festivals'. It is usually when everyday life resumes after three weeks of festival days, which include both religious events and public holidays. Everyone returns to school, work and daily routines. But in 2023 that was not the case. That year during the 'after the chaggim' period, no aspect of real life resumed. Across the country, and especially for those living in the north and south, people fled to safer places or enlisted for reserve duty, and stranded sukkah huts became a symbol that we never reached 'after the chaggim'. As rocket sirens continued to blare in the following days and weeks, our homes and our entire sense of security felt like a sukkah – fragile, temporary and subject to forces beyond our control.

The greatest number of Jewish deaths in a single day since the Holocaust

The first news on casualties I read that Saturday was in the *Times of Israel*, which reported 22 dead from the Hamas infiltration.

I remember being horrified by that number, not yet knowing it would grow so significantly.

A Facebook friend who lives in Sderot posted, 'Bodies in the streets of Sderot, vans of Hamas driving around everywhere. There has been no IDF on the streets for more than two hours. Failure on the level of Yom Kippur. Pray for us.'

I was shocked. Where was the IDF? How did Hamas penetrate one of the most secured walls on earth – the one that separates Gaza and southern Israel? What happened to the hundreds of cameras, motion sensors and soldiers guarding it 24/7? I was sad and angry. I couldn't look away from the news channel.

Over the coming days, more details emerged, each more horrific and gruesome in nature. Hila Fakliro, a 26-year-old fitness instructor who was at the Tribe of Nova festival, explained in an interview that at daybreak on October 7, she looked up to the sky, away from the vodka and Red Bull cocktails she was mixing. 'Oh, my God,' she said. 'Look! There are fireworks!' Fakliro was drawn to trance music festivals as a means 'to disconnect [her] mind from all the tension in Israel'.

The festival, held on the final day of the Jewish holiday of Sukkot amid groves of eucalyptus trees only two kilometres from Gaza, seemed particularly well organised, so the fireworks struck her as no more than an extravagant flourish. Her fellow bartender, whom she had met just hours before, turned to her and said: 'I don't think those are fireworks.'[1]

They were not. They were, in fact, the white flashes of Hamas rockets fired from Gaza, the fire at dawn signalling an attack that would turn fields full of dancing young people into a slaughterhouse. Within hours, 364 ravers were gunned down and dozens more were taken as hostages to Gaza.

Kfar Azza, one of the kibbutzim most devastated by the attack, sits on the border with Gaza and carries the Hebrew name of the strip. Until October 7, the kibbutz was home to 800 people. One survivor from Kfar Azza shared with reporters that: 'Hamas came into every home, into every room, every place. They would burn each house with people inside so they would die. They shot children, babies, old people, anyone. No one was safe from it. The first victim was a 90-year-old woman who was sitting on her porch. She saw them coming and she got shot.'[2]

Another resident described hours spent hiding from the gunmen: 'We were in this panic room for I think over thirty hours. Then they broke windows and started shooting everywhere. At some point they shot at the door of the panic room.'[3]

In Jerusalem, the updates continued to roll in. A new WhatsApp message every few seconds revealed more details. A tweet of condemnation, a horrific video on Instagram, videos from the rave on TikTok and lengthy cries of pain on Facebook.

Enough.

I couldn't read it anymore. But like passing a horrific car crash with many dead and bloodied bodies lying on the road, I couldn't look away – even though I knew it would be better for my mental health not to see it all. The moment I turned off my phone, I went to the TV. I turned on Channel N12's rolling coverage live from the Gaza border and saw more interviews with survivors and military experts, and endless panel discussions that shed far more heat than light.

Enough.

Then I went to my laptop and read long op-eds in multiple newspapers and Substacks from Jewish authors in Jerusalem and Melbourne, including Daniel Gordis, Julie Szego and Michael Gawenda, each sharing their own anger and heartbreak from the massacre.

Enough.

I went back to my phone. And the calls came in from around the world. And so this became my life for the first two weeks of the war. Moving in and out of bomb shelters, switching from screen to screen, from Zoom call to media interview. All the while surrounded by grief, pain and shock like never before.

The comfort of last week's news

Beyond the love of my wonderful and resilient family, one of the few comforts that first week after October 7 was reading the news of the week prior. Despite being a compulsive news follower, the only physical paper I read is the weekly Shabbat edition of *Haaretz*. Reading a newspaper published on October 6 was a surreal experience. The analysis of almost every article seemed wrong, the predictions of every column ridiculous. All the stories about the proposed reform to the Supreme Court, the heated debates between the secular and ultra-Orthodox Haredim over gender segregation in public places, and the corruption scandals of various government ministers were all irrelevant. I could have been reading a paper from a hundred years ago. Nothing mattered anymore. Not a single story that received several column inches the day before was a topic of public conversation by the next day, and wouldn't be for months to come.

A nation united

Within days of the massacre, the country I lived in was no longer the same place it had been.

A week before October 7, Israel had been riven with internal strife between the religious and secular, with levels of animosity so intense that some felt we were on the verge of an ideological civil war.

A week before October 7, on the holy day of Yom Kippur, Dizengoff Square in Tel Aviv had been the scene of clashes over a mechitzah, which is a partition or a divider used in Orthodox Jewish prayer spaces to separate genders. Liberal Israelis strongly oppose any form of gender segregation in public spaces, so the mechitzah in a public square caused a furore.

A week after October 7, the resilience of Israelis shone through as the same square was filled with hundreds of young Tel Aviv residents sorting through thousands of donated boxes of clothing, toiletries and food for soldiers and residents of the south.

A week after October 7, the war had a slogan: 'B'yachad nenatzeach – Together we will win'. It became ubiquitous, appearing in the corner of every TV news broadcast, on giant billboards, and even on shopping bags and supermarket receipts.

A week after October 7, in Dizengoff Centre and Ichilov Hospital in Tel Aviv, the Pais Arena in Jerusalem and many other places across the country, thousands of people lined up for hours to donate blood. Bnei Akiva youth group volunteers were lining up to dig graves.

Thousands of WhatsApp groups offered free babysitting for parents whose partners had been called up to the army reserves, free transport for the elderly to medical appointments, or just company for anyone who needed mental health support.

My friend Rabbi Joe Wolfson lives in Tel Aviv and was involved in organising many volunteer efforts. He summarised the dramatic shift powerfully in a single sentence on Facebook: 'I have lived 100 years in 5 days. If there is one thing I know it's this. If we are like this, we are truly undefeatable.'

After October 7, despite remaining in my home, I felt that I too lived in a different country. The solidarity between so many different parts of society was remarkable. Yet, while this unity is a blessing that so many Israelis dream of, it can also be a curse.

Another friend, Dr Elana Sztokman, observed in her Substack that week:

> Calls for unity almost always attach to language suggesting
> that certain people should stop talking. Now is a perfect
> example. Bibi's talk of unity – which is perfectly mimicked
> by so many people in Israel right now – is precisely an
> instruction to protesters to cease and desist. This man is
> leading Israel off a cliff. And now all these calls for unity
> are basically shutting down opposition.[4]

Elana was right. In the days following October 7, right and left ceased to exist. A unity government was formed that included 76 of the 120 members of the Knesset, ranging from complete secularists to the ultra-Orthodox, unified in working together for Israel's security, all differences set aside. After 39 continuous weeks, Saturday-night anti-government protests stopped. The judicial overhaul was over. A new Israel was coming into existence.

The future of peacebuilding

Since moving to Jerusalem from Melbourne in 2018, I've been the education director at the interfaith youth movement Kids4Peace (K4P) Jerusalem, facilitating dialogue and trust-building activities between Israeli and Palestinian teens.

On October 9, 2023, the father of a Jewish child at Kids4Peace sent me a message. 'Ittay, this message is going to be hard to hear,' he wrote. 'My daughter, who has gained so much from your program over the years, has shared with me that some of her Arab friends from Kids4Peace have posted celebratory messages. She cannot see herself returning to K4P. It is like a punch in the gut to find out that K4P is an illusion.'

I called him immediately. A long conversation with him and then his 16-year-old daughter followed. Her brother had been called up to the reserves. She was justified in her rage. I didn't have much to say, but I could listen. I encouraged her to contact her Palestinian friends and share how these posts made her feel. Perhaps hearing from someone they knew and cared about would move them. Isn't that ultimately Kids4Peace's whole theory of change? Humanise the other to build bridges of tolerance and understanding?

But even I was starting to question the truth of this. Though I couldn't vocalise it then, I too was beginning to wonder whether Kids4Peace was an illusion after witnessing the horrors of October 7.

The following day, while messaging an acquaintance from a different Israeli–Palestinian peacebuilding organisation, I noticed he had changed his WhatsApp profile picture to an image of a paraglider.

Paragliders were one means by which Hamas terrorists had infiltrated Israel, over the Gaza wall, on their mission to kill and burn hundreds of Jewish families in their homes.

I was shocked. Absolutely floored. I looked at the profile picture for ten minutes. Stunned. So many thoughts raced through my head. Do I ignore this? Can such a person be reasoned with? But they know me and care for me. And I for them too.

I called him, knowing full well that the conversation could end our friendship. But what kind of role model would I be if I couldn't follow the advice that I had just given to my young Kids4Peace participant?

Heart racing, I started the conversation. 'I want to ask a personal question. Is that OK?'

He said, 'Yes.'

'I can see you changed your profile picture to a paraglider. Knowing what the men in those paragliders did to my people two days ago, I found that very hurtful. Why did you do this?'

'While I'm against the killing of women and children, Israel has kept my people under siege for so long,' he responded. 'I have family in Gaza. You can't keep people in prison for decades and not think a day will come when they try to break out. For me, this picture represents freedom. I want my people to be free.'

I told him that I am all for Palestinian freedom. It is something I advocate for wherever possible both as a journalist and peace educator. But not like this. He said it was unfair that the world always stands with Israel when it is attacked, as happened after October 7, but never stands with Palestine when Gaza is attacked.

It was then that I was reminded of my mission – peacebuilding and the promotion of nonviolent solutions to bring justice and equality for all. I asked, 'Why do you still work in a peacebuilding organisation?'

He responded, 'I do this because it's a job, but really it's all bullshit.'

For a few more minutes, I did my best to express solidarity with him, reiterating my opposition to both Hamas and any IDF operation that would harm innocent civilians, including his loved ones in Gaza. I told him I prayed that both our people could one day find a way to share this land.

At the end of the call, I looked at my phone. The conversation had lasted eight minutes. It had felt like hours. I lay in bed for a long time afterwards, thoughts rushing through my head.

The next day, I noticed that my friend had changed his profile picture.

Faith and tears

I always thought the aphorism 'there are no atheists in foxholes' was a brash claim by those with deep religious faith. And yet, on the first Shabbat after October 7, for reasons I couldn't quite explain to myself because I am not religious, I had a strong urge to be in a synagogue, in prayer with my community. My wife was reluctant for me to go because rocket attacks were still frequent. Even though it's taboo in the Jewish tradition to bring a phone to a synagogue on Shabbat, I took mine with me and kept it on so I could let my wife know I was OK in case of a siren. To keep everyone at ease, the Progressive Jerusalem synagogue Kol Haneshama had moved its service that night from its beautiful stained-glass-windowed prayer space to an underground bomb shelter. The prayers were led by my friends Rabbi Oded Mazor and Rabbi Debi Shua-Haim. As Yedid Nefesh, the first psalm of Kabbalat Shabbat, began, the room was quieter than I had ever heard in a synagogue before. While chanting the words 'ana el na, ref ana la', meaning 'O God, please let us be healed', Oded burst into tears. Behind me, another friend began to cry. Within minutes the grief in the room was overwhelming. It then dawned on me: I wasn't at a Kabbalat Shabbat service; I was at a shiva.

In the Jewish tradition, after a person dies, there is a mourning period of seven days, which we call 'shiva'. During that time we set ourselves apart from the world, refraining from work, entertainment, music and sex. We cover the mirrors in our homes so we can focus on grief and remembrance rather than appearance. We also tear our clothes over our hearts, to make public the pain we feel at those torn from our lives.

In that first week in Israel, after 251 people were kidnapped and 1195 people were killed in a wave of indescribable brutality by Hamas, an entire country, and indeed almost the entire Jewish world, was in shiva.

In the following days, when someone from abroad asked me what it was like in Jerusalem, I would answer in just one word.

Shiva.

Response from the left in the United States and Australia

In the days after October 7, many in the global left – from Bernie Sanders to the entire Australian Labor Party – expressed strong opposition to Hamas's attack and offered heartfelt condolences to Israel's victims while cautioning against a disproportionate response.

Yet after the decision in Australia to light up the Sydney Opera House in blue and white in solidarity with Israeli victims, a small group of men gathered, waving Palestinian flags and chanting 'Where's the Jews?' and 'Fuck the Jews'. This incident concerned and terrified many Jewish Australians, leaving them wondering, 'How can this be happening in a place like Australia, a country we know and love that has been so good to us?'

Jewish artist Anita Lester shared her dismay at the silence of Australian creative communities in the first week after the Hamas attack:

> Imagine if a Coachella, a Falls Festival, a Strawberry Fields, or a Glastonbury had been the subject of a massacre – can you imagine how the global creative community would rally around them? Remember the terrorist attack at the Bataclan – every artist I know rallied in support. And wars and natural disasters provoked concerts and fundraisers. But when it's in Israel … This creative community has remained disturbingly quiet when it comes to supporting the Jewish people. This isn't about politics; it's about being an ally, and I fear this lengthy silence has broken our trust. This is something we will never forget.[5]

On the other side of the ocean, some prominent leftists didn't just remain silent, they justified the Hamas attack. Numerous American scholars and writers cited postcolonial thinkers like Franz Fanon and CLR James to justify violence as an act of 'decolonisation'. Others placed the term 'unprovoked' in ironic quotation marks when referring to the massacre of young people at a music festival and entire families murdered in their homes.[6]

Najma Sharif, an American writer, tweeted, 'What did y'all think decolonization meant? Just vibes?'

In addition to individual voices, a joint statement from 35 Harvard student groups placed the responsibility for October 7 entirely on Israel, saying it was 'the only one to blame'. Columbia University students put out a statement without even acknowledging Hamas crimes against humanity, while the head of the New York University Law Student Bar Association sent a note to students saying she would 'not condemn Palestinian resistance'.[7]

Responding to this disturbing phenomenon, a statement was released on October 16 by several leading anti-Occupation and leftist groups in Israel. It called out their peers on the left who refused to speak out against the rape and murder of innocents:

> This array of responses surprised us. We never imagined that individuals on the left, advocates of equality, freedom, justice, and welfare, would reveal such extreme moral insensitivity and political recklessness.
>
> Let us be clear: Hamas is a theocratic and repressive organisation that vehemently opposes the attempt to promote peace and equality in the Middle East. Its core commitments are fundamentally inconsistent with progressive principles, and thus the inclination of certain leftists to react affirmatively to its actions is utterly absurd. Moreover, there is no justification for shooting civilians in their homes; no rationalization for the murder of children in front of their parents; no reason for the persecution and execution of partygoers. Legitimizing or excusing these actions amounts to a betrayal of the fundamental principles of left-wing politics.

It concluded by noting that there is 'no contradiction between staunchly opposing the Israeli subjugation and occupation of Palestinians and unequivocally condemning brutal acts of violence against innocent civilians. In fact, every consistent leftist must hold both positions simultaneously.'[8]

Memories of historic traumas

For Israelis and Palestinians alike, October 7 evoked our darkest memories of national suffering.

For many Jewish Israelis, the repeated refrain in the media that this was 'the darkest day for the Jewish people since the Holocaust' rang true. The haunting footage of armed men storming homes to murder Jews and of parents cradling their children as they lay in hiding brought back decades-old memories and trauma.

Despite the army being one of the most trusted national institutions with formidable military prowess, it failed the promise of 'Never Again'. Once more, Jews were killed indiscriminately or were abandoned for many hours without protection.

On the other side of the wall, there was also a huge trauma. Within a week of the attack, 1.1 million people were given 24-hours' notice to evacuate their homes in Gaza. Memories of the Nakba in 1948 flooded back for many Palestinians. Within a month, over 10,000 Palestinians had been killed in Gaza by Israeli airstrikes allegedly targeting Hamas leaders and infrastructure. Thousands of those killed were children. Many felt and feared that the catastrophe of 1948 – when over 750,000 Palestinians were displaced from their homes during the war – was repeating itself.

Just as the trauma of the Holocaust lives on through generations of survivors' children and grandchildren in Israel, most Palestinians in Gaza today are descendants of those 1948 Nakba refugees, largely expelled from Al-Majdal, which is today called Ashkelon.

To the people of Gaza, and to Palestinians around the world, Israel's vow that residents would be allowed to return to the north of Gaza once Hamas was eliminated was impossible to trust.

In the following weeks, many Arab Israelis and East Jerusalem Palestinians were attacked on the streets, in their college dorms, or just as they were doing their jobs while speaking Arabic. This affected many people, as 37% of Palestinians who live in East Jerusalem work in West Jerusalem.[9] Many Arabs were fired from their employment for liking social media posts that expressed support for Palestinian resistance. Others were fired just for expressing sadness at the loss of innocent lives in Gaza. My son's former school sent a letter to all the parents noting that while they see themselves as a tolerant education facility, they had requested that the Arab cleaner only work after-hours to accommodate the fears of the students and parents. As that wasn't possible due to her availability, the school then wrote that she would be under 'supervision' when doing her job. This was concerning a person who had been on the school staff for over a decade.

All the stories combined to make Arabs question their place in Israel like never before, fearing greatly that it was only a matter of time until calls for a mass expulsion would be repeated.

Even before October 7, from Silwan and Sheikh Jarrah in East Jerusalem to Masafer Yatta and Al-Baqa'a in the West

Bank, Palestinians in 2023 were facing forced displacement in a growing number of communities.

For years I had heard from Palestinian friends that the Nakba was not a single event but an ongoing process. It was not exclusively the trauma of the 1948 refugees, but the emotional inheritance of all Palestinians. Ultimately, for both Palestinians and Israelis, the traumas of the Holocaust and the Nakba – two of the most foundational events in their respective histories – came back to life as horrific re-enactments. Whole buildings flattened in Gaza with several generations of families wiped out in an instant. Dozens of Jewish children taken hostage in dark tunnels. Scenes that should only ever appear in nightmares or horror movies were the pictures of the nightly news. It was as if the roots of the conflict from 75 years ago were coming back to torment us, all who were privileged and cursed to live in this so-called holy land, as if we hadn't already suffered enough.

The fog of war

War is the realm of uncertainty; three-quarters of the factors on which action in war is based are wrapped in a fog of greater or lesser uncertainty. A sensitive and discriminating judgement is called for; a skilled intelligence to scent out the truth.

– Carl von Clausewitz, 1780–1831[10]

In the days leading up to Israel's ground invasion of Gaza on October 27, there was 24/7 media coverage. Every Israeli news channel was filled with analysis and bluster from former generals and military experts. These were interspersed with regular press statements from politicians. Prime Minister Benjamin Netanyahu was clear in his intentions: 'we will win', 'we will strike them', 'we will annihilate terrorism', 'we will take a mighty vengeance' and 'the enemy will pay an unprecedented price', suffering 'return fire of a magnitude that the enemy has not known'.

On October 9, Defence Minister Yoav Gallant announced he had 'ordered a complete siege on the Gaza Strip. There will be no electricity, no food, no fuel, everything is closed … We are fighting human animals and we are acting accordingly.'

On October 12, Israel's President Isaac Herzog was asked what steps Israel was taking to reduce harm to civilians in Gaza. He replied, 'The entire nation is responsible. This rhetoric of "unaware, uninvolved civilians" is not true. They could've resisted, they could've fought this evil regime that took over Gaza.'

Live on Instagram, former Israeli prime minister Naftali Bennett shared, 'We are a nation of lions. They must fear us. If Hamas pays a heavy price right now, they will never mess with us again. We will win if the world is on our side. Just keep reminding all your friends: Hamas are Nazis.'

There were hundreds more statements, from both left and right and from Jews across the world, all expressing a similar sentiment.

Suddenly, many Australian Jews whom I knew personally – especially those on the left who had, on October 6, been ashamed of Israel's far-right government – changed their tune. From being Israel's most ardent critics, or just indifferent to the Jewish state, they put their qualms with Netanyahu aside to become ardent defenders of the IDF's conduct in Gaza. War can do that to people. I felt it in me too. But it seemed to me that one thing was missing in all these calls for revenge, deterrence and defeating Hamas.

A plan.

Israel had no plan for the day after.

In the first week after October 7, I spoke with friends in media and politics to try to find out whether Israel had a plan. Like all those around me, I deeply wanted Hamas defeated, knowing that there could not be real peace for either Palestinians or Israelis under Hamas's theocratic and repressive rule. But what was the plan? Who would replace Hamas? There is no opposition party in Gaza. The Palestinian Authority, which is widely viewed by Palestinians as corrupt and ineffective in both opposing Israel and governing Palestine, would certainly not be welcomed there, and Israeli occupying forces remaining permanently would turn this event from Israel's 9/11 into Israel's Vietnam.

One friend who had recently started working for the prime minister's office countered, 'Did the Allies have a plan in World War II before they attacked Hitler? Don't worry, a plan will come after we defeat Hamas.'

I wasn't comforted. I knew that without a plan, without Israel saying that after it defeated Hamas it would work towards building a free and democratic Palestinian state, international support for the Jewish state would evaporate immediately.

Sadly, that prediction was correct.

As the war against Hamas dragged on, many of the countries that had openly shown their support for Israel now called for Israel to stop its bombing of Gaza. Leaders who had proudly lit up iconic national landmarks in blue and white –

including Niagara Falls, the Sydney Opera House, 10 Downing Street, the Brandenburg Gate and the Eiffel Tower – were now calling for a ceasefire, sanctions, and even boycotts of certain Israeli companies and individuals. For many Israelis, the word 'ceasefire' was code for failure, as it meant letting Hamas stay in power and leaving the hostages for dead in Gaza.

Watching this unfold, I kept thinking of the words from Ami Ayalon, former chief of Israel's internal security service, Shin Bet, who tellingly quoted the Prussian military theorist Carl von Clausewitz: 'Victory is the creation of a better political reality.'

The deadly Hamas conception

Two weeks into the war, former Hamas leader Khaled Mashal gave a rare interview, which aired on the Al-Arabiya news network. The interviewer, Rasha Nabil, challenged him with several statements about the size and scale of the massacre on October 7. Mashal denied these statements of fact. I'd never seen such an interview before. It was fascinating to watch a Hamas leader facing critical questions. But it also revealed a fundamental flaw in the Hamas conception of Israelis.

Nabil pressed Mashal on the expected sympathy for the Palestinian cause, citing comparisons between Hamas and ISIS in Western media. She questioned how the group could justify actions that led to the deaths of over 1200 Israelis, and highlighted the responsibility Hamas holds for the 'great human tragedy' in Gaza.

Mashal admitted to anticipating the IDF response, but justified the massacre by drawing various parallels with other historical struggles. 'The Algerians managed to repel French colonialism, the Afghans managed to expel the Americans and the Soviets, the Viet Cong won the Vietnam War,' he said. When asked about the impending suffering of innocent Gazans, he stated that the Soviets sacrificed 30 million victims to repel the Nazi invader. He called Israelis 'Ghuzza' – the invaders – a nickname for external enemies of Islam.[11]

Khaled Mashal was not making rhetorical claims. Like many Palestinians, and many in the West, he truly believes that the Israeli Jews are a foreign invader sent from distant empires. He believes that, given the appropriate amount of pressure and sacrifice on the part of the Palestinians, the Jews will simply give up, pack their bags and return to their countries of origin from Poland to Iraq.

This message was also espoused by Hezbollah, a Shia Islamist political party with strong ties to Iran, which was founded in 1982 by clerics in response to the Israeli invasion of Lebanon. Classified as a terrorist organisation by Australia, it is driven by opposition to Israel and resistance to Western influence in the Middle East. Hezbollah had been firing rockets into northern Israel on an almost daily basis since October 8.

In January 2024, Hezbollah Secretary-General Hassan Nasrallah proclaimed in a long speech from Beirut, which was watched closely throughout the West Bank, Gaza and East Jerusalem, 'Everything Israel has touched since October 7 is doomed to fail. They lack security, and without security, Israel will lose its right to exist. I call on the Zionists – pack your bags and go to another place that will accept you. After all, every Israeli has a passport from another country.'[12]

Nasrallah was assassinated by an Israeli airstrike on Hezbollah's central headquarters in Beirut on September 27,

2024. Perhaps both his replacement in Hezbollah and Mashal require an awakening like that of Palestinian Authority President Mahmoud Abbas from the secular Fatah political party. He too once proposed the establishment of an 'Arab National Fund' to encourage the return of Mizrachi Jews to their Arab countries of origin. However, in the 1980s, after meeting with left-wing Israeli activists, Abbas was forced to shift his perspective. He formed an understanding that Jews truly see the Land of Israel as their historical and religious homeland, and therefore understood that they are not going anywhere.

Mashal's inaccurate conception of Israelis encompasses a complete lack of understanding of the nature of Israeli society and the deep motivations of the Zionist movement. He would therefore be wise to heed the words of Palestinian academic Rashid Khalidi, who explained that just as Israelis need to change their perception, so too would Palestinians 'need weaning from a pernicious delusion … that Jewish Israelis are not a "real" people and that they do not have national rights'.[13]

Israeli Jews believe there is a strong case of historic justice in our return to our ancient homeland, despite the tortured impact that has had on the Palestinians. Palestinians, by the same token, feel a deep connection to the terraced mountains and olive groves of that same land – a land they also see as their national homeland. This desire for self-determination may appear to some as no more or less legitimate than the Zionist movement. Both sides often view their own claims to the land as historically justified, while questioning the historical basis for the other's.

Without seeing Jews and Palestinians as equally connected to this land, there is no way for the wars between us to end.

The deadly Israeli conception

'Anyone who wants to thwart the establishment of a Palestinian state has to support bolstering Hamas and transferring money to Hamas. This is part of our strategy – to isolate the Palestinians in Gaza from the Palestinians in the West Bank.' This is what Prime Minister Benyamin Netanyahu told a Likud party meeting in 2019.[14]

On October 2, 2023, Israeli National Security Council chief Tzachi Hanegbi said in a radio interview that 'Since Operation Guardians of the Wall in May two years ago, the Hamas leadership has taken a decision to exercise unprecedented restraint'. With great confidence, he admitted, 'For more than two years, Hamas has not fired a single missile from Gaza. It is restraining itself, and knows the repercussions of another provocation. Hamas has been very deterred for at least 15 years. It is not heading towards escalation.'[15]

That entire worldview collapsed when Hamas launched its attack five days later. The decades-old Israeli strategy of weakening the Palestinian Authority (which has recognised Israel) and believing that the IDF's overwhelming military force in previous wars could deter future Hamas attacks was entirely flawed.

Yet it wasn't Netanyahu who invented the idea of strengthening Palestinian extremists in the face of Palestinian moderates to ensure Israel would never have a partner for peace. He also wasn't the first to believe that a state of unending war was the only possible status quo between Israelis and Palestinians. The conception has a long history.

In 1956, the IDF chief of staff, Moshe Dayan, delivered a powerful eulogy that has endured in the public memory. Dayan was honouring 21-year-old security officer Roi Rotberg, who was murdered in Kibbutz Nahal Oz in an ambush by attackers from Gaza, which was then part of Egypt. His body was mutilated. Public outrage in Israel was fierce, leading Dayan to speak at his funeral.

> Yesterday at dawn Roi was murdered. The quiet of the spring morning blinded him, and he did not see those who sought his life hiding behind the furrows. Let us not today cast blame on his murderers. What can we say against their terrible hatred of us? For eight years now, they have sat in the refugee camps of Gaza and have watched how, before their very eyes, we have turned their land and villages, where they and their forefathers previously dwelled, into our home.

Despite acknowledging the hatred caused by the Nakba, Dayan went on to argue that Israeli military strength was the only way to deal with such enmity across the border.

> We are the generation of settlement; without a steel helmet and the muzzle of the cannon, we will not be able to plant a tree and build a home. Our children will not have a life if we do not dig shelters, and without barbed wire and machine guns we will not be able to pave roads and dig water wells ... This is the destiny of our generation. This is the choice of our lives – to be ready and armed and strong and tough. For if the sword falls from our fist, our lives will be cut down.[16]

The eulogy echoed themes from a 1923 essay by Ze'ev Jabotinsky, the leading revisionist Zionist thinker at that time. His key message revolved around the concept of an 'Iron Wall' of Jewish military strength as the only viable means of securing Jewish aspirations in the region. Jabotinsky argued that peaceful coexistence with the Arab population is not feasible in the short term due to deep-seated hostility and mistrust. He claimed that Arab resistance to Jewish settlement will persist as long as Arabs perceive a chance of defeating or displacing the Jewish population, asserting that only when the Arabs realise that Jewish sovereignty is unassailable, and that further resistance is futile, will they be willing to negotiate a peaceful coexistence.[17] This ideology still lies at the heart of Israel's Likud party, where Jabotinsky is viewed as both a founding father and an ideological hero.

In 2024, many Israelis viewed Palestinian enmity as eternal and unchanging. This is why extreme solutions offered by the Religious Zionism party have found a growing audience in their calls for the expulsion or transfer of Palestinians from Gaza so that their land can be annexed and settled by Israelis.

Others claim that Dayan's fierce, and enduring, 'live by the sword' philosophy has prevented many Israelis from believing in any possibility of coexistence through negotiation and compromise, as occurred in other conflicts such as in Northern Ireland.

The anticipated investigation into the events of October 7 will likely reveal a disturbing similarity to a past intelligence failure prior to the Yom Kippur War in 1973, when Israeli intelligence failed to anticipate attacks from Egypt and Syria due to assumptions that led to the misinterpretation or disregard of the many warning signs. Tragically, over 2600 Israeli soldiers lost their lives in that war as a result.

The October 7 misconception rested on greater hubris: believing that Hamas could be safely managed with Qatari 'money for quiet' and increasing worker permits for Gazans into Israel, while deepening the occupation of the West Bank indefinitely. Most Israelis today are sure that the inquiry will find that the government's manifest neglect of security on the Gaza border that cursed morning was the key reason why help came far too late for so many innocent people who needed protection.

The problem with these two conceptions

The dominant Palestinian and Israeli conceptions – that Israelis can 'go back to where they came from' and that a fragile peace with Hamas can be 'bought' – both remind me that at the core of the 120-year tragedy between the river and the sea is a deep and reciprocal misreading of the other. Too many Palestinians think Israelis are colonists who'll return to some imagined metropole in Russia if the violence is bad enough. Too many Israelis think Palestinians can be subdued, bribed, pacified or demoralised to accept anything less than freedom and equality.

Both analyses are grounded in lazy stereotypes and ill-fitting precedents. If Israel holds on to its conception of the Palestinians, it will ultimately lead to further erosion of the democratic values outlined in Israel's Declaration of Independence, which will come to be superseded by the theocratic Jewish vision expressed by extremist cabinet ministers Itamar Ben Gvir and Bezalel Smotrich. It will also lead to the resettlement of Gaza and permanent military occupation of all Palestinian cities, and endless wars with Israel's neighbours.

If Hamas and Hezbollah hold on to their conception of Israel and continue to fight for liberation using extreme acts of violent resistance, this too will lead to endless wars and misery.

There are today two rooted and indigenous national identities, which each will fight to the last man to preserve. Mirrored identities, with each stubbornly committed to ignoring the other.

Therefore, we must make a choice. Either we will fight forever and suffer the tragic consequences, or we will stop this pain and horror by moving towards a political process that allows us to share this land as equals. This book was partly written to give hope to those who want to break free of both conceptions.

The meaning of freedom

On October 10, in an interview with Channel 7 in Australia, I described how the rockets from Hamas had been frightening my children, and that my wife and I had a friend whose son had been taken hostage; it was an unthinkable situation causing immeasurable distress to his family. I then acknowledged that the suffering across the border in Gaza for innocent civilians was no less distressing. 'My war is not with the Palestinian people,' I said. 'My war is with Hamas and the people who are trying to kill me and my family.'

Even though I wasn't asked about my vision for the future, I concluded the interview by saying:

> The people in Gaza have the right to be free. I want to see the Gaza siege lifted. I want to see a free Palestine, but not

like this. Not by Hamas taking innocent people hostage and gunning down so many people indiscriminately [at the Nova festival]. I hope that one day, we will find a way to share this land. For this to be my home, it must also be the home of the Palestinian people. And we need to find a way to share it in justice, peace and equality for everyone.

The Channel 7 journalist, quite surprised by an Israeli speaking in that manner just three days after October 7, responded by saying, 'That's a remarkably balanced take, given what you are up against right now.'

Reflecting on that interview a year later, I still feel that it is essential to condemn both the brutality of Hamas and the horrific destruction of so many innocent lives in Gaza by Israel. Affirming the humanity of both Israelis and Palestinians shouldn't be considered remarkable. That tightrope I walked, and have continued to tread since October 7, was the only way my conscience could find a modicum of peace.

CHAPTER 2

Holocaust, Hashem and Israel: Reflections on my school education

Before Jerusalem became my home, I lived for 37 years in Australia. In the heart of Melbourne's southeast lie the suburbs of Caulfield, St Kilda East and Elsternwick – home to a quarter of Australia's Jewish population and most of the city's Jewish community. The area is affectionately known to Melbourne Jewry as the Bagel Belt, the Shtetl and sometimes even the Ghetto. In 1981, my Israeli parents, Reuven and Carmella, moved me and my brother from Ramat Gan, the Israeli city where I was born, to Melbourne. And so when I was two years old, this far-flung corner of the Jewish world – the edge of the diaspora – became my home too.

My father was born in 1948 at the dawn of the State of Israel. Having fought in both the Six-Day War of 1967 and the Yom Kippur War of 1973 – two military conflicts that changed the course of Israel's trajectory as a state – he came to Australia looking for a new opportunity to establish himself. A diamond trader and gemmologist by profession, he eventually opened his own business, and what started out as a short-term work sojourn turned into a permanent relocation.

My parents wanted me to have a good Jewish education, and there was an abundance of choice; Melbourne was fortunate to have a strong network of Jewish schools. In 1981, about 80% of Jews in Australia attended private schools with ideologies ranging from Bundist and secularist to the most fervently Orthodox and Hasidic.

From Years 1 through 12, I attended Mount Scopus Memorial College, a Modern-Orthodox, Zionist Jewish school. In the 1990s, more than half of Melbourne's Jewish community was educated at Scopus, which was then one of the largest Jewish schools in the world.

Some of its more high-profile graduates include federal members of parliament such as Michael Danby, Josh Frydenberg and Josh Burns, music producer Michael Gudinski, businessman Anthony Pratt, publisher Louise Adler and AFL footballer Harry Sheezel. Mark Regev was the Israeli prime minister's senior adviser for foreign affairs and international communications and is one of over 600 Scopus graduates living in Israel.

As a result of being an immigrant and a Scopus graduate, I have always had a sense of living simultaneously in two worlds, one Australian and the other Jewish-Israeli.

As a young boy, I spoke Hebrew at home and spent a lot of time in the company of other Israeli expat families. As a teenager, I worked at two fast-food places – Kosher Express on Carlisle Street and Deveroli's on Acland Street. Both eateries also doubled as social hubs and parliaments where middle-aged Jewish men would sit for hours solving the world's problems over cakes and café lattes. But I also competed in track and field at Little Athletics in the decidedly non-Jewish timeslot of Saturday morning. I also became a footy umpire in the South Metro league, where I was exposed to the beer-drinking, footy-loving, umpire-haranguing, meat-pie-eating cliché of the stereotypical Australian male. Yet despite these diverse experiences growing up, I never really felt Israeli, nor did I ever feel Australian. I was wedged between two very different worlds; at home in neither.

After graduating in 1996, I undertook a service gap year in Israel, followed by a two-year commitment as a leader in a Jewish youth movement called Hineni. Realising how much I enjoyed being involved in the education of young people inspired me to pursue a teaching career. At university, I was drawn to the Jewish studies department, focusing on Israel, Hebrew and global politics. I completed a bachelor degree, followed by a graduate diploma of education.

From 2003 to 2017, I worked as a teacher at various Jewish schools in Melbourne. These included the Hasidic Adass Israel School, the Progressive King David School and Modern-Orthodox Mount Scopus Memorial College. I have taught thousands of students about Jewish history and identity, with a lens on our texts, traditions and music. I also taught Israel studies and Indigenous Australian history, while co-leading an interfaith dialogue in schools program called 'Building Bridges' for Jewish, Muslim and Christian teenagers. This would come to have a profound influence on the direction my life took.

In 2018, my wife and I took the opportunity of long-service leave to move to Jerusalem with our two children. We were meant to stay for two years, but we fell in love with the city, its people and the dynamic life here that never failed to challenge and inspire us.

From 2018 onwards, using the skills I had acquired facilitating Building Bridges in Australia, I have been employed at Kids4Peace Jerusalem, an interfaith youth movement for Jewish, Muslim and Christian teenagers. My experiences as a peacebuilder have informed much of this book, which is the product of the insights I gained after facilitating over 1000 hours of dialogue between Israeli and Palestinian youth in my role as education director. I also work as the Jerusalem correspondent for *The Jewish Independent*, writing biweekly columns about the Australia–Israel relationship, culture, music, war and peace.

The questions of war

'Hi Ittay. Hope you and your family are well at this time. I'm an Australian Jew, and I care deeply about Israeli and Palestinian lives. Can I ask you a question about what's happening in Israel and Gaza right now?'

So began more than 50 messages I received in the first month following the October 7 attacks.

As I responded to each question, I quickly realised that what most people were asking was less about what was happening today in Gaza and far more about the events that led up to this war – and about their identities as Australian Jews. These included questions about the definition of antisemitism and how it differs from criticism of Israel, the issue of intersectionality, how to manage respectful disagreement about the war with people we care about at work or in our family, and the ability to verify and process the many different stories we see on social media.

One of the people who asked me a variation of this question on WhatsApp was Hannah Baker, a family lawyer in Melbourne. Like me, Hannah is also a graduate of Mount Scopus Memorial College. After many messages back and forth, we decided to turn our conversations into a podcast called *From the Yarra River to the Mediterranean Sea.*

I remember Hannah saying to me in our first episode, 'There's so much stuff that I'm learning now through Instagram, asking questions and having conversations with other people. I was never taught this during twelve years of Jewish day-school education. So now I'm thinking, "Why do we only learn one narrative?"'

I responded that there were three reasons the Israeli narrative was given precedence over the Palestinian one, and all of them led directly to why we are having this conversation about Israel and Gaza today.

The three pillars of education in Australia's Jewish Zionist schools

There are three pillars of education in Australia's Jewish Zionist schools. The first has nothing to do with the conflict and everything to do with the greatest tragedy that ever befell the Jewish people, which came about as a result of not having a Jewish national home with safe and secure borders – the Shoah. The second is to do with our relationship with Hashem (God), and the third is Israel and Zionism.

These three pillars have shaped my identity and that of many Australian Jews. They have shaped the ways we view the Israeli–Palestinian conflict, our relationships with our tradition and our roles as citizens of Australia.

Pillar one: Shoah

As a child, I shied away from learning about the Shoah – the Holocaust – because unlike many other Melbourne Jews, none of my four grandparents was in Europe during the war. For some of my friends at Scopus, the Holocaust was learned not through movies or history books but from the stories their grandparents shared after Friday-night Shabbat meals; stories sometimes illustrated by numbers tattooed on their arms if those grandparents were among the few to have survived the hell of Auschwitz.

As a sensitive child, learning the details of how Hitler's plans unfolded caused me immense grief, sometimes to a level I just couldn't bear. Even though I taught Holocaust history in Australian Jewish schools, there was always a small part of me that couldn't accept it had happened because it felt too horrific to be true, and because I wanted to believe that humans are inherently good.

All this changed in 2008, when I was a fellow in the Hebrew University Senior Educators program, which included a week-long trip to Hungary and Poland. My first memory of the Auschwitz–Birkenau concentration camp wasn't the gas chambers or the barracks. It was the car park. There were hundreds of buses, filled with school students and families from all over Europe. I had no idea that Auschwitz was so big, so vast, and that so many people wanted to see it. There was even a gift shop selling books in dozens of languages about the rise and fall of the Nazi regime.

Inside the gates, famous for the heinous lie 'Arbeit Macht Frei' – 'Work makes one free' – the camp was seemingly endless. I couldn't believe humans could build something so enormous and grand for the primary purpose of killing people. But what really struck me on the trip was the museum. There were several large glass cabinets: one filled with hair, another filled with spectacles and a third filled with shoes. I remember my horror as I wondered what kind of person would not only murder people in such enormous numbers but then also steal the very hair on their heads to use in mattresses for Nazi soldiers. What kind of depraved ideology would compel such an atrocity?

During our group reflection that night, many educators shared that, after the Holocaust, their survivor family members no longer believed in God. For me, after going to Auschwitz, I began to lose my faith in humanity. Bearing witness to the horror challenged my belief that humans are fundamentally good at heart, and I have been desperately struggling to find that faith again ever since.

How most Australian Jews remember the Shoah

In August 1945, Australia's minister for immigration, Arthur Calwell, introduced a close relatives reunion scheme, allowing Holocaust survivors with family in Australia to immigrate. As a result, after World War II Australia took in more Holocaust survivors relative to its population than any country other than Israel. By 1961, despite challenges such as shipping shortages, passenger quotas on Jewish immigrants and local prejudice towards non-British immigrants, around 35,000 Jewish refugees had settled in Australia.[1] Australia has more Holocaust-survivor descendants than any other Jewish community on earth, outside of Israel. In 2024, Australian Jews comprised just 0.4% of the total Australian population. Despite the tiny size of the community, its members have made extraordinary contributions to the Australian way of life in many fields including the arts, philanthropy, law and Indigenous-rights advocacy.

Observant Jews are obligated to live by 613 commandments from the Bible, yet in the Melbourne Jewish community that was my home as a child, it was clear that there were 614. German Holocaust survivor and eminent philosopher Rabbi Emil Fackenheim formulated the concept of the '614th commandment', the moral imperative that Jews never use the Holocaust as a reason to give up on God, Judaism or the continued survival of the Jewish people. Doing so would give Hitler a posthumous victory.

Although the education I received taught me that Hitler committed suicide in a bunker at the end of World War II, it simultaneously taught me that the forces of antisemitism that the war unleashed were very much alive in the deeds of Jew-haters throughout the world. I was also taught that if I ever forgot, even for a moment, the evil that Hitler did to my people, this act would give him his posthumous victory from the grave.

Also embodied in this commandment was the ideal of 'Jewish unity'. This principle posited that when dissent and disagreement among Jews is minimised, antisemitism will also be diminished.[2] This desire for unity also comes out of fear, based on past experiences where dissenting voices critical of the Jewish mainstream legitimised the targeting of Jewish communities in hostile countries. The ideal of unity rests on the ethical precept that 'all Jews are responsible for one another' – a principle that has been embedded in our tradition for generations as a result of being a tiny minority that has often been persecuted.

Therefore, the mainstream Melbourne Jewish community, many of whom are descendants of Holocaust survivors, take seriously the call for Jewish unity and show considerable concern about antisemitism, anti-Zionism and assimilation.

Antisemitism, anti-Zionism and assimilation

Antisemitism is the hatred of Jews, usually based on a conspiracy theory connected to nefarious Jewish power and influence that subverts the will of the wider population. Jews are not a race, instead identifying as a religious group, ethnicity and, for some, a nationality.

Antisemitism is part of the intergenerational trauma that many Jews carry. The ways it manifests in Australia include doxing,[3] vandalism of Jewish institutions such as schools and synagogues, and, occasionally, physical attacks. The fear of antisemitism sometimes causes Australian Jews to hide their identity; for example, since October 7, many children at Jewish schools have feared wearing their identifiably Jewish school uniforms in public. For others, online campaigns undermining core Jewish beliefs have encouraged them to be more visibly Jewish or increase their participation in Jewish events as a sign that they would not let the hatred of others minimise their love and identification with their people.

For me, antisemitism is a fear in the back of my mind that the place where I feel safe now may not be safe in the future. For example, I have calendar notifications six months before the expiry dates for the passports of all my family members, so I can begin the renewal process. I do this because our history reminds me that wherever we live, home can be as fragile as the teetering fiddler on a roof, so having a valid passport is essential.

Anti-Zionism has long been of great concern to many in the community where I was raised. It's a view that holds

43

that Israel shouldn't exist due to the negative consequences on the Palestinian people of the state's creation and ongoing existence. A Gen08 survey of Australian Jews conducted by Monash University in 2008 asked, 'Do you regard yourself as a Zionist? By the term Zionist, we mean that you feel connected to the Jewish people, to Jewish history, culture and beliefs, the Hebrew language and the Jewish homeland, Israel?' Eighty per cent answered in the affirmative.[4] While many non-Jews and Palestinians understand Zionism as quite different from this definition (a point I will return to later in this book), this high level of Zionist identification helps explain why many Australian Jewish schools incorporate Zionist education into their curricula.

Assimilation is a process whereby Jews stop practising their religion/culture or connecting to their Jewish identity. Assimilation can be explained as disinterest or disconnection, not valuing and passing down Jewish customs and traditions, not participating in Jewish events and festivals, or marrying someone of a different faith.

Assimilation is very different from integration. I am very much in favour of Jews integrating into the wider Australian society, because I think living in a vibrant multicultural space both enhances our Jewish identity and allows others to embrace our culture. While many Melbourne Jews feel the same way, some on the more Hasidic end of the spectrum are very concerned about assimilation, feeling that too much leaning into the culture of Australia could lead to a reduction in the number of practising Jews and, at worst, the elimination of Jewish people from Australia. In some sectors of the Jewish community, if a member left the fold and chose not to marry a Jew, their parents would not attend the wedding because they would see their child's choice as an act of betrayal of a 4000-year-old tradition.

A deep understanding of Jewish texts and cultural heritage requires an immense amount of knowledge that takes years to acquire and, for some, also includes the study of Aramaic, Hebrew or Yiddish. Jewish schools are very popular in the community as a means to combat assimilation and foster solidarity with fellow Jews, our culture, land and literature. These aspects of our tradition have formed over generations of struggle to practise Judaism freely.

In summary, if I had to describe the purpose of Melbourne Jewish-Zionist education in three statements, they would be:

1. Love your Jewishness and Jewish people, honouring and celebrating our beautiful culture and traditions as a source of inspiration to do good in the world.
2. Care for the people of Israel, and especially stand up for them in their hour of need.
3. Fight antisemitism wherever it appears and remember the Holocaust to ensure it never happens again.

Holocaust Memorial Day

Known in Hebrew as Yom HaShoah, Holocaust Memorial Day is one of the most important days for the community and is held each April. Even the most disconnected Australian Jew will often share something on social media highlighting the importance of 'Never Again', and thousands will gather for memorials where the testimonies of survivors will take centre stage.

At Scopus, the central focus of this day was a two-hour memorial assembly that was compulsory for all staff and students from Years 7 to 12. I have formative memories of tattooed survivors of Auschwitz sharing their harrowing stories with all those gathered in the school's enormous Rose Hall. Many of the students' parents would also come to be a part of the moving memorial. It always concluded poignantly with the ceremonial lighting of six candles by survivors with their children and grandchildren, representing the approximately six million Jews who perished.

Soon after I started teaching Judaic studies at Scopus in 2010, the head of Jewish studies, Avi Cohen, approached me to take on the coordination of the school's Yom HaShoah ceremony, a position I held for the next six years. Before my time, the deeply moving, highly researched and informative assembly had been coordinated by some of Australia's most experienced Holocaust educators: Miriam Munz, Sue Hampel and Frances Prince. Having this role in the school as the shaper of Holocaust memory on Yom HaShoah was humbling and, at times, overwhelming.

During the first months of the school year, from February to April, I would spend hundreds of hours researching and coordinating an assembly about a specific theme ranging from the Warsaw Ghetto Uprising to the plight of Hungarian Jewry. I would write a very detailed script breaking down the dense historical details into relatable human experiences, prepare a slide show filled with archival photos and videos from the genocide, rehearse music in Hebrew and Yiddish, and meet with survivors to help them tell their stories in a way that teenage students could absorb. Finally, I would rehearse the whole presentation several times with the students.

The assembly was deeply personal for many of the students because most had a relative, close or distant, who had been murdered or who had survived. Every year, the assembly would conclude with a seven-minute honour roll listing the names of every family member of a Scopus student murdered by the Nazis. It numbered over 1000 names. The whole auditorium then stood while a choir led the singing of the 'Partisan Hymn' in Yiddish, which concludes with the triumphant words 'Mir zaynen do', meaning 'We are here!'

Communal celebration controversy

Back in 2012, there was a significant controversy within the Melbourne Jewish community in response to a speech on Yom HaShoah from Gary Samowitz at the general Jewish Community Council of Victoria communal commemoration. At the time, Samowitz was the CEO of Jewish Aid Australia, a non-governmental organisation that was very active in supporting Sudanese refugees in Australia. He had been invited to speak at the Yom HaShoah memorial by organising committee member Bram Presser.

Standing in front of 1500 people on the night of Yom HaShoah, Samowitz used his time on stage to call the Jewish community to join the Sudanese community in an act of protest against Omar al-Bashir and his persecution and genocide of the Darfuri and Nuba Mountains peoples. He concluded, 'When we say "never again", we are not only talking about never again to the Jews. We are choosing not to be bystanders. Never again means never again.'

Despite having submitted his speech to the committee before the event, the backlash was fast and furious. Gary told me later that it came from all directions. He was criticised for speaking at the event as someone who was not the descendant of survivors, and some even criticised him for not wearing a kippa (head covering) during his speech, despite Yom HaShoah not being a religious event.

Outrage flared in the letters page of the *Australian Jewish News* the following week, with writers expressing disgust that a modern-day event was being compared to the Holocaust, which many in the community felt was a unique calamity in human history.

I was reminded of this incident in 2024 when the same thing happened again, but this time on a global platform. After winning the Oscar for Best International Feature Film for the Holocaust film *Zone of Interest*, Jewish director Jonathan Glazer stood before the world holding his golden trophy and read a speech, which included this line: 'We stand here as men who refute their Jewishness and the Holocaust being hijacked by an occupation which has led to conflict for so many innocent people, whether the victims of October the seventh in Israel or the ongoing attack on Gaza.'

Thousands of posts were written by Jews across the world angrily accusing Glazer of refuting his Jewish identity entirely. But that was a selective misreading of what he was trying to say. He certainly wasn't denying his Jewish identity. What he was doing was defining his Jewishness in his own terms, as I think all Jews should.

It's clear to me that the language Glazer used in his acceptance speech, however clumsy his phrasing, was chosen as a statement against the brutality of the October 7 attack and Israel's destruction of so many lives and homes in Gaza in response. Neither event could have happened without the horrific process of dehumanisation that has occurred in both

Palestinian and Israeli societies over generations. I don't want my Jewishness and the Holocaust being used to justify the war in Gaza, either. Yet for most Israelis, the war wasn't about the Holocaust at all. It was justified by the need to prevent Hamas from ever again having the ability to harm Jewish life in the way it did on October 7.

Reflecting on this moment, I was initially upset that Glazer didn't use his minute in the global spotlight to share a speech like the one Branko Lustig gave in 1994 at the 66th Annual Academy Awards after winning the Oscar for Best Picture for *Schindler's List*. He stood before the world as a survivor of Auschwitz, recalling the immense spiritual journey from the hell of that concentration camp to the Dorothy Chandler Pavilion in Los Angeles, reminding all gathered of the final words of his friends and family who perished in the camps, which were an exhortation to tell the world how they died, to witness and to remember.

In the 30 years that have passed since then, so much of the world has changed, especially its relationship to the horrors of World War II. Today, it has become almost impossible to speak about the Holocaust on its own terms; instead, it has become a reference to which every other atrocity is compared. No longer will it stand alone in history as a symbol of what happens when people forgo their consciences to follow orders.

Today, it will be misappropriated to draw attention to many causes, such as animal liberation, Zionism, Palestinian freedom and the need to combat climate change.

I, for one, would prefer to let the Holocaust be the Holocaust. I don't want it to be a central pillar of my Jewish identity, nor do I want it to be the reason I tell my students or my children to be Jewish. I also don't want it to be a comparison point to every other injustice. I wish for people to relate to world events on their own merits and not use 'it's not as bad as the Holocaust' as an excuse to justify inaction about them. I want humanity to look to visions such as the Universal Declaration of Human Rights, written while the ashes of the Shoah were still smouldering, to provide a framework for ensuring that the atrocities of World War II never happen again – to anyone.

As the last survivors sadly pass from this earth, and the Holocaust becomes more of a historical event and less of an immediate family story for most Australian Jews, one wonders whether this will remain the pillar that it is for the Melbourne community.

Using the Holocaust to remind teenagers that they must not be the weak link who stops being Jewish, breaking the chain that has lasted since Moses led our people out of Egypt, is compelling for many. Yet employing guilt as the prime motivator for Jewish solidarity will always be limited in the kind of Judaism it will produce.

Pillar two: Hashem

The second pillar in my Modern-Orthodox Jewish school education was Hashem.

Literally meaning 'the name', Hashem is the Hebrew word for God. It is used as an honorific like Sir or Your Majesty, reflecting the ideal that one never addresses royalty by their personal name. The idea that the Jewish people have a special relationship with the creator that is unlike that of any other people was deeply embedded in me as a child.

When I was in Year 11, my Scopus year level attended a compulsory week-long camp called Counterpoint, held at Candlebark Farm near Healesville in rural Victoria. It was led by hip Orthodox camp counsellors from Yeshiva University in New York, who were there to help us youngsters answer the question, 'Why be Jewish?' We all thought they were exceptionally cool in their baseball caps, especially Moishe, who was an awesome singer and could play the *Seinfeld* theme on an electric keyboard.

Of the many educational programs they facilitated, one related to something called the Bible codes, which I had never heard of before. A Bible code is an alleged collection of hidden words found within the Hebrew text of the Torah that predicts important historical occurrences. Think of it as the Jewish version of Nostradamus.

What followed was several hours of discussion during which the camp staff presented a great deal of evidence for the existence of Bible codes. This included a 1994 paper written by Doron Witztum, Eliyahu Rips and Yoav Rosenberg called 'Equidistant Letter Sequences (ELS) in the Book of Genesis'. Published in the peer-reviewed journal *Statistical Science*, the paper offered what seemed to be compelling evidence that the Bible codes foretold names and places of events from throughout history, including information about notable rabbis long before those rabbis lived.

The message from our camp counsellors was quite clear: there was no way possible that the Bible had a human author, because no human of flesh and blood, especially without the help of computers, could write a book with so many hidden codes predicting the future leadership of the Jewish people with such accuracy. They then went on to argue that, given the Bible's unquestionably divine origin, its laws and commandments should be followed with love and commitment.

Sixteen-year-old me was completely won over.

On that same camp, we also had to watch a harrowing play, a monologue told by one of the leaders who was dressed in rags and standing in a cage. Written by Rabbi Dr Johnny Krug, a specialist in the field of creative drama and theatrical technique in informal Jewish education, it was called *The Last Jew* and began with these words:

> Who am I? I am the last Jew. The year is 2124, the place
> is the Smithsonian in Washington DC. I am in this
> museum, in a cage on exhibit. People pass my way, day in
> and out, staring, pointing, and even sometimes laughing.
> On the walls surrounding my exhibit are the remnants of
> a Jewish culture; a talit, a Torah, the books of the Talmud.
> Each day, as I sit here watching the people pass, I wonder
> to myself how six and a half million people who existed
> as Jews a little over a century ago could have possibly
> vanished.

As the monologue was read in anger, pain and tears, the normally rowdy students fell totally silent. It concluded with this message:

> Little over 150 years ago, a man in World War II
> slaughtered six million Jews, and my father told me that
> people swore they would never forget ... How forgetful
> a people can be! When the people lost their pride in

themselves, their religion, and their Israel, they lost
everything. As it was once said, 'If I am not for myself,
who will be for me?' I am the last American Jew. In less
than twenty years, I too, will die. And never again will
another Jew set foot on this planet.[5]

After the performance, we split up into small groups and
discussed the meaning of the play until the early hours of the
morning. The message from our educators was unmistakable:
if you don't remember the Holocaust, if you don't fight
antisemitism, if you don't donate to Israel and keep the
commandments of the Torah, your fate will be the same as
that of this man in a cage at the Smithsonian. As a 16-year-
old, swept up in the euphoric combination of charismatic camp
leaders, 'irrefutable' Bible codes and some heavily laden guilt
from *The Last Jew*, it was that night that I decided to start
believing in God.

For the next few years, I became more religiously observant,
lest I betray my people. I was also convinced that the person I
would marry could only be Jewish.

I learned later that there was hardly a generation in the
diaspora that did not worry about becoming the final link in
the chain of Jewish history. As it turns out, worrying about the
Jewish future is a very Jewish pastime.

Today, I would have fact-checked our counsellors' claims
about the Bible codes and found an immediate rebuttal, but
Google didn't exist back then. If it had, I would have quickly
discovered that the same equidistant letter sequence codes,
which I was told only appeared in the Bible, could also be found
in books of similar extensive length such as *Moby Dick* and *War*

and Peace. I no longer believe in the power of any supernatural being to intervene in human affairs. My relationship with God has evolved over the years since high school, primarily as a result of two experiences.

The first was reading *The God Delusion* in my early twenties. Expecting to prove the book wrong, I was surprised by how compelling an argument it gave that one could be good without God. In the book, Richard Dawkins's concept of the 'moral zeitgeist' refers to the general moral consensus of a particular time or place, in contrast to the traditional Jewish view that morality is absolute and unchanging. His claim in the book is that 'morality is not innate'. It is not written in our genes. It is not God-given. It is not a gift from on high. It is something we have made for ourselves, slowly and painfully, over the course of millions of years.

The second experience was studying the Bible at Jerusalem's Hebrew University in 2007. In the semester course for Jewish educators, Dr Yair Zakovitch went through every book of the Bible and showed how each was influenced by, or sometimes even a direct copy of, prior ancient Near Eastern texts. These ranged from the Epic of Gilgamesh to the Code of Hammurabi, showing rather convincingly that the Bible was written by human authors.

For these two reasons, in addition to the tragedy of the Holocaust, I no longer believe in an interventionist God. While this lack of belief hasn't stopped me from attending synagogue regularly, teaching Jewish studies or feeling connected to Israel, it has made me much more open to seeing and hearing multiple voices on issues of religion, faith, tradition and Zionism.

For example, as a child, whenever I would say the Kiddush (blessing) over wine on Friday night, I would always read the words directly from the siddur (prayer book) liturgy that praised God for choosing the Jewish people *from* all other nations. Yet as an adult, I changed the way I said the blessing, replacing the word *from* to *with*. I did this as an affirmation of my desire to be connected to the Jewish story and God, yet also to imagine a creator that had chosen every nation for a specific purpose in the world, making my religion much more universalist.

Perhaps this lumps me together with many other Jews who don't believe in God but feel connected to the idea that the Land of Israel was promised by God to the Jewish people. To understand how this contradiction came to be, one needs to understand the place of the third pillar of Jewish education: Zionism.

Pillar three: Israel and Zionism

Parents who send their children to Zionist schools in Melbourne such as Scopus, Bialik, Yavneh and the King David School, do so for many reasons. Scopus and Yavneh both follow the teachings of Orthodox Judaism, King David is Progressive, and Bialik is a pluralist school, giving space to the religious expression found in multiple denominations. All these schools strive to foster a sense of community and service by instilling values and skills in their students that prepare them to actively participate in social change for good – be that in their Jewish circles, their local networks as Australians, or more broadly as global citizens.

Parents choose these schools to help their children make Jewish friends, support them to do well academically, set them up successfully for work and university entrance, develop their notions of community and service, and encourage them to love Israel.

To achieve these goals, each school – in balance with their religious ideology and specific student backgrounds – chooses what to add or omit from their school experience.

To generate love for Israel, they teach Hebrew, place Israeli flags around the school, and run camps around Zionist themes led by engaging educators from both Australia and Israel.

Two of the most moving and memorable days commemorated at Zionist schools, only a day apart from each other, are Yom HaZikaron, on which the schools stop regular learning to mourn the fallen soldiers of Israel, and Yom Ha'atzmaut, on which the schools celebrate the birth of Israel through dancing, live music and many joyous activities ranging from jumping castles to special assemblies. On these days, students are reminded of the painful price we pay to secure safety in a Jewish homeland, emphasising the current existence of one as both a privilege and a blessing that must be celebrated.

In Year 10, students go on a special month-long trip to Israel, which is often deeply transformative for the participants in building a love for Israel and her people. The huge excitement and euphoria that accompany every day of these Israel tours, between the waterfalls, desert hikes and dramatic moments of prayer at holy places, are unforgettable.

When the students return home to Melbourne, they sometimes express their love for Israel by joining a Zionist youth movement, as I did. Others stay connected to Israel by following Israeli news and joining WhatsApp groups, sharing Israeli content on their social media and attending synagogues that have many Israel-related activities.

To generate love, the schools also teach their students about Israel very differently from the way they teach science, maths or English. None of these schools will ever have a dedicated camp or hours-long debate about whether one should love algebra, wonder at the marvel of English grammar or appreciate the wisdom of the periodic table. Yet most of these schools have informal Jewish education departments staffed by relatable young educators who use experiential techniques to teach about Israel on a deeply personal level. When successful, their education transforms the Jewish state from just another foreign country on the other side of the world to a place students come to consider a second home.

I know this because I was the head of the middle-school informal education department at the King David School for four years, having also taught at Bialik, Yavneh and then later Scopus over a period of 15 years. I observed how effectively these talented educators brought Israel to life through their many creative and emotive programs for youth.

For many Australian parents who choose to send their children to Jewish schools in Melbourne, Sydney or Perth, these informal education departments are the jewel in the crown in helping their children see the beauty of Israel, which is a central pillar of their Jewish identity.

How October 7 changed Jewish schools

From October 7 onwards, Jewish schools became much more than places of education. They also became a safe haven where young Australian Jews could express their identity in a safe place amid growing hostility towards Israel and, in some cases, Judaism itself, from opponents of Israel's actions in Gaza.

On Saturday, May 25, 2024, in the middle of the night, a lone man on a bicycle rode to Scopus and wrote 'Jew Die' on the gates with spray paint. The shock and rage felt by the students and their parents on seeing this hateful graffiti was palpable across the Melbourne Jewish community. Even Prime Minister Anthony Albanese tweeted, 'No place for this in Australia or anywhere else.' Some parents feared sending their children to school the following Monday.

In response, Principal Dan Sztrajt gathered together all the secondary-school students to share words of reassurance. He did so by reminding them that the college was founded in 1949 and that this attack had happened in the same year it was celebrating its 75th anniversary.

> Seventy-five years ago, the founders of this school chose a motto at a time when the horrors of the Holocaust were closer in their memory than Covid is to us today. There are many statements from the Torah about memory or learning, which would have been the obvious choice for a place of education. But instead, they chose the motto 'Be strong and of good courage', perhaps knowing that at some point in the future, our sense of security may be questioned and that the most important message for future generations like you is to be courageous in your beliefs, not allowing the actions of one racist to dictate who you are, remaining steadfast as proud Australians and proud Jews.

This message wasn't just about how to respond to antisemitism. It was also the motto that shaped the relationship of many young Australian Jews to Israel during the war, affirming their resolution to stand firmly with the Jewish state.

Three weeks later during Shavuot, a Jewish festival where people traditionally stay up late learning about Jewish themes, a huge event for young people was held by the Jewish youth movement Habonim Dror in Elsternwick. Hundreds of people, mainly Jews in their twenties, gathered to hear a panel featuring principals from several Jewish schools talking about the mission of their different schools in the current climate. At the end of the panel, Hannah Baker asked the night's only audience question. It was the same question she asked me in the first episode of our podcast – why don't Jewish schools teach the Palestinian narrative with the same time and attention they teach the Israeli narrative?

To varying degrees, each principal, in turn, explained why it is important to offer a nuanced education and spoke about criticism of Israel as an expression of love. Dan Sztrajt added that learning the Palestinian narrative adds volume to the understanding of his students, but that he felt students shouldn't identify with the suffering of the Palestinian Nakba of 1948 to the extent that it makes them question whether they want to celebrate Israeli Independence Day on Yom Ha'atzmaut.

Perhaps due to my belief that peace was and is possible with the Palestinians, I always tried to include more context in the Israeli education I delivered as a teacher at Scopus, bringing in many diverse voices through YouTube videos and documentaries that went beyond the classic Zionist narrative. At the same time, I have a great deal of understanding for the choices made by educators who give more time to mainstream Israeli narratives, especially during a war where the legitimacy of Israel is so under attack.

As a graduate of Scopus, I received an education in which I learned almost nothing about the suffering of Palestinians in the Nakba of 1948, atrocities such as the massacres of Kafr Qasim in 1956 and Sabra and Shatila in 1982, or how the Israeli military occupation of the territories captured in 1967 harmfully impacts so many Palestinians on a daily basis and denies millions of people democratic representation in the Israeli parliament, the Knesset. Just as US schools don't teach the Vietnam War from the perspective of the Viet Cong, and Australian schools give less voice to the perspective of Turks than they do to the Diggers when teaching Gallipoli, Jewish schools make the choice to focus almost entirely on one half of the story as a means of affirming all I have written above.

Even though this may sound odd to some today, I am deeply grateful for the education that in some ways left me blind to the complete picture. It's precisely this education that taught me to love and care for the humans who call Jerusalem home and that has led me to where I am today.

When I turned 18 I stopped learning science, maths, French and many other subjects I studied at school. While I once knew the periodic table by heart, I no longer remember the names of many of the elements. I have no ability to ask for directions in Paris, and I can't even help my daughter complete her algebra homework because I have long forgotten what the x and y are meant to do for one another. I think the reason for this is that I was never taught to love these subjects. I was never taught to care about them beyond being marks on a report or end-of-year exam.

On the other hand, because I was taught to love Israel, my love for and interest in Israel didn't end when I finished school; rather, it was only just beginning. On this subject, I was given both the skills and desire to be a lifelong learner. So maybe I was fooled, maybe I wasn't given the full picture, maybe my education was biased and one-sided, but without that start to my life, I would never have become the teacher and peace educator and journalist I am today.

CHAPTER 3

Where it all began: Two nations, one homeland

After moving to Jerusalem in 2018, I started exploring the Palestinian narrative through my feet and eyes and not just in my head through books, podcasts and news articles as I had done up to that point. I realised I had huge gaps in my knowledge, even though I had been teaching the history of Israel for over two decades.

One of the ways I loved learning the chronicles of Palestinian history was through museums. A well-curated museum is an exceptional place to see and experience the history of a culture that is not your own, because every part of the story has been intentionally chosen to craft a certain historical narrative. For this reason, museums are often important tools for building national identity and telling a collective story.

One of the most impressive museums I visited was the Palestinian Museum in the West Bank city of Birzeit. A vast edifice on the top of a mountain, it's filled with beautiful art galleries and an enormous collection of traditional Palestinian thobes – customary garments adorned with detailed embroidery, known as tatreez; the hues within each thobe typically denote the wearer's geographical origin, with distinct colours representing various regions of Palestine. Outside the museum, imposing outdoor sculptures, including a staircase breaking out of a metal cage, overlook the olive trees and parched desert landscape surrounding the north of Ramallah.

Before I arrived, I was expecting that the museum would begin its narration in 1948, as that's when I always thought the Palestinian story began – as a resistance movement to Zionism. As it turns out, the first panel in the museum begins the story 200 years prior, in 1748.

This was the year Daher al-Omar al-Zaydani came to power in the northern city of Akka (or, as Israelis today call it, Akko), by the Mediterranean Sea.

The first panel on the timeline explained that before nationalism as we know it today developed, Palestine had political groups that were somewhat independent of the Ottoman Empire. These groups played an important role in shaping the urban centres that later became Palestine's coastal cities. The most significant effort at self-governance was led by Daher al-Omar, who began his rise to power in the Galilee and made Akka his capital in 1748. His rule continued for over four decades, during which he consolidated his authority despite the presence of the Ottoman Empire. He oversaw the construction of coastal towns and restructured the country's interior, laying a solid foundation for the cities' prosperity that was reliant upon agriculture and foreign trade, especially in relation to cotton production.

The sculpture of backhoes on the terrace of the Palestinian Museum in the West Bank city of Birzeit was created by Jerusalem artist Nida Sinnokrot. The museum describes the lifted arms of the backhoes as being 'raised up to the skies in a primal gesture that recalls despair as well as prayer, absolution and defiance'. These are the same kinds of backhoes that are used for demolishing homes in Palestine, and rebuilding new ones for Jewish settlers.

Palestinian academic Nur Masalha describes Daher as 'the founding father of early Palestinian modernities and social renewal'.[1] At the time of his death, Daher had been the governor of most of the land from the Jordan River to the Mediterranean Sea for over 40 years.

I knew none of this before entering the museum. While I had heard a great deal about Jewish leaders from King David to King Herod, how had I not learned about this towering figure? Why didn't I know of this important history that existed over a century before the birth of Theodor Herzl, the founding father of political Zionism?

The more I researched the history of Palestine before 1948, the more I realised the falsity of an old saying used by Christian Zionist Lord Shaftesbury in his argument for a return of the Jewish people to Palestine. He claimed in the 1850s that Palestine was 'A land without a people for a people without a land'. By this, he meant that Palestine was 'empty' and waiting to be filled by a Jewish state. While this phrase has often been misinterpreted to mean that the early Zionists didn't register that the Arab people of Palestine were there, the way I understand it is as an expression of disbelief in the *peoplehood* of Palestine, and a lack of recognition of their separate history, culture and legitimate claim to national self-determination. In the words of Ian Black, author of *Enemies and Neighbours: Arabs and Jews in Palestine and Israel, 1917–2017*, Palestine contained people, but not *a people*.[2] It is as if Daher al-Omar and his unifying reign over the land, which formed a distinct identity among its inhabitants, never existed.

When I looked up the demographics of the land, I was even more surprised. On the eve of the first Aliyah (wave of Jewish immigration from Russia, Eastern Europe and Yemen) in 1882, the three Ottoman districts corresponding to modern Palestine had a total population of 462,465 citizens.[3] Of this number, 87% were Muslim (including Druze), 10% were Christian (mostly Greek Orthodox) and just 3% were Jewish. Since many of the Jewish residents were not Ottoman citizens, some scholars place the Jewish total a bit higher than the census figure, yet whatever the exact number, it's clear the Jews constituted only a small proportion of the population at the time.[4]

In my school education I had learned about the four holy cities of Jerusalem, Tzfat, Hebron and Tiberias, where most of the Jews of Palestine lived in 1882, but no one had ever told me they were only 3 to 8% of the total population of the land. This means that while it's true that for thousands of years there has been an unbroken Jewish presence in Eretz Yisrael (the Biblical Hebrew term used for the Land of Israel, whose borders are more expansive than the modern State of Israel), it's also true that at the time the first Zionists began to settle the land through the first Aliyah, Jews were a tiny minority.

By the end of the 1948 war, due to the Nakba, Jews constituted 82.1% of Israel's population. In 2024, that figure was 73.2%. Israel's official population statistics include Jews in the West Bank, but exclude Palestinians there and in Gaza, who do not have citizenship. For most Jewish members of Knesset, maintaining Jewish majority of the state is a primary national objective that shapes everything from the government's stance on immigration and asylum seekers to its policies on education and housing.

As someone who is deeply grateful that a Jewish state exists but is deeply saddened by the fact that it came at the expense of the Palestinian people, all this talk of demographics – which is still so much a part of the Israeli discourse to this day – makes me very uncomfortable. Perhaps this is because I feel that the most important characteristic of the Jewish state I want to live in is not the number of Jews it holds but rather the manner in which it secures the personal, religious and national rights of all who may choose to live there.

The Nakba

For Palestinians, the Nakba represents the violent and catastrophic displacement of at least 750,000 Palestinians at the hands of Zionist militias in 1948. At the time, this represented around 65% of all Palestinians. They were either forcibly removed from their homes or fled from land that would become Israel. It is seared into their collective memory, and its consequences have defined all Palestinians' lives, in the West Bank, Gaza Strip, inside Israel and in the diaspora.

I began to teach Jewish students about the Nakba in 2020 when I was invited to do so in Jerusalem by the organisers of several different gap-year programs. Sometimes I taught these programs as standalone seminars and sometimes as dual-narrative lectures, which involves teaching history from multiple perspectives.

It troubled me that Palestinian educators were rarely invited to teach these same groups, especially when I taught Israelis in Hebrew, but I knew why. In many cases, the institutions were taking a brave step by even giving a platform to a narrative other than the Zionist one. Having faith that I could teach this story in a manner that would inform the students rather than turning the lesson into a political argument is perhaps why they offered this opportunity to me frequently.

Despite my qualms, I believed that giving the students access to these narratives was more important than the teacher's identity. To accommodate my not being Palestinian, I would try to avoid the dry timelines and slide-show dot points many people lean on when teaching history, instead filling my classes with the personal stories of displaced Palestinians. The one I would often begin my classes with was that of Ghada Karmi.

Ghada grew up in the south Jerusalem neighbourhood of Qatamon. (Palestinians spell the neighbourhood Qatamon, while Israelis spell it Katamon. This comes from the Arabic letter Qaf, which has a guttural sound that doesn't exist in Hebrew, where there is only the letter Kaf.) Today, it's a neighbourhood popular with French- and English-speaking immigrants, known for its top-ranking religious Zionist schools and a mixture of spacious old Arab houses and upmarket apartments. You can tell the Arab houses because they are the ones that still have the ocean-blue or olive-green shutters and tiled verandas. In the 1940s, when Qatamon was a predominantly Christian Palestinian neighbourhood, many houses were enveloped by leafy gardens planted with lavish fruit trees and flowers.

Three days before Greek Orthodox Christmas, on the night of January 5, 1948, Ghada went to sleep as usual. It was raining heavily, and the sky was filled with thunder and lightning. At some point in the night, she awoke from a nightmare. For a few seconds, she could not distinguish dream from reality.

When Ghada got up in the morning, she found no one in her house. Almost the whole street was deserted. She ran frantically and found her family at the scene of an explosion that had happened during the night at the Semiramis Hotel located in the street behind her house.[5]

In the months preceding the bombing, there had been much fear and instability. The British had been given the mandate to govern the Palestine region in 1922, after driving Ottoman forces out of the Levant in World War I. After the Holocaust, large numbers of Jewish refugees from Europe had arrived there seeking refuge. In November 1947, the United Nations passed a partition plan to divide Palestine into two states, one Arab and one Jewish. In January 1948, partition was imminent – and so was war.

The bomb at the Semiramis Hotel was planted and detonated by the Haganah paramilitary group (a precursor to the IDF). The Haganah suspected that the hotel was one of two Arab headquarters in Qatamon and that it was an important meeting place for Arab fighters who distributed arms to villages in the Jerusalem area. The Haganah was also motivated by reports that Palestinian resistance leader Abdul Qader al-Husseini's distinctive white Jeep had been seen on that block. The group justified the bombing as self-defence following Arab attacks.

The enormous blast claimed the lives of about two dozen innocent civilians. Hardest hit among the casualties was the Lorenzo family, who managed the hotel. Eight coffins from one family. Manager Raouf Lorenzo and his wife, Irma, were killed alongside their eldest son, Hubert. Eyewitnesses reported that Hubert's dog, Brackie, would not leave the rubble until his master's body was recovered. Raouf and Irma left behind five surviving children. Raouf's four sisters – Nazira, Labibe, Marie and Eleonore – and Eleonore's husband, Lutfi Aboussouan, were also killed. Cooks, waiters and hotel staff and guests numbered among those killed and injured.[6]

British authorities strongly condemned the bombing. David Ben Gurion, who served as the chairman of the Jewish Agency Executive from 1935 to 1948 and would later become Israel's first prime minister, dismissed Mishael Shaham, the Haganah officer in charge of the Jerusalem area.

In the days that followed the bombing, there was a panicked exodus from Qatamon towards Jordan. The months of fear and instability, culminating in the incident, had finally broken the people's resistance. The Arabs who remained felt great anger towards those who left, feeling that they were making the choice the Jews wanted. What was left of the local Arab leadership tried to persuade people not to go. But the tide was impossible to halt.

Ghada Karmi's family fled to Damascus in April 1948 and later ended up in London. Her memoir about this period of her life, *In Search of Fatima*, is still read and studied across the world as an introduction to the Nakba.

The site of the Semiramis Hotel today

On January 5, 2021, I walked by the spot where the hotel once stood and found a plaque acknowledging the bombing by the Haganah, and listing the number of people killed and injured, but not their names. The bombing is framed as an 'apparently mistaken' defensive strike, amid a wider campaign against Arab violence in the area. The plaque made no reference to the desire stated by Yisrael Amir, the Jerusalem field commander of the Haganah, to 'strike a major blow in Arab Qatamon … that might force the Arabs out of the quarter and change the psychological climate in the city'.[7]

I posted about the place and what it means on my Facebook page, which has a large following among south Jerusalem residents:

Passing by this house today in Katamon, I must reflect on the tragedy that happened here on this very day in 1948.

Before the new apartment that you see in this picture on the corner of Hachish and Mehalkei Hamayim was built, this was the site of the three-storey Semiramis Hotel that operated during the Mandate period and was managed by two Palestinian Christian families, the Lorenzos and Aboussouans.

On March 27, 2002, 54 years after the Semiramis Hotel bombing, thirty Israelis were tragically murdered in the Passover bombing at the Park Hotel in Netanya. It was the deadliest attack against Israelis during the Second Intifada. Among the dead, the oldest was Chanah Rogan, 90. The youngest was Sivan Vider, who was 20.

Abbas al-Sayed, a grandson of one of the survivors of the Semiramis Hotel bombing, recruited and trained Adbel Basset Odeh who carried out the Park Hotel massacre. When Abbas was caught and imprisoned, he claimed that the attack in 2002 was to avenge the killing at the Semiramis Hotel in 1948.

I first learned about the connection between these two attacks on a tour of Katamon led by my Arabic teacher Anwar Ben Badis. I was shocked that al-Sayed had waited 54 years to take revenge, and even more so that the victims of his vengeance were all civilians enjoying a festive meal on the Jewish festival of Passover.

When I walk past this building today in Katamon, I mourn the loss of life which took place here and in the Park Hotel in Netanya. I pray that all the families who lost their loved ones in both attacks can find the courage to honour the memory of their loved ones by turning away from revenge and embracing life.

May the memories of all be a blessing for peace.

The responses to the post were mixed. Some residents who had lived in the neighbourhood for their whole lives thanked me for sharing this little-known history of their childhood streets, which had never been taught in Israeli schools. Others were furious at the comparison I made between the two hotel bombings, as if I were trying to justify one because of the other.

I explained that I abhor all forms of violence and was simply sharing what I'd learned from a guide when I toured the neighbourhood. I also hoped that no more houses or hotels filled with people might ever be blown up in the name of any ideology, or historical or recent trauma.

Writing this in 2024, I can say it is, sadly, a wish that never came true.

The road untravelled

Studying history, one often comes across fascinating ideas and plans that were never realised. As the United Nations debated how to prevent the inevitable war in 1948, Rabbi Judah Magnes, who was the president of the Hebrew University of Jerusalem, presented an idea to the United Nations Special Committee on Palestine (UNSCOP) that never generated much interest or support. It's probably what I would have supported had I been

Before this new apartment in Katamon was built, this was the site of the three-storey Semiramis Hotel that operated during the Mandate period, managed by two Palestinian Christian families, the Lorenzos and Aboussouans.

alive then. Magnes advocated for a unified, binational Jewish–Arab state, instead of splitting the land between two states or between a Jewish state and Jordan.

During his testimony before UNSCOP, Magnes asserted that cooperation between Jewish and Arab communities was not only possible for achieving peace in the region but also the ideal. He proposed a binational state in which all citizens would enjoy equal rights, regardless of demographic majority or minority status. According to his plan, Jews and Arabs would each have their own separate 'national committees' overseen by a supreme governing council. In his vision of the shared state, Magnes emphasised that each community would maintain its religious practices, customs and cultural values, including their respective educational and legal systems. He envisaged the binational state as akin to a federation of two states without territorial division.

Furthermore, Magnes contended that the land of Israel does not exclusively belong to either Jews or Arabs. He argued that Arabs have substantial ancestral rights to the land, having inhabited and cultivated it for generations. What he said was true. Palestine has no fewer graves of significant Palestinians than Israel has graves with significant Jews; heroes to both nations are buried here.

Magnes also warned against the impracticality and consequences of one group dominating the other, foreseeing conflicts, unrest and rebellions.

Despite knowing that the concept of a binational state had little support among Jews and none among Arabs, Magnes persisted in his pursuit of this vision until the end of his life.

His actions reminded me of a similar Palestinian leader who also called for sharing the land but never obtained much support from his people for the idea. Raghib al-Nashashibi was a civil engineer with much political talent, and he was the mayor of Jerusalem from 1920 to 1934. During an election in 1927, most of the Jews in the city voted for him because he directed many badly needed public-works projects, such as new roads, a sewerage system and new water pipes. He also initially supported the British proposal to partition Palestine in 1937 and opposed armed rebellion against the British.

I often wonder what my life would have looked like today if the dreams of Magnes and Nashashibi had become realities. How many lives would have been saved? How many children that were never born could have done wonders for this place had Jews and Palestinians shared this land in peace from day one?

Magnes's ideas were built on the thinking of fellow Hebrew University professor Martin Buber. Buber was a resident of Jerusalem's Rehavia neighbourhood and famous for his book *I and Thou*, published in 1923. Buber's critique of objectification in human relationships with both other humans and God was a philosophy that appealed to me greatly and was the subject of my academic research when I was a student at the Hebrew University in the same building where he once taught.

At the Twelfth Zionist Congress in 1921, Buber proposed a resolution committing the Zionist leadership to 'establishing a just alliance with the Arab peoples'. It read: 'We do not aspire to return to the Land of Israel with which we have inseparable historical and spiritual ties to suppress another people or dominate them. In this land, whose population is sparse and scattered, there is room for us and its present inhabitants.'[8]

Sadly, for the future of those who believe in a different form of nationalism, the dreams of Buber, Magnus and Nashashibi are no more than footnotes in history today.

In 1947, their vision for a shared future on this land was rejected by the majority of Palestinians. It was also shunned by the majority of Zionists. As I reflect on our situation today, it feels like the issues that started our wars in 1948 are the furthest away they have ever been from being resolved.

One can only hope that our future leaders learn from the mistakes of the past. That they will avoid all-or-nothing solutions that cause so much death and destruction, embracing instead a middle path of moderation and compromise, sometimes sacrificing the dream of the perfect so that all can live in the reality of the good.

CHAPTER 4

The first Palestinian–Zionist dialogue

Dialogue is always preferable to war. That's something I believe today and a truth I have known for many years, despite how often I'm called delusional for believing that the most bitter of enemies can one day find compromise around a negotiation table. In understanding the history of Jewish–Arab interactions in this land, there is still one exchange of letters that, for me, stands out more than any other.

The first meaningful correspondence between a Palestinian leader and a Zionist leader happened in 1899. It was a pair of letters written in French and sent across an ocean. So many of the sentiments contained within them would be rare to hear today, yet others feel like they were written yesterday.

Yusuf Diya al-Din Pasha al-Khalidi wrote the first letter. As the mayor of Jerusalem, al-Khalidi had firsthand experience of the tensions among the local population that had been triggered by the arrival of the first European Jewish settlers in the 1880s.

His great-great-nephew Rashid Khalidi, an esteemed academic of Palestinian history, wrote of his ancestor that he had a deep understanding of the foundations of Zionism, particularly as a reaction to the intense antisemitism in Christian Europe.

Mayor al-Khalidi was familiar with *Der Judenstaat*, written by Theodor Herzl, the Viennese journalist who founded the modern Zionist movement. He was aware of the debates between Zionist leaders about whether a Jewish state should be established in British East Africa (Uganda) or Palestine, and in 1899 he penned the following letter to Theodor Herzl.

Dear Theodor Herzl,
I flatter myself to think that I need not speak of my feelings towards your people. As far as the Israelites are concerned, I really do regard them as relatives of us Arabs; for us they are cousins; we really do have the same father, Abraham, from whom we are also descended. There are a lot of affinities between the two races; we have almost the same language. Politically, moreover, I am convinced that the Jews and Arabs will do well to support each other if they are to resist the invaders of other races. It is these sentiments that put me at ease to speak frankly to you about the great question that is currently agitating your people.

You are well aware that I am talking about Zionism. The idea in itself is only natural, beautiful and just. Who can dispute the rights of the Jews to Palestine? My God, historically, it is your country! And what a marvellous spectacle it would be if the Jews, so gifted, were once again reconstituted as an independent nation, respected, happy, able to render services to poor humanity in the moral domain as in the past!

Unfortunately, the destinies of nations are not governed solely by these abstract conceptions, however pure, however noble they may be. We must reckon with reality, with established facts, with force, yes, with the brutal force of circumstances. But the reality is that Palestine is now an integral part of the Ottoman Empire and, what is more serious, it is inhabited by people other than only Israelites.

This reality, these acquired facts, this brutal force of circumstances leave Zionism, geographically, no hope of realisation. Jews certainly possess capital and intelligence. But however great the power of money in this world, one cannot buy millions all at once. To achieve a goal like the one that Zionism must propose, other, more formidable blows are needed, those of cannons and battleships. And even the nations best disposed towards the Jews, like the English and the Americans, I do not believe that they will ever agree to go to war against other nations to help the Jews settle in Palestine.

Therefore, in the name of God, let Palestine be left alone.

Whenever I teach students about this letter in my dual-narrative history classes, the first point I highlight is the respect and understanding al-Khalidi has for both the Jewish people in general and Herzl personally. He also knows enough about Jewish history to write, 'Who can deny the rights of the Jews to Palestine? My God, historically, it is your country!'

This isn't something Jews hear often today from advocates for Palestine. At the same time, he also concludes by noting, 'Therefore, in the name of God, let Palestine be left alone,' which is certainly something Jews often hear from advocates for Palestine today.

A week later, the following letter was written by Dr Theodor Herzl in reply.

Carl Ludwigstrasse 50
Währing district, Vienna
19 March 1899

Excellency,
Let me tell you first of all that the feelings of friendship
which you express for the Jewish people inspire in me the
deepest appreciation.

    The Zionist idea, of which I am the humble servant,
has no hostile tendency toward the Ottoman Government,
but quite to the contrary this movement is concerned
with opening up new resources for the Ottoman Empire.
In allowing immigration to a number of Jews bringing
their intelligence, their financial acumen and their means
of enterprise to the country, no one can doubt that the
wellbeing of the entire country would be the happy result.
It is necessary to understand this, and make it known to
everybody.

    As Your Excellency said very well in your letter, the
Jews have no belligerent power behind them, neither are
they themselves of a warlike nature. They are a completely
peaceful element, and very content if they are left in peace.

Therefore, there is absolutely nothing to fear from their immigration.

The question of the Holy Places?

But no one thinks of ever touching those. As I have said and written many times: These places have lost forever the faculty of belonging exclusively to one faith, to one race or to one people. The Holy Places are and will remain holy for all the world, for the Muslims as for the Christians as for the Jews. The universal peace which all men of good will ardently hope for will have its symbol in a brotherly union in the Holy Places.

You see another difficulty, Excellency, in the existence of the non-Jewish population in Palestine. But who would think of sending them away? It is their wellbeing, their individual wealth which we will increase by bringing in our own. Do you think that an Arab who owns land or a house in Palestine worth three or four thousand francs will be very angry to see the price of his land rise in a short time, to see it rise five and ten times in value perhaps in a few months? Moreover, that will necessarily happen with the arrival of the Jews. That is what the indigenous population must realize, that they will gain excellent brothers as the Sultan will gain faithful and good subjects who will make this province flourish – this province which is their historic homeland.

When one looks at the situation in this light, which is the true one, one must be the friend of Zionism when one is the friend of Turkey.

I hope, Excellency, that these few explanations will suffice to give you a little more sympathy for our movement.

You tell Jews that we would do better to go somewhere else. That may well happen the day we realise that Turkey does not understand the enormous advantages that our movement offers it. We have explained our aim publicly, sincerely and loyally. I have submitted to His Majesty the Sultan some general propositions, and I am pleased to believe that the extreme clearness of his mind will make him accept in principle the idea of which one can afterwards discuss the details of execution. If he will not accept it, we will search and, believe me, we will find elsewhere what we need.

But then Turkey will have lost its last chance to regulate its finances and to recover its economic vigour.

It is a sincere friend of the Turks who tells you these things today. Remember that!

And accept, Excellency, the assurance of my very high consideration.

Reading this letter today the part that surprises me most is Herzl's offer to seek to establish a Jewish national home elsewhere if the Zionist movement didn't win the favour of the Ottoman Empire. This is something no Zionist would say today. I also appreciate the respect and esteem Herzl had towards al-Khalidi, and his promise to ensure holy places would be sites of brotherly union. Sadly, in the reality of today, the two most disputed holy sites – the Temple Mount/Al-Aqsa Mosque in Jerusalem and the Cave of the Patriarchs/Sanctuary of Abraham in Hebron – are also two of the least safe and most violent areas of the Holy Land. Every time I hear about unholy discord around these two places of prayer, I feel the opposite of the 'brotherly love' their physical presence is supposed to represent according to the sacred texts of both Judaism and Islam.

Rashid Khalidi reads Herzl's letter as a 'colonial document', especially the part where he refers to the Palestinians, then approximately 92% of the population, as the land's 'non-Jewish population'. He also notes in an article published in *The Intercept* that the letter simply glossed over the fact that Zionism was ultimately meant to lead to Jewish domination of Palestine: 'Herzl employed a justification that has been a touchstone for colonialists at all times and in all places and that would become a staple argument of the Zionist movement: Jewish immigration would economically benefit the indigenous people of Palestine.'[1]

Most revealingly, to Khalidi, the letter addresses a consideration that al-Khalidi had not even raised. 'You see another difficulty, Excellency,' Herzl wrote, 'in the existence of the non-Jewish population in Palestine. But who would think of sending them away?' Yet in order for Zionism to reach its goal of establishing a Jewish majority in the land with defensible borders, this is exactly what happened in 1948 when 750,000 Palestinians were expelled from their homes in the Nakba.

To me, these two letters are the first warning signs that Jewish and Arab self-determination will not be realised peacefully if the vision of one comes at the expense of the other. Herzl's dream ultimately came true. In 2021, Israel was for the first time listed among the top 20 global economies by GDP per capita.[2] His vision of a Jewish state becoming the economic powerhouse of the Middle East, or as some call it today, a start-up nation, has now been realised.

Al-Khalidi was right that no amount of economic advancement could ever remove the desire of Palestinians to be a free people in their homeland. He was also right that Zionism would only eventually achieve its goals of Jewish self-determination through 'formidable blows from cannons and battleships'. However, he was wrong about the English and the Americans, who have many times gone to war siding with Israel and against many other nations to help the Jews remain safe in the land they have made their home again.

Beyond their historical intricacies, these two letters allude to a deeper tension that lies at the heart of the conflict today. Beyond this being a dispute over land, holy places and the right to build and live safely on ancestral land, this conflict is also a battle of narratives. It's a battle of stories we tell ourselves, of pain we have caused one another that may never be forgiven and of the dreams that must be fulfilled.

This battle of narratives, of who has the greatest right to the land, is not just fought in Palestine and Israel. It is also being fought on the other side of the world in Australia.

CHAPTER 5

Indigenous Australians, Jews and Palestinians

Before the Dreaming, the Australian continent was a flat, featureless place, devoid of life.

Then, giant beings came down from the sky, came from across the sea and emerged from the thin earth. With their arrival, the Dreaming began, and life was born.

In the north of Australia, one of many beings, the Djang'kawu sisters, gave birth to humanity.

In central Australia, Itakawarra broke the marriage laws and, as punishment, was turned into stone, forever entombed in the landscape.

On the east coast, Biame shaped the landscape, and when his work was complete, he stepped onto a mountain and back into the sky.

These beings, part animal, part human, travelled the country, dancing, hunting, making love and war. As they moved across the land, their bodies shaped the earth, creating the rivers and mountain ranges. In everything they touched they left their essence, making the landscape sacred to those who honour the dreaming, the First Australians.

– Rachel Perkins and Marcia Langton,
The First Australians[1]

I begin this chapter by sharing this creation story because I assume most Australians don't know it. For many of us over 40, myself included, our education informed us that Australian history began when Captain Cook 'discovered' Australia in 1770. Growing up as a child in the 1980s, I still have vivid memories of 'Colonial Day' at school, when all the boys dressed as British sailors and the girls wore large dresses or court gowns as we played old-time English games, drank tea and sang 'Bound for Botany Bay'. At one point in the day, a tall, barefoot Aboriginal man showed us how to light a fire without matches, which we all thought was incredible. He rubbed two sticks together over a handful of straw until there was smoke, then fire. He then showed us how to throw a large, oddly shaped stick that could magically turn mid-air and come right back into his arms. Both the fire-starting and boomerang-throwing were strangely fascinating for all the youngsters at school that day. But these events also stereotyped Indigenous people as cavemen, living without knowledge of modern luxuries, still walking around in loincloths with no shoes. While I later learned much more about Aboriginal culture, that's the most powerful memory from my education about Australian history.

After I finished school, I spent many years researching the First Nations people of Australia through books, movies, podcasts and conversations with them. I undertook this learning because I felt that, as an immigrant, I could never really understand or connect to the land where I was living without this knowledge.

One person I spoke to was Bruce Pascoe, professor of Indigenous agriculture at Melbourne University. I was amazed to learn that before colonisation, the Australian continent had supported over 1.6 billion lives over 60,000 years. Aboriginal and Torres Strait Islander peoples were able to make a land with unreliable rainfall, on the driest continent on earth, a place for life to flourish. In the words of Pascoe, 'Sixty thousand years makes Aboriginal people the longest-living civilisation on earth. If you can't learn from people who are that successful, then you are really defying your own intelligence.' That quote opens the excellent SBS documentary *The First Australians*.

Then came the horror. Without listing here all the terrible crimes committed against the Aboriginal people, the first entry in Captain Cook's diary on April 29, 1770, says so much. Cook describes trying to come ashore off Botany Bay and encountering two Aboriginal men who threw darts and stones at the British, whereupon Cook fired his musket at them three times until they withdrew.

From the first contact between the British and Indigenous people, the scene was set for catastrophic relations.

A Jewish balanda in Yolngu country

Six in ten white Australians claim they have never met an Indigenous person.[2] My first contact with someone Indigenous happened a long way from Botany Bay. In 2011, I spent five days on Galiwin'ku (Elcho Island). An hour's flight northeast of Darwin, this tiny island is home to around 2000 people. Today it is the largest and most remote Aboriginal community in northeast Arnhem Land and the second-largest Aboriginal community (in terms of concentrated population) in the Northern Territory. Most of the island's population are children. Only 7% are aged over 50.

I visited there as part of a five-day program for students from Mount Scopus Memorial College, where I was a Jewish studies teacher. Throughout our time there, the locals referred to the people in our group as 'balanda', which means 'white person' in the Yolngu language.

The experience shaped me profoundly. Learning about the law and ceremony of the Yolngu people and seeing how they practise their culture, despite all the pressures from the modern world that undermine their traditions, was remarkable.

One afternoon, an elder took us to the beach. We followed him on the soft sand until he stopped at a very specific location. He told us to walk a few metres into the sea, where there was a small sinkhole. As every student took two steps into the water, they suddenly dropped about half a metre into the sandbank. He then told us, 'This is the place from which the world was created by the Djang'kawu sisters.' It reminded me of the Islamic stories around the Kaaba in Mecca, and the Jewish stories around the stone that lies at the heart of the Temple Mount. Standing in that very spot where the story transpired felt surreal.

According to the Dreaming, the Djang'kawu sisters once stood at that exact location. They descended from the sky in a canoe and then journeyed across the land, singing and naming what they encountered. They carried sacred objects known as rangga, and digging sticks. As they touched the ground with their sticks, different landforms, water wells and plant and animal life sprouted forth. The sisters were constantly pregnant, and their children populated the world. One night while the sisters slept, their brother stole the sacred objects from them. Initially, the sisters had both male and female sexual organs, but their brothers cut off the male parts.

The Djang'kawu story is about fertility and the creation of life on earth. It also emphasises that men hold the power to perform sacred rituals.

For me, the story had so many echoes of the one I grew up with about Adam and Eve in the Garden of Eden, and how the sin of eating the fruit cursed women to forever suffer in childbirth and men to make bread through the sweat of their brow. Unlike the Yolngu, it had never occurred to my Jewish Studies educators to teach the story of the Garden of Eden through re-enactment. Instead, we learned through books. That afternoon on Elcho Island, the elders invited us into a ceremony to re-enact their creation story.

The girls in the group were invited to participate in the Yolngu ceremony. It included a combination of sets, props, body painting, dancing to the music of clapsticks and beautiful singing.

The re-enactment of the story of the ancestral beings who created the land served as both a way of handing down the tradition and an affirmation of tribal customs and laws.

Yorta Yorta Beyachad

Following my experience on Elcho Island, I requested that our school introduce a subject called Teaching Australian History through Aboriginal Eyes. After much consultation with Jewish social-justice organisation Stand Up, which specialises in facilitating education and advocacy for Indigenous rights, a new Year 9 elective was born: Aboriginal studies. The first cohort in 2014 had just ten students. The course included two lessons a week over a semester, culminating in a three-day trip to Shepparton and Cummeragunja on the border of New South Wales and Victoria. The trip up north was called Yorta Yorta Beyachad, with the final word meaning 'together' in Hebrew. We chose the name in recognition of the longstanding relationship between Jewish people and the Yorta Yorta nation, from the time of William Cooper (see further on) to the present.

Teaching this elective was both a privilege and an enormous challenge. Finding space for any new subject in an already crowded curriculum is difficult, so I was thrilled that my school trusted me and saw the importance of greenlighting the project. The challenge I faced at the time was trying to teach a subject that had no textbook, no professional subject association where other teachers could network, and no other educators at the school teaching it.

I spent almost my entire summer break reading excerpts from various books and articles, attending conferences, compiling education materials, visiting museums and editing film clips that could be suitable for Year 9 students. One of the most powerful resources I encountered was an ABC miniseries called *The Secret River*. It's based on the 2005 historical novel by Kate Grenville about an early 19th-century Englishman transported to Australia for theft. With exceptional beauty and heartbreak, it brings the viewer into the life of its central character, William

Thornhill. Like many parents, Thornhill sees Australia as a land of growth and opportunity for his young family. However, the story ends horrifically, with him joining a British militia that carries out a brutal massacre of Indigenous people. In the end, the few Indigenous survivors become workers on his farm, subdued and broken.

Based on true events that took place on the majestic Hawkesbury River in the area now known as Wisemans Ferry, near Sydney, *The Secret River* captured much about the Frontier Wars that I had been reluctant to face to that point. When I lived in Australia, I would watch the miniseries every year on January 26, as an act of recognition of the pain that so many Aboriginal people still feel on that day. I would spend the rest of the day with friends, having a barbecue, listening to triple j's Hottest 100 and enjoying the sunshine, but always knowing that the independence and freedom I was celebrating was not a universal experience.

For many of the students in the Yorta Yorta Beyachad program, their experience of watching *The Secret River*, and learning about Aboriginal history from the Dreaming to Mabo and beyond, also gave them a great deal more empathy with First Nations peoples.

Students would often note in their class evaluations that the course was life-changing for two reasons. For many, it was the first time they'd had the opportunity to meet and hear Indigenous people on country, such as Shane Charles, whose Dreaming tour of the Barmah Forest left them feeling connected to the earth and trees in ways they had never imagined. In a school that has an abundance of seminars and learning activities to explore their Jewish or Zionist identities, for most students it was also the first time they had ever seriously contemplated their Australian identity and been asked to consider what responsibilities came with their newfound knowledge.

The fact that Yorta Yorta Beyachad still exists as a program at Scopus, having run every year since 2014, is one of the achievements I am most proud of as an educator.

Jewish solidarity with First Nations people

Many Jewish Australians have a strong sense of solidarity and support for Aboriginal people, far beyond the rate of the general population. These people include Ron Castan AM QC, who was the senior counsel on the 1992 Mabo case – in which the High Court overturned the fiction of terra nullius, the British claim that the continent belonged to no one before they arrived – and philanthropist Sandra Bardas OAM, who helped create Worawa College, Victoria's first fully independent Indigenous secondary college.

Explaining his motivation for his activism, Castan once said, 'My determination not to stand by and see the Jewish people downtrodden and persecuted was meaningless if I was standing by and seeing another oppressed people downtrodden and persecuted within my own country.'[3]

Beyond sharing a history of discrimination that many Jews and First Australians carry with them, almost all stories of Jewish–Aboriginal solidarity begin with the courage of William Cooper. A revered Yorta Yorta leader, Cooper dedicated his life to advocating for the rights of his people and all marginalised communities. In December 1938, he led a march to the German Consulate in Melbourne to protest the Nazi mistreatment of Jewish people.

The story of Cooper's stand on behalf of the Jewish community deeply moved Mark Leibler AC, a prominent Melbourne lawyer and Zionist leader, when he learned about it in the 1990s. He explained in a piece published in the *Australian Jewish News* that when he was a young boy, he learned almost nothing about Australia's Indigenous history. 'I was not aware of having met an Aboriginal person until the 1990s, when my firm started to advise the Yorta Yorta peoples in their epic struggle for native title,' he wrote. 'Three decades later, they remain our clients and friends, alongside many other Indigenous businesses and community organisations.'[4]

After meeting with Yorta Yorta claimants Monica Morgan and Uncle Henry Atkinson, Leibler was amazed to learn that William Cooper was Morgan's grandfather. He felt he finally comprehended the ongoing injustice faced by Indigenous Australians, whose story is scarred by dispossession, prejudice and racism, as is the story of the Jewish people. He promised that his firm would stand by the Yorta Yorta people for as long as necessary.

These two motivations of Ron Castan and Mark Leibler, namely remembering our common history of persecution and honouring the memory of William Cooper, are shared by many Jewish Australians. For example, in the 2023 referendum on the Voice to Parliament, only 39% of Australians voted in favour of the constitutional amendment that would have recognised Aboriginal and Torres Strait Islander people in the constitution and given them a voice in the passing of laws that would affect their lives. Yet in the electorate of Macnamara, which has the highest Jewish population in Australia, the YES vote was 64% overall, and an incredible 81% in the St Kilda polling booth.[5]

Aboriginal solidarity with Palestinians

Despite the examples above, for the vast majority of Indigenous Australians, there is far more solidarity with the Palestinian cause of freedom than the cause of Zionism.

Some of the most prominent Indigenous Australians for Palestine include Senator Lidia Thorpe, Malyangapa and Barkindji rapper Barkaa, GetUp CEO and Widjabul Wia-bul woman from Bundjalung Country Larrisa Baldwin, Celeste Liddle, Emily Wurramara, Darumbal and South Sea Islander journalist Amy McQuire, and Aboriginal historian and activist Gary Foley.[6]

According to Australian Palestinian community organiser Noura Mansour, support for First Nations' justice and self-determination has also become an integral part of the movement for Palestine in Australia. The solidarity stems from a shared identity as victims of colonisation and dispossession. This connection became so intrinsic that by January 26, 2024, the Invasion Day rally had so many green, black and red flags that it appeared indistinguishable from a Free Palestine rally.[7]

On the other hand, there are also some prominent Indigenous leaders who are sympathetic to Israel such as Noel Pearson, Nyunggai Warren Mundine and Marcia Langton. Most prominent among them is former Olympian and Labor Senator Nova Peris who explained on a podcast in 2024: 'As an Aboriginal woman, I'm one of four generations that lived under Australia's greatest lie of terra nullius. The Jewish community was instrumental in overturning that lie. I want to reciprocate by helping overturn a similar lie which is being told against the Jewish people – that they have no connection to the land of Israel and are settler-colonialists.'[8]

Truth and reconciliation

Many Australian prime ministers in the modern era have recognised the suffering of the Aboriginal people, the first being Paul Keating, who acknowledged in his famous Redfern speech of 1992:

> It was we who did the dispossessing. We took the
> traditional lands and smashed the traditional way of life.
> We brought the diseases and the alcohol. We committed
> the murders. We took the children from their mothers.
> We practised discrimination and exclusion. It was our
> ignorance and our prejudice and our failure to imagine
> that these things could be done to us.

Today, it's hard to imagine a process of recognition happening between Israeli and Palestinian leaders.

In Australia, it is not disputed that First Nations peoples are indigenous to the land. But in Israel–Palestine, the question of who holds a stronger claim to being indigenous is both complex and highly debated. Both Jewish Israelis and Palestinians possess deep historical ties to the land. However, focusing on these competing claims of indigeneity is unlikely to foster peace. The national identities that led to a demand for statehood for both groups were largely formed around the same period, starting with intellectual movements in the 1880s and expanding into mass movements in the 20th century. As with all nations, their identities are constructed rather than inherent, shaped by choices about how to define themselves.[9] But this does not make them any less real.

Unfortunately, both sides often challenge the legitimacy of the other's national identity. Palestinian leaders, for instance, often characterise Jewishness solely as a religion, therefore denying the legitimacy of a Jewish nation-state. Similarly, many in Zionist circles dismiss Palestinian national identity, claiming that Palestinians are a completely modern and invented people with no history before the formation of the PLO in 1964.

Yet for there to be peace, there must be a reconciliation process to support Israelis and Palestinians who are ready to acknowledge the place of the other on the land and the hurt caused over so many years of war. Such a process can begin by acknowledging that the pain of the victims and the families who ultimately bury their loved ones is always the same.

From that pain, whether it be felt by an Israeli or a Palestinian, an Indigenous or immigrant Australian, one can only hope the desire for revenge and hatred is overcome by movements that build justice, security and equality for all.

On the night following Israel's 75th Yom Ha'atzmaut – Independence Day – a documentary was screened by Emet, a new collective of young Jews in Australia who 'envision a community that stands for freedom and justice by ending our community's support for the Occupation'. The documentary *Tantura* explores the 1948 massacre in the Palestinian village of Tantura and ponders the question of whether Israel has anything to learn from the Australian experience of reconciliation, which is still ongoing.

There is a scene in the film where a Jewish-Israeli man compares the situation in his homeland with Australia. Noting that despite the inherited inequality towards Indigenous Australians that still exists today, he remarks that at least Australia has matured to the level where it can acknowledge the injustice done, through acts like the 1992 Mabo decision of the High Court, as well as former prime minister Kevin Rudd's national apology of 2008, and the Acknowledgment of Country affirmations made at most public events.

He then compares the Frontier Wars in Australia from 1788 to 1934 to the Nakba, noting that acknowledgment of the latter 'doesn't even glitter on the horizon of public life in Israel'.

In the documentary, we also meet four elderly members of Kibbutz Nachsholim, located where Tantura once stood, who discuss whether it would be appropriate to erect a monument on the kibbutz in honour of those from Tantura who were killed. One said that it wouldn't be appropriate because 'if it's important to them, it harms me'. Another supported building a monument, saying, 'They have the right to remember.'

Reflecting on this reality, one can't help wondering what would happen to relations between Israelis and Palestinians if a peace process existed that didn't just talk about borders on maps, but also included a truth and reconciliation process that involved understanding the historical narrative of the other.

A September 2024 report by the Palestinian–Israeli pollster team of Khalil Shikaki and Dahlia Scheindlin explored this possibility and found that among Israelis initially opposed to a comprehensive agreement, support for peace increases most if the Palestinian government combats incitement against Israel (60%) and the Palestinian State recognises Israel as the State of the Jewish people with equal rights for Arabs (59%). Support for peace among Palestinians increases from 34% to 49% if Israel acknowledges Palestinian historic and religious links to historic Palestine and 54% if Palestinian refugees receive monetary compensation for what they lost in the Nakba.[10]

Together with other confidence-building measures, the survey highlighted the impact that acknowledging one another could have on populations that currently oppose any form of compromise.

Voting in the Voice referendum from Israel

Australia is geographically at the end of the earth for most Israelis. Seeing the island continent continue to struggle with its legacy of settlement 235 years after Captain Arthur Philip first declared the area in Sydney where he landed as belonging exclusively to King George III, one can only hope that Israelis and Palestinians won't have to wait that long for our reconciliation process to begin.

I had this thought very much at the forefront of my mind when I lodged a pre-poll vote on October 3, 2023, from the Australian Embassy in Tel Aviv. While I voted YES, I couldn't help but feel that it was deeply unfair that whether or not Aboriginal and Torres Strait Islanders would have a voice in parliament on laws that affect them was up to me and the other 97% of Australians who had no history in the country prior to 1788. I asked myself, why should we, who came by boat or by plane, be the ones to determine the rights of those who have survived and thrived on one the driest continents on earth for over 60,000 years?

On the other hand, voting from a location overlooking the Mediterranean Sea, which many of my Jewish ancestors passed by boat or by plane on their way to Palestine from 1882 onwards to build and be rebuilt, added another dimension. At that time, Jews were only approximately 5% of the total population here. Today, the character of Israel is one that privileges my people over the historic Arab and Palestinian population in so many ways that could be different if they had a voice that was heard in the laws passed by the Zionist government that affects their lives.

So, while I voted only once that day, deep down I wanted to vote twice. Once for the First Nations of Australia who deeply deserve a voice, and once for justice and equality for all peoples who share this land between the river and sea.

Putting that slip of paper into the ballot box, I also said a little prayer for the future, hoping that at the end of a meaningful truth and reconciliation process, a government may one day exist on the shores of the Mediterranean that hears and represents the voices of every person under its jurisdiction so that laws no longer favour one specific group at the expense of another, but rather are made for the common good.

When I moved to Jerusalem in 2018, I was privileged to work in an organisation that had this vision as their goal.

CHAPTER 6

Keeping hope alive:
Inside Jerusalem's youth
movement for peace

Since August 2018, I have been the education director of
Kids4Peace Jerusalem, an interfaith youth movement that
brings together Jewish, Muslim and Christian children for
biweekly dialogue programs, overnight seminars and summer
camps. Kids4Peace is a member of ALMEP, the Alliance for
Middle East Peace, comprising over 160 member organisations.
Kids4Peace merged with Seeds of Peace in 2020.

Until January 2024, Kids4Peace Jerusalem operated out of
an office located in the heart of Sheikh Jarrah. Its very existence
in the most disputed neighbourhood of Jerusalem, amid one of
the most intractable conflicts of our generation, was something
I found remarkable. Working there with our community
manager, Suma Qawasmi, and education co-director, Angham
Hussein, I have learned a great deal about Jerusalem that one

could never discover in any other way. When Suma and I speak to groups from abroad about our work, she often says that our organisation is a place for youth to meet in a healthy way. Unlike her experience of Jerusalem, where Palestinian interactions with Jews mainly happen at checkpoints in a hostile environment, Kids4Peace gives kids a positive atmosphere for interaction, allowing them to see one another from a different perspective and accept that we all need to feel at home here and live side by side.

In Neil Postman's 1982 book *The Disappearance of Childhood*, he wrote: 'Children are the living messages we send to a time we will not see.'[1] This quote reminds me that children are not simply our progeny but also our cultural messengers, and we will not be around to see the world that our children create. We can only partially judge our success as parents and educators based on the messages we send them. If we raise them to be empathetic, humble and compassionate, we can be confident that they will make the world fairer and more just. But if we don't, then the society that the children of Jerusalem will create will sadly appear not much different from the tense and polarised city that exists today.

Henry Ralph Carse: Refusing war to discover peace

The founder and first executive director of the Kids4Peace movement ('Kids4Peace International') was Dr Henry Ralph Carse, a native of Vermont in the United States, who made the Holy Land his home in 1970. Raised in the Roman Catholic tradition, Carse was inspired by the spirituality of Thomas Merton and Mahatma Gandhi, and he left his home country rather than be drafted to fight in the Vietnam War. His pilgrimage of dissent brought him through many adventures to his new home in Jerusalem, a city he saw as a symbol of hope and peace.

In the 1980s, Carse married a Jewish-Israeli woman and started a family. In accordance with the laws of Israel, he had citizenship conferred upon him due to his marriage to a Jewish person. He soon received a call-up notice and was drafted into the IDF in 1985. His early pacifist leanings were deeply challenged during his active service in the IDF, especially as this was a time of increased tension between Palestinians and Israelis – an escalation called the First Intifada. After witnessing horrific human rights abuses against Palestinians in the Occupied West Bank, and especially in the El Arroub refugee camp, he felt devastated and betrayed. He came to believe that the promises of Zionism that he had listened to, so hopefully, did not have integrity in real life. He now felt complicit in the wrongs perpetuated by the IDF on Palestinian land and the humiliation of Palestinian society. From this emotional low point in his life, Carse crossed a threshold, committing himself to transforming the status quo.

By 2001, Carse was teaching and guiding pilgrims at St George's College in Jerusalem, a continuing education centre of the Anglican Communion. As a peace activist and interfaith scholar, he was deeply concerned for the children of Israel and Palestine – Muslims, Christians and Jews – once again caught in the crossfire as the conflict escalated yet again in the Second Intifada.

Carse's work as a guide and teacher brought him into contact with Christian pilgrims from the world over, including many Episcopalians (Anglicans) from the United

States. Moved by the distress of Palestinians and Israelis in conflict, these pilgrims often asked what they could do to help. In September of 2001, Carse first suggested a dialogue initiative for children from both sides of the conflict. The idea was wholeheartedly approved by Carse's employers at the Episcopal Diocese of Jerusalem, and the first Kids4Peace group was collegially formed the very next year.

Around them, the violence of the Second Intifada continued. Even though I wasn't living in Jerusalem at the time, I still remember my shock and horror in August 2001 when I learned that a Hamas suicide bomber had carried out an attack at 2 pm on a warm summer's day in the popular Sbarro pizzeria in the centre of Jerusalem. Given the heat that day, more people than usual were eating inside to get cool from the air conditioning, with most patrons being mothers with children. Fifteen Israelis were murdered, and over 130 were injured. One of the victims was Malki Roth, a 15-year-old Australian.

In June 2002, 19 people were killed and 74 injured by a Hamas suicide bombing in a bus travelling from Gilo to the centre of Jerusalem. Many of the passengers were students on their way to school.

In September 2003, seven people were killed and over 50 wounded in a suicide bombing at Cafe Hillel on Emek Refaim Street, the main thoroughfare of the German Colony in Jerusalem, which is the neighbourhood I live in today.

Each of these suicide bombings was followed by intense attacks by the IDF against Hamas in the West Bank, often resulting in the killing of innocent bystanders – many of them children. Palestinians in Jerusalem often encountered restrictions on their movement. A growing number of checkpoints and barriers limited their ability to travel freely within the city and to other parts of the West Bank. Many had their homes demolished, a common occurrence due to Israel's restrictive building-permit policies for Palestinians.

For many years, grassroots dialogue initiatives involving Palestinians and Israelis, with a view to effecting peace in the Middle East, had focused entirely on political solutions. Each of these had, in its turn, failed to deliver on its promise of enduring peace; as a result, people on both sides now felt betrayed and disheartened. By contrast, Carse and his Jewish, Muslim and Christian colleagues in Kids4Peace asked what tools for peacemaking are embedded in the spiritual traditions of their respective faiths, and how these tools might be used to forge a unified youth movement for peace, with a strong basis in faith and spirituality.

The Kids4Peace movement was born. The first full-fledged dialogue experience was generously hosted by an Episcopal summer camp near Houston, Texas, in the summer of 2002. This was followed by Kids4Peace chapters opening in Georgia, Vermont, North Carolina and Canada. Meanwhile, at its point of origin, Jerusalem, Kids4Peace encounters and dialogue continued, bringing together more and more diverse Israeli and Palestinian youngsters and their families.

From an Australian classroom to a Jerusalem youth movement

In July 2018, six months after leaving Melbourne for Jerusalem, I applied to work at Kids4Peace. Until that point, my two main experiences doing this type of work came from my five-year stint as the regional coordinator of the interfaith dialogue in schools program, Building Bridges, which brought together Jewish,

Christian and Muslim high-school students in Melbourne, and coordinating the Yorta Yorta Beyachad program at Scopus, which facilitated encounters between Jewish students and Aboriginal elders. Yet neither experience adequately prepared me for facilitating dialogue between Jerusalem youth, who not only saw or experienced violence on a regular basis but didn't even have a language in common.

Jerusalem is unlike any other city in the country, and its conflicts are unlike those of any other place. Until the Six-Day War in 1967, its eastern side, including the Old City, was part of Jordan and its western side was part of Israel. Today, there is no marker on the old 1967 borderline that divided east and west, with part of it now being the route of the light rail, which is the most popular form of public transport in the city. Yet the city has no shortage of walls, checkpoints and fences that divide its Jewish and Arab inhabitants both between and sometimes even within certain neighbourhoods.

As opposed to residents of Haifa or Jaffa, which are within the 1967 borders of Israel, 95% of Arab residents in East Jerusalem are not citizens of Israel. Many Palestinians in Jerusalem don't want Israeli citizenship, as they reject the sovereignty of the Jewish state over a city they see as the capital of Palestine, preferring residency instead. Those who do seek Israeli citizenship face endless bureaucratic obstacles.[2]

Unlike children from Gaza and the West Bank, East Jerusalemite children who attend Kids4Peace from places such as Beit Hanina and Beit Safafa don't need to go through checkpoints and security checks to visit the western part of the city because these neighbourhoods are on the Israeli side of the wall. Most of the Arab children from East Jerusalem don't speak

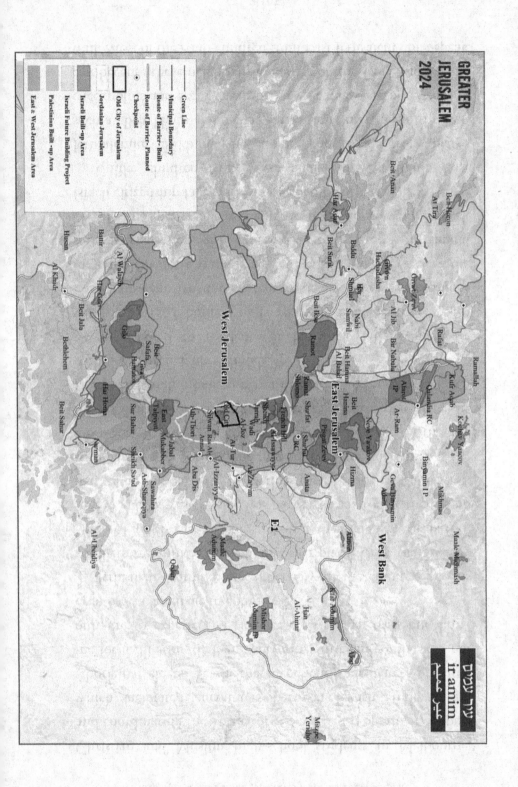

GREATER
JERUSALEM
2024

Green Line
Municipal Boundary
Route of Barrier- Built
Route of Barrier- Planned
Checkpoint
Old City of Jerusalem
Jordanian Jerusalem
Israeli Built-up Area
Palestinian Built -up Area
Israeli Future Building Project
East & West Jerusalem Area

West Jerusalem

East Jerusalem

West Bank

E1

ir amim
עיר עמים

Old City

Beit Hanina
Ramallah
Kufr Aqab
Kochav Ya'acov
Mikhmas
Maale Mikhmash
Qalandia RC
Ar-Ram
Binyamin IP
Geva Binyamin
Adam
Anata
Hizma
Neve Ya'akov
Pisgat Ze'ev
Shu'fat
Shu'fat RC
Beit Hanina
Beit Iksa
Al Jib
Bir Nabala
Al Balad
Givon Hachadasha
Nabi Samwil
Nabi Samuel
Biddu
Beit Surik
Har Adar
Beit Anan
Bet-Horon
At-Tira
Giv'on
Ofran Zevi
Rafat
Atarot
Atarot IP

Husan
Battir
Al Walaja
Har Gilo
Beit Jala
Bethlehem
Beit Sahur
Al Khidr
Beit Safafa
Givat Hamtos
Gilo
Har Homa
Sur Bahir
Umm Tuba
Numan
Al U'beidiya
Ash-Sharqiya
Sawahira
Sheikh Sa'ad
Abu Dis
Al-Izzariyya
Al-Za'ayim
Abu-Thon
Al-Tur
At-Tur
Wadi Joz
Sheikh Jarrah
Issawiyya
French Hill
Shlomo
Ramot Shu'fat
Mt. Scopus
Silwan Ras Al-Amud
East Talpiyot
Jabal Mukaber
Ramot

Ma'ale Adumim
Mishor Adumim
Mishor Adumim IP
Kfar Adumim
Nofei Prat
Alon
Kedar
Hizma
Han Al-Ahmar
Mitzpe Yericho

Hebrew. Most of the Jewish children of West Jerusalem don't speak Arabic.

Jerusalem contains many of the most significant holy places of the three monotheistic faiths. This means that, unlike other cities in the country, for a peace organisation to thrive in Jerusalem it must have staff that speak Hebrew and Arabic, must be incredibly sensitive to religious differences, and must constantly remember its place in a holy city that is a symbol for the Palestinian and Jewish diasporas, yet is also a home for all its residents.

Jerusalem doesn't have what Australians call 'public schools' that are open to children of all faiths, races and beliefs, teaching a pluralist education. Instead, the vast majority of students in Jerusalem are enrolled in one of the following four school systems, each subsidised to various extents by the Jerusalem Municipality and the ministry of education.

Stream	Ideology	Percentage of Jerusalem students enrolled in Year 1
Haredi Jewish	These schools are all separated by gender and also mostly by ethnic background between Ashkenazim and Mizrachim, with girls' schools being more inclusive and neighbourhood-oriented. About 5% are publicly run and teach the core curriculum of maths, English and science in exchange for full government funding and oversight. The majority of the remaining 95% are private but state-funded to various degrees, depending on their rate of inclusivity and declared level of education. Girls' schools provide a similar level of education to the publicly run schools, with some exceptions, while the boys generally learn Jewish-studies subjects with little to no core education in primary school and absolutely no core education in high school.	40%

Stream	Ideology	Percentage of Jerusalem students enrolled in Year 1
Palestinian Arabic	This is the only stream that delivers instruction exclusively in Arabic. Approximately a third of these schools are under the auspices of the Jerusalem Municipality, which offers Bagrut (matriculation) and the Israel-approved curriculum and even Tanach (Bible studies) in exchange for more funding and better-paid teachers. The other two-thirds are private but partially state-funded, and teach a curriculum that comes out of Ramallah offering the Tawjihi matriculation. Israel censors the curriculum for history and civics in these schools in exchange for partial state funding. Sometimes, two models can operate in the same school. Since 2018, Israel has only licensed new schools in East Jerusalem on the condition that they teach the Bagrut system. There are also a small number of private schools that offer international programs such as the IB, GSCE, Baccalauréat, and AP courses. Almost all schools are separated by gender.	36%
National Religious Jewish	Separated by gender in high school but not primary, these schools emphasise both religious observance and Zionism, with a strong encouragement of nationalist values and serving in the IDF.	13%
Secular Jewish	All co-ed, these schools have no prayers or religious instruction classes taught by rabbis, instead emphasising liberal humanistic values such as egalitarianism, LGBT rights and environmentalism. These schools also strongly encourage IDF service but include a greater range of opinions in lessons taught about the conflict than the National Religious stream.	11%

Figures are based on enrolments from 2019[3]

While many outsiders would view these diverse and competing school systems as a weakness, fostering ideological divisions and tribalism, for many Jerusalemite parents, the ability to choose the exact kind of education they want, including the ability to restrict who their children will mix with, is the primary reason why they stay in the city. It also poses one of the most significant challenges to the Kids4Peace youth movement, which operates after school hours and actively seeks dialogue between the students of these four very different streams and ideologies.

Challenging fear and ignorance

Before coming to Kids4Peace, every time I heard someone speaking Arabic on the light rail, I would tense up hearing the language of a nation I had been taught to fear. Now that I am so used to hearing Arabic as the language of games, dialogue and words spoken during meals at festivals, I feel as though this is the language of someone who could be my friend.

– Fifteen-year-old Jewish participant at Kids4Peace

More than the physical and language barriers that divide the city, more than our challenges fundraising for our programs, and more than our difficulties in finding the right staff, our greatest challenge to being successful at Kids4Peace is ignorance.

Before working there, I remember telling a few friends that I had a job interview at Kids4Peace in Sheikh Jarrah, hoping they would give me some advice. One said, 'A peace organisation in Jerusalem? It's a nice idea, but it's never going to achieve anything.' Another said, more bleakly, 'Try not to get stabbed.'

Sadly, that's how many Jewish Israelis see Sheikh Jarrah, due to its history as a strife-riven Palestinian neighbourhood. At its heart lies an ancient tomb, which is believed by some to belong to the former Jewish Temple high priest Shimon HaTzadik.

Since the Knesset passed a law in 1970 that allowed Jews to reclaim land in East Jerusalem if the land had ever had a prior Jewish owner, extreme settler groups have launched several legal cases to remove Palestinians from their homes, or in the case of the home belonging to Muna and Mohammed Kurd, actually moved into the front part of their existing home in 2009. No such law exists in Israel today that allows Palestinians to reclaim land where they lived before 1948 in what is now Israel.

As I began working at Kids4Peace, Sheikh Jarrah slowly transformed from a place I would never set foot in to a neighbourhood I visited several times a week. I came to know its streets, cafes, holy sites and tombs as well as my own neighbourhood in West Jerusalem, often taking visitors there on tours.

It was a huge eye-opener for me to hear Suma's stories. She has lived in Sheikh Jarrah her whole life and has seen her family and neighbours dragged to court hundreds of times to justify their presence there against hostile settler groups.

Ultimately, Sheikh Jarrah is the eye of the storm in the unsolved question of who will own Jerusalem in the future and what its status will be.

I remember the first program I facilitated in our Sheikh Jarrah office, which was once also the home of the pirate radio station All for Peace. About 30 teenagers came that Thursday evening. I introduced myself and started to explain why I had left Australia to live in Israel when a Muslim youth interrupted me and said, 'You now live in Palestine.' I was a bit taken aback, but then I thought about her reaction. In her narrative, the borders of Palestine extended from the Jordan River to the Mediterranean Sea, and indeed over 138 countries recognise the

East Jerusalem neighbourhood of Sheikh Jarrah, where we were meeting, as part of Palestine.

Realising that I had to adapt my language, from that day on, whenever someone has asked me where I live or work, I have almost never answered Israel or Palestine, stating instead that my home is Jerusalem, which is a name agreeable to all.

When asked by friends, 'Why do you work there?' I answer that Jerusalem is a city where everyone is a minority: Haredim, secular Israelis, religious Zionists and Palestinians. Yet each group acts and feels as though it should be the majority. I am therefore drawn to a place such as Kids4Peace that models a Jerusalem based on the foundations of justice and equality for all its inhabitants.

What happens at Kids4Peace

Kids4Peace programs always happen on Thursday evenings, the day before our Friday–Saturday weekend, when kids are less likely to be stressed about homework or an upcoming assessment. Just as several kids always come late due to issues with traffic, there are always a handful that come over an hour early, precisely to avoid the clogged roads.

Some come in twos or threes from a carpool; others come on their own. Less obvious but equally important: some come from just around the corner while others have to travel an hour or two through the stress and uncertainty of military checkpoints. Some of the Jewish boys wear a kippah on their heads, while some of the Muslim girls wear a hijab. For those who know how segregated Jerusalem is, the likelihood that any of these kids would have had any meaningful contact with each other if not for Kids4Peace is likely zero.

The kids are split into two groups: Juniors, who are in Years 6 and 7, and Seniors, who are in Years 8 and 9. Volunteer murshideen (Arabic for counsellors), who are in Years 10 or 11, are assisted by paid leaders.

One Thursday evening in 2022, Avi Meyerstein, the founder of the Alliance for Middle East Peace, visited Kids4Peace. He wrote movingly for the *Times of Israel* about this typical night.[4] The aim of that night was to teach the Juniors about the impact of labels and stereotypes connected to their beliefs. The atmosphere was relaxed and cosy. As the kids began to trickle in, they got a high five or a 'How's it going?' from one of the murshideen. True to their age, they all reacted to these greetings differently. Some offered a nonchalant shrug or a quiet look around the room. Others returned a wide smile or made an enthusiastic gesture.

The evening launched with icebreakers. The younger kids began a game in which each person had a word taped to their back – they had to find out their identity and a partner who matched their identity. Everyone else would walk around the room and give them clues to help them guess. Some examples included Superman and Batman, Anna and Elsa, Corona and Pfizer, Messi and Neymar. As the kids stumbled around in search of clues, they laughed hysterically.

On the surface, these kids were having a blast. They navigated the room and interacted without regard to who they were, where they came from or how the wider society would label them. People in the community might have been shocked to see this, but there it was just plain fun.

However, the game wasn't solely about laughs – it was full of meaning too. It was a reminder about the identities we carry inside versus the ones we wear on the outside, not to mention how we sometimes need a community to help us figure out who we really are. What community we choose can make a big difference to who we become. These kids had found a community like none other.

Tel Aviv vs Ramallah

That same night, the Seniors participated in a program about how to debate respectfully. They began by sitting in a big circle, with two chairs facing each other in the centre, one marked 'agree' and the other 'disagree'. The first question the leaders posed generated raucous excitement: Barcelona or Real Madrid?

The kids in the centre were debating each other, and everyone around the room was listening and cheering them on. When someone in the larger circle thought they could add to the debate, they would tap a shoulder and take one of the places at the centre. And that was just the start. The next hot topic: Instagram vs TikTok. And then: Tel Aviv vs Ramallah.

Yarden and Mohammed, the Israeli and Palestinian grade leaders, provided help with real-time translation into Hebrew and Arabic when necessary. As the game went on, they gradually introduced new rules into each round of the debate.

Round 1: No shouting.
Round 2: No interrupting the other person.
Round 3: Before you respond, you have to first repeat
what your debate partner just said.
Round 4: Always refer to your opponent respectfully.

More topics followed in debates for or against: Everyone should be vegetarian! Mixed-gender schools are better! Parents should be able to read everything on their kids' phones!

As I observed the program I had written being facilitated by my staff and volunteers, it was clear what was happening. First, the kids were realigning themselves, not along national or religious lines but based on their ideas. Second, they were learning tools for engaging in respectful debate. Third, they had a chance to reflect on how it felt to play alternate roles and interact with each other differently.

Even the kids who remained in the outer circle through the whole program without saying a word were reflecting on why it was hard to tap the shoulder of a peer to enter the debate. I could see their minds processing the thrill and fear of vocalising a strong opinion among a mixed group of Palestinian and Israeli teenagers.

After the activity, the murshideen led a debrief, posing questions for discussion. How did it feel to sit on the chairs in the middle? How did it feel to sit on the outside? What did it feel like to argue for something you don't believe? How did the debate change after we added the rules? What would your life be like – what would the world be like – if everyone debated this way?

A little later, the kids took on more issues. They broke into small groups to consider various ethical dilemmas they might encounter in their teenage lives. Should you invite your whole class to a party? What do you do if you find money on the street? What should happen if a student cheats on an important test?

Again, a thoughtful conversation followed. How did it feel to disagree with people? Was it harder or easier to disagree with someone of your own religion or a different one? Do you learn more from people with whom you agree or disagree?

These were just a few segments of a lively two-hour program, which concluded with talk of Hanukkah and Christmas celebrations and everyone singing the Kids4Peace song. Before parting ways, the students exchanged hugs and high-fives and said goodbye as they filtered out of the room.

What these young people do every week at Kids4Peace Jerusalem is not easy or popular. Yet those who participate – and their parents – seem to have discovered its rewards and know what an opportunity it presents. They walk away with relationships and skills that are simply unheard of in today's Jerusalem.

And if they have a little more hope than most, it's not from naivete. Quite the contrary – it's because they're grounded in reality. Unlike most of their peers in the wider community, they enter adulthood prepared for the toughest issues. They become adult community members, having had this experience of building trust, exchanging ideas respectfully and confronting a generational conflict together.

When I step out into the cool Jerusalem air after an evening at Kids4Peace, I often think, 'What would the next generation of voters and leaders look like in this city if they all experienced what I saw tonight?'

Most Kids4Peace graduates leave prouder and more secure in their political and national identity. Perhaps this may surprise many people who think peace programs aim to diminish these parts of one's worldview in favour of some kind of idealised shared narrative. This rarely happens, because explaining your religion and beliefs to others often strengthens your connection to your faith.

For example, at Kids4Peace summer camps, prayer times are a powerful and connecting experience. On a Friday, we hold the Jum'ah prayer in the morning, where the Muslim participants prostrate in rows, saying 'Allahu Akbar' – 'God is great' – followed by a Khutbah, a sermon. For many of the Jewish and Christian kids, it is not only the first time they have seen Muslim prayer but also the first time they heard the words 'Allahu Akbar' in this context, rather than how they may have encountered them in the media. This is followed in the afternoon by Christian participants facilitating a dialogue about the Sermon on the Mount, where Jesus taught that 'Blessed are the peacemakers, for they will be called children of God'. Finally, in the evening, there is a Jewish Kabbalat Shabbat service with joyous singing for the Lecha Dodi prayer and students of all faiths invited to join in the dancing. When I showed Henry Ralph Carse, the founder of Kids4Peace, a video of this day from our 2019 camp, he said, 'This is the heart of Kids4Peace. Children should grow up not being terrified by each other's moments of prayer, but rather being vulnerable enough to share and even celebrate them together.'

The parents of Kids4Peace

In addition to running regular programs throughout the year for the kids, we also run dialogue programs for their parents twice a year. At a parents meeting in 2021, around fifteen Jewish and Palestinian parents came to an introductory session about the activities their children were participating in. Rather than explain the program through a slide-show presentation, I wanted them to experience what we do, so together with fellow education director Angham Hussein, I seated them in circles of five and gave them several conversation prompts:

What's your religion?

What neighbourhood do you live in?

Why did you sign up your child to Kids4Peace?

What's a challenge you face in life at the moment?

What do you hope for Jerusalem in five years from now?

We allocated 30 minutes to discuss these questions, but they could have easily talked for hours. The parents entered the room as strangers, but by the end of the night they were chatting away like old high-school friends. One Palestinian parent revealed that he enrolled his son in Kids4Peace because he had never experienced anything like it during his own childhood. He didn't want his son to grow up without meaningful interactions with Jews, as he had.

I remember one Jewish mother telling me privately afterwards, 'Even though I have lived in Jerusalem for many years, this is the first time I have ever had a personal conversation about something other than directions with a woman wearing a hijab.' She later shared with me that from that meeting on, whenever she saw a woman wearing a hijab around Jerusalem, she no longer saw that person as a stranger but as a potential friend. All of that from just a two-hour meeting.

Another parent shared this reflection with over a hundred youth and their parents at the closing celebration of our 2023 program:

We enrolled our 12-year-old [Jewish] daughter in
Kids4Peace for the obvious reasons. Jerusalem is such a
beautifully diverse city full of rich culture and religious
expression. However, as you kids learned and witnessed

with your own eyes here, your daily lives tend to be segregated, offering precious few opportunities for meaningful encounters with people from different backgrounds than you. As we've all seen, it's so easy to be afraid and feel suspicious of people you've never really spent time with.

We enrolled our daughter in Kids4Peace because we want to surround our children with real experiences of the better and more equal world we dream of. In this imaginative work, education is a radical act. We want to make it impossible for our kids to be able to dehumanise any person or group of people.

I want to bless all of you at Kids4Peace and say that these friendships help you dream bigger, more compassionate futures in this place we call home. That when you hear someone in your school or at the park making mean or condescending comments against someone different from you, you remember the encounters you've had here and find the courage to stand up and call out all hatred.

It was incredibly moving.

Angham and I then came to the stage to share a speech. We both spoke in Arabic and Hebrew about the growth we had seen in the kids over that year. I concluded my speech by talking about why I love my job:

Every time a parent or a child comes to Kids4Peace, I want two things to happen to them. The first is, I want you to hear one thing that you find troubling. It could be a fact about inequality, a story that challenges your own biases, or just the existence of an injustice you never knew about. After that, I want you to hear one thing you find comforting. A story of resilience, an idea you never heard of before that could make life better, or a personal story of someone speaking out against racism and injustice that gave you hope. If that happens to you each time you enter the doors of this building, then our mission is being realised.

Ultimately, the purpose of this place is to create conversations that comfort the troubled and trouble the comfortable.

The evening ended with a Jewish staff counsellor and an Arab youth participant singing the song 'Hallelujah' together in Arabic and Hebrew, bringing together the holy and the broken, united and dreaming of peace.

After October 7

At the end of the summer in 2023, just as we were preparing our opening meetings for the new school year, October 7 unfolded. Despite the raw shock our leadership team experienced, we called or messaged every one of our staff and volunteers individually, knowing that the care and concern conveyed in a personal message of 'Hope you are well, I'm thinking about you' would be infinitely more appreciated that any press statement we could have issued as an organisation.

We then made the difficult decision to postpone our start date for fears of safety, as there were still rocket attacks on our city, and no one knew how the war down south would impact the very volatile Jerusalem.

After a very sombre Ramadan passed in peace, we decided to renew our programs. We spent considerable time contemplating the first meeting. What could we possibly do to encompass all that these children had endured seven months into the war? We imagined that the bank of trust and friendship we had spent years building between these children would have depleted, just as we had witnessed in the wider community. It was a joy and surprise, therefore, to find that the foundations remained, and the youth returned enthusiastically, albeit in smaller numbers than before.

When we shared the news that we were reopening, one of the Israeli parents wrote in the WhatsApp group:

> We felt the unique value of your work with the kids over
> the last year gave our daughter the ability to honestly and
> bravely empathise with the residents of Gaza from the
> first moments of the war, to be interested and distinguish
> between those involved and those not involved, and to
> empathise with the suffering of both sides. We attribute
> this ability in her to the time she spent at Kids4Peace. She
> is so excited to hear your programs are resuming. I hope as
> many parents as possible in this group will send their kids
> to your programs. You are doing holy work; we must not
> lose hope.

In May 2024, our first meeting back centred around an art activity expressing feelings. It was very special, not just because of the fact that it was happening during a war, but because it had much the same warmth of interactions and engagements that we saw in our programs before the war. In our second meeting back, which had around an equal number of Israelis and Palestinians, we played an auction game where groups of kids had Monopoly money that they could use to buy 'attributes' that they wanted to include in their ideal Jerusalem. The items they could bid for included security, religious freedom, equality, good weather, parks and sports arenas, food and entertainment, effective public transport and a mall. In their heated discussions about what to bid for with their limited funds, what was most moving was to see them not in grief and pain about the reality of our present but excited to dream and build a Jerusalem of our future.

As our programs continue, we are extra sensitive to the different needs of the staff and participants, who are each at different stages of grief, despair and hope. Yet by far the most memorable and hopeful experience I have ever had at Kids4Peace was one that didn't even happen in Jerusalem. It happened in Northern Ireland.

CHAPTER 7:

'Peace is possible': Lessons from Belfast

These days, not many people ask – let alone try to answer – the question of what our lives might look like had the Oslo Accords of 1993 led to genuine peace between Israelis and Palestinians.

Yet, as a peace educator, it's a question I ask myself all the time while I try to design programs to inspire optimism and even a little bit of hope for our participants.

In 2019, I accompanied a group of 12 teenagers from Kids4Peace Jerusalem to Belfast, the capital of Northern Ireland, for a program that aimed to explore the process that resulted in the 1998 Good Friday Agreement between the British and Irish governments, which was facilitated by United States President Bill Clinton and Special Envoy George Mitchell. While not perfect, it built much more positive rapport and understanding between the Protestants and Catholics than did the failed 1993 Oslo Accords between Israel and the PLO.

Our goal was to see what we could learn from people plagued by sectarian hatred in their city – a legacy of violence dating to the Norman invasion of 1169.

At the height of the Troubles – a rather understated word for the horrific violence that took place between 1968 and 1998 – there were years such as 1972, which included Bloody Sunday and Bloody Friday, in which Belfast experienced a terrorist attack, on average, every 40 minutes. Belfast was surrounded by a ring of steel. High walls divided the city's Catholics and Protestants, neighbourhood by neighbourhood, street by street.

Yet in 1998, when the Good Friday Agreement was put to the vote in two referendums, 71% of the people of Northern Ireland voted for it. The peace agreement instituted a government in which power was carefully balanced between Protestant loyalists and Catholic nationalists. It also stipulated that Northern Ireland could be reunited with Ireland if majorities on both sides of the border favoured it. This has yet to happen, meaning that the British loyalists could claim it as a win for now and the Irish republicans could claim it as a win for the future.

Most importantly, it put an end to a lethal guerrilla war. The Irish Republican Army (IRA) and pro-British paramilitary groups agreed to give up their weapons, while Britain and Ireland freed about 400 people jailed for their involvement in violence.

In 2023, on the 25th anniversary of the Good Friday Agreement, the Irish Foreign Ministry shared a moving reflection by Gail McConnell, a poet and academic. 'I was seventeen in the spring of 1998,' she said. 'Had I had a vote, I would have ticked the "yes" box, and I would have done so in the knowledge that I was voting for the early release from prison of one of my father's murderers.'[1]

Such a statement seems unimaginable to most Israelis and Palestinians – let alone bereaved families who have lost loved ones to the conflict.

In 1993, when the Oslo Accord was signed, not only was there no follow-up referendum for Israelis and Palestinians, but the agreement itself was largely a secret, even to the cabinet members of the Israeli government and to many in the PLO, until a few short weeks before the historic signing on the White House lawn. According to the Alliance for Middle East Peace, the lack of grassroots work required by civil society to build a constituency for peace before Oslo, as happened in Northern Ireland, is one of many reasons for its failure.

Tony Blair, former prime minister of the United Kingdom and co-signatory to the Good Friday Agreement, has echoed this view:

> The Good Friday Agreement in Northern Ireland didn't begin or come to fruition in a vacuum. There were many great things that happened before we even got to the negotiations that set the context, laid the groundwork, and created the environments for the negotiation to succeed. One of those things was the International Fund for Ireland.[2]

Established in 1986, the IFI has received generous contributions from various donors, including the United States, European Union, United Kingdom, Australia, Canada and New Zealand, securing an impressive $US982 million to date for dialogue and peacebuilding initiatives. Participation in these programs started as a privilege for a select few and then gradually became a right and, eventually, a rite of passage for young Catholics and Protestants across Ireland.

One of the most influential initiatives was the Northern Ireland Women's Coalition, led by Mary Blood. Her tireless dedication to integrated education and understanding of its potential to unite children from diverse backgrounds was essential in helping people believe peace was possible. Her advocacy raised millions of pounds in support of mixed Catholic and Protestant schools across Northern Ireland.

Organisations like Tar Anall and the Ex-Prisoners Interpretative Centre (EPIC) worked to involve former combatants in peace efforts, offering vital services such as counselling, education, discussion groups and inter-community mediation. These initiatives encouraged ex-paramilitary members from both sides to engage in dialogue with their political opponents, helping to humanise each other and break down stereotypes. Programs were also aimed at guiding former prisoners and activists towards nonviolent contributions to their communities, while welfare support services were extended to both ex-prisoners and the broader public.

The Belfast YMCA was another key player, promoting dialogue and mutual understanding among young people from different backgrounds. Peer-mediation programs in schools, introduced as early as 1987, aimed to reduce violence by fostering empathy and understanding among students. These initiatives stressed the importance of informal face-to-face interactions between conflicting groups.

Collectively, these programs created valuable opportunities for Catholics and Protestants to connect, breaking down barriers and fostering trust. By focusing on shared experiences and common objectives, they helped people move beyond sectarianism in order to recognise their shared humanity.

I remember our trip leader and peacemaker Reverend Gary Mason telling the Kids4Peace staff about this peace fund in Ireland, saying, 'If you want peace today, you should have started building it twenty years ago. And if you don't feel like working for peace today, then you better not complain to me in twenty years that the conflict is ongoing and affecting your children.'

Due to the lack of meaningful contact between Jewish Israelis and Palestinians, and the polarising nature of social media, if Israelis and Palestinians were invited to vote on a referendum today for something similar to the agreement outlined in the Geneva Accord hammered out by Israeli and Palestinian moderates in 2003, it's likely neither side would reach anywhere near 50%.

That's because in the Middle East, past experience has led both sides of this intractable conflict to feel incredibly pessimistic about the intentions of the other. It seems that all the solutions ever implemented are always short-term, to stop or respond to the violence of today, rather than long-term solutions that could prevent the violence of tomorrow.

What, if anything, can we learn from Northern Ireland?

An important part of the Kids4Peace trip to Belfast was a meeting with Nichola Mallon and Mike Nesbitt, two politicians from opposing sides who rejected violence and embraced dialogue and negotiation.

Mallon, an Irish nationalist from the Social Democratic and Labour Party, told us, 'There was a time here when people told us that politics didn't work, and you were considered weak if you thought that the political constitutional route was the way

Within the mural:

EVERYONE, REPUBLICAN OR OTHERWISE HAS THEIR OWN PARTICULAR ROLE TO PLAY

...OUR REVENGE WILL BE THE LAUGHTER OF OUR CHILDREN

Bobby Sands MP

POET, GAEILGEOIR, REVOLUTIONARY, IRA VOLUNTEER

A mural of IRA member and hunger striker Bobby Sands, Belfast.
Credit: Evan McCaffrey / Shutterstock.com

to go. But it's come full circle. And what we have learned is that the killing didn't advance the change that we wanted. Politics has, and politics [still] is.'

Speaking of the violence, she said, 'I am sure that of the people who did engage in acts of political violence, not many of them would say to you, with hand on heart, that violence was counterproductive to their goals, but in their hearts they all know it was.'

She then added: 'Things have changed much more through the democratic process than by us killing each other.'

A Palestinian student spoke about the frustrating failure of politics to achieve peace back home. Mallon said the key to ending the violence in Northern Ireland was the building of deep personal relationships and trust across the political aisle. 'At the end of the day,' she said, 'this is my home, and this is Mike's home.'

The situation in Jerusalem today feels like everything that happened in Belfast, but in reverse. There is no faith here in politics. There is no trust among the people – let alone significant connection with 'the other'.

In July 2024, a joint Palestinian–Israeli survey found that among Jewish Israelis, support for the two-state solution had dropped to its lowest level since polling on the matter began in the early 1990s. Furthermore, a record-high 94% of Palestinians and 86% of Israelis said that the other side could not be trusted.

One of the greatest obstacles to peace in Jerusalem is the Border Police. As a unit of the Israeli army, they do the lion's share of policing in East Jerusalem, as opposed to the regular police. Being much more heavily armed than the police, and staffed by younger men and women with more extreme political views than the general population, they are known for using excessive force against Arab demonstrators – far in excess of the force they would use against Haredi, Jewish-settler or secular liberal anti-Netanyahu or pro-hostage demonstrators. Arab kids are asked to show ID, frisked for weapons and moved along from public places far more often than any other population, creating significant tension and a climate of fear for many East Jerusalem residents.

The deeply unequal manner in which Israel's Border Police operate in Jerusalem, plus the fact that the various school systems are almost completely segregated on both inter-religious and national lines, means that there is almost no opportunity or desire for youth in the city to meet or understand one another.

The dominant approach of the Israeli security establishment, as expressed by Prime Minister Benjamin Netanyahu in 2023, is to stand as 'a powerful iron wall against our enemies … ensuring that whoever tries to harm us on one front, or more than one front, needs to know that they will pay the price'.[3]

Today in Israel, both the government and seemingly most of the Jewish population believe that force, rather than politics or negotiation, is the factor that will bring peace for them.

What if our public narratives before Oslo had taught us to see our history in a manner that didn't delegitimise the narrative of the other?

What if, on our memorial days, we remembered not only the pain caused to us but also the pain we caused to one another?

What if we promoted nonviolence and compromise as signs of strength rather than weakness?

On my final day of that summer trip in Northern Ireland with Kids4Peace, I walked past the Garrick Bar in Belfast. Pubs in Belfast are almost as ubiquitous as falafel shops in Jerusalem,

Ittay Flescher outside The Garrick in Belfast, 2019.

open all hours and appearing on most street corners. Written in huge letters on the outside wall of the pub are words that sum up so much of what we can learn from how the Troubles ended: 'A nation that keeps one eye on the past is wise. A nation that keeps two eyes on the past is blind.'

Those words felt like a revelation.

Imagine what Jerusalem would be like if that sentiment was etched more deeply on both the walls of the city and the hearts of its residents.

Imagine if those words could become a guiding light for both Israelis and Palestinians – so that we wouldn't go another 30 years missing the opportunity to build grassroots connections that can, together, call for justice and equality for all, as they did for those in Belfast and across Northern Ireland.

Of course, there are major differences between Belfast and Jerusalem. In Northern Ireland, the minority had the military power over the majority. In Jerusalem, it's the majority over the minority. We also speak different languages and are fighting over one land that we each want exclusively, in its entirety.

As I'm writing this in 2024, four of the Jewish youth who participated in the Belfast trip are serving in the IDF. The Palestinians are studying various degrees in Jerusalem and abroad but are also glued to their phones, watching in fear and horror as their loved ones are being bombed in Gaza.

Any good that may come out of this program is unknown. As Neil Postman said in 1982, 'Children are the living messages we send to a time we will not see.' Here's hoping the messages they deliver will be different to the ones they inherited from the generations before them.

CHAPTER 8

Daring to dialogue: How supporters of Palestine and Israel can talk to one another

During the time Hannah Baker and I were recording our podcast, *From the Yarra River to the Mediterranean Sea*, in early 2024, we interviewed several peacebuilders who had participated in interfaith dialogue programs similar to Kids4Peace. This led to many requests to facilitate similar interfaith dialogue groups in Australia between supporters of Palestine and Israel.

As I was helping to coordinate a Jewish–Muslim encounter group in Sydney, one of the potential Jewish participants said to me, 'I love the idea of this group, and think it's so important, but I will only feel comfortable attending if I know in advance that all the Muslims in the group have publicly condemned Hamas and have not in any way justified their hostage-taking or atrocities on October 7.' Later, a potential Muslim participant said to me that she might find it hard to encourage other Muslims to join the group unless all the Jewish participants, in advance, unequivocally condemned the Israeli destruction of Gaza and called for a ceasefire.

While it's natural to want to hear these condemnations before gathering in a circle, after hearing these two participants' requests, I understood that the group was unlikely to form. It encapsulated for me why it's so hard for supporters of Israel and Palestine to talk to one another these days.

The meaning of Zionism and 'Free Palestine'

Have you ever been sure that a certain word, phrase or idea means something particular, but the rest of the world seems to think it means something completely different? This experience happens all the time to Israelis and Palestinians.

In a post on Threads in 2023, Palestinian–American writer Mo Husseini put it this way:

> When a Palestinian says, 'Zionism is racism,' their
> understanding of the word 'Zionism' is anchored in a
> definition of a Zionism that is by definition exclusionary
> and racist and dehumanizing – an exceptionalist view
> of the Jewish people's right to a homeland in a way that
> abnegates the rights of the Palestinian people and elevates
> the primacy of ethnic Judaism above all others.
>
> On the other hand, when a Jewish person says, 'I am a
> proud Zionist,' their understanding of the word 'Zionism'
> is anchored in a very real history of discrimination,
> persecution, and genocide, and that foundation focuses

on the creation of a homeland and nation where Jews can finally control their own destinies and be safe.

Which means that when a Jew hears a Palestinian use the phrase, 'Zionism is racism,' what they hear is 'I do not believe in the right of the Jewish people to have a nation where they can finally control their destinies and be safe.'

Which means that when a Palestinian hears a Jew use the phrase, 'I am a proud Zionist.' what they hear is 'I believe that the Jewish people's right to a state is more important than your right to a state and that being Jewish means I am better than you.'

One simple word carries completely different meanings & each of those meanings is loaded with historical, cultural, and emotional baggage that can't easily be unpacked or set aside.

The same is true of a phrase like 'Free Palestine' which a Palestinian might use as a call for justice, human rights, and self-determination for the Palestinian people but a Jewish person will hear as a refusal to accept Israel's right to exist and a negation of the Jewish people's right to a Jewish homeland.[1]

The rise of nationalism: A blessing and a curse

Nationalism is a profoundly important value for both Israelis and Palestinians. For many of us, the sight of our national flags, anthems and cultural symbols being venerated or desecrated can evoke emotions as intense and passionate as those stirred by witnessing harm or disrespect to our own families.

Throughout the history of this region, various men – mainly foreign but also a few locals – have drawn lines on maps to create political entities, regions of autonomy and even countries in what is now called the Middle East. While I'm far from being a nationalist, it's hard for me to ignore how meaningful the creation of modern nation-states has been for the vast majority of people in the world. This is primarily because the nation-state has become the principal and, some would say, most effective vehicle in granting individual human rights, housing, education, health and welfare benefits.

Nation-states, or at least the strong ones, have also shielded their citizens from the ravages of war, preserved ancient cultures, traditions and languages, and given many people an ideal to live by. But nation-states and the lines that divide them on maps can often cause two people who are neighbours and friends to become the fiercest of enemies in an instant.

The other outcome of these lines and borders on maps is that they teach us all to play a psychological game, one which says that the people on my side of the line are worth more than those on the other side. This includes their health, wellbeing, safety and even their very lives. To me, as a humanist, this is the curse of nationalism.

Acknowledging that nationalism plays a huge role in the identity of both Israelis and Palestinians, two highly patriotic societies, I have often wondered how to facilitate dialogue about nationalism in a manner that could be constructive and meaningful. Given how triggering flags are to both sides, I knew that even having them in the room during any such dialogue would always be out of the question. Many Israelis see the Palestinian flag as the flag of the PLO, which, until the Oslo Accords, was deemed a terrorist group in Israel. Many Palestinians see the blue-and white Israeli flag emblazoned on the shoulders of soldiers and police all around them as a symbol of oppression and brutality.

For this reason, we never bring Israeli or Palestinian flags to Kids4Peace. We do not shy away from difficult conversations around nationalism, but we use less confronting symbols than flags to open these conversations. A tool we find to be very useful is the use of the symbols of 'Srulik' and 'Handala'.

Srulik and Handala

Srulik is a cartoon character who first appeared in the weekly Israeli newspaper *HaOlam Hazeh* in 1951. He was created by Kariel 'Dosh' Gardosh (1921–2000), whose whole family was killed in Auschwitz during the Holocaust, and who moved to British-ruled Palestine in early 1948.

The character's epithet is a nickname for Israel (Yisraelik – Srulik), and he is often drawn as a young man wearing a kova tembel, the hat worn by the pioneers who built Israel, often called 'kibbutznikim'. Wearing biblical Teva sandals and khaki shorts, he loves the land of Israel and its soil. Srulik's outfit – the sandals, the hat, the shorts – was common attire for many Israelis both in the city and in rural areas at the time the state was born. His image is the opposite of the age-old antisemitic caricatures that portray Jews as sorrowful and hunched, with exaggerated facial features and banknotes in their pockets.

Former Israeli member of the Knesset Tommy Lapid once said, 'Dosh's Srulik is the symbol of Israel, like Marianne is the symbol of France, John Bull is the symbol of Great Britain and Uncle Sam is the symbol of the United States.'[2]

Dosh (Kariel Gardosh) and his creation Srulik.[3]

Handala was created by Naji Salim Hussain Al-Ali (1938–1987), who was born in the Palestinian village of Al-Shajara, situated between Tiberias and Nazareth. In 1948, when he was ten years old, he lived as an exile in the Ain al-Hilweh refugee camp of southern Lebanon. A political commentator, he worked for several different newspapers in different countries. During his life, he created over 40,000 drawings depicting the life of the Palestinian people: both their suffering and the resistance. He also harshly criticised Palestinian leadership, Arab regimes and the Israeli Occupation.

Al-Ali was shot to death in London in 1987, some say by Israel's Shin Bet intelligence agency, others say by the PLO. After Al-Ali's death, his son said, 'Many people were unhappy with his cartoons throughout his career: that could range from, obviously, Israel as the enemy, and Arab leaders and Arab governments, including the Palestinian leadership. There were always threats, and there were always problems with his cartoons. But this did not stop him from actually drawing.'[14]

His most famous creation, Handala, first appeared in a Kuwaiti paper *Al-Siyasa* in 1969. Handala is a ten-year-old who was forced to leave his home in the Nakba, who will always remain a ten-year-old until he can return home. His turned back and clasped hands symbolise a rejection of 'outside solutions'. His ragged clothes and bare feet symbolise an allegiance to the poor.

Instead of Israeli and Palestinian flags, the educators at Kids4Peace use the images of Srulik and Handala in many programs that touch on the issue of national identity.

After showing the kids the two cartoons, we ask the Israelis: 'How do you feel about Srulik as a portrayal of your people? What would you change?'

Naji Al-Ali's Handala in downtown Ramallah on Rukab Street outside
Handala Cafe and Museum. Credit: Chris Whitman Abdelkarim

Many say that while Srulik may have represented their grandparents' generation, none of them today wear khaki shorts or that silly hat, although many still do wear Teva sandals. They say a more accurate cartoon representation of an Israeli today would be a secular woman living in a city, maybe working in tech or an office job, and she would be doing something that shows her liberal values.

We then ask the Palestinian kids: 'How do you feel about Handala as a portrayal of your people? What would you change?'

Without hesitation, all the kids say Handala is a very accurate representation of the Palestinian struggle, and none of them would change anything.

One of the youth leaders then notes that many of the kids in the room don't look like Handala: 'You have shoes, we can see your faces, and thankfully they are not bruised and battered.' The Palestinian kids respond that even though they don't physically look like Handala, they are deeply moved by the distress they see him in, and this makes them believe that the current situation must change.

We then do an art activity where the children draw additional symbols for their Israeli and Palestinian identities – from Magen Davids (stars of David) to olive trees, each adding a deeper layer to how they are connected to this land. Many Palestinian kids draw a single key, representing a desire to return to their pre-1948 homes, or a watermelon, which has the colours of their flag. Many Israeli kids draw peace signs, candles or the Menorah candelabra, which appears on the emblem of Israel.

In the end, we hang all these pictures on the wall and make a little museum. The young people stand before each other and share the meaning of the art they have created.

Every time I conduct this program, which we have done many times at Kids4Peace, I am amazed. Seeing the honesty and openness the young people have in sharing their stories, the compassion and empathy with which their peers listen, and knowing that this may be the only space in Jerusalem that night where such an encounter is possible, gives me immense hope for the future. It also makes me think – if this can happen here in Jerusalem, maybe it can happen in other places around the world too.

Inside the mind of the Jewish/Israeli and Palestinian diaspora

When I share the work I do at Kids4Peace with Jewish friends in Melbourne, especially those on the left, they are often moved and inspired. A common response I hear is, 'I wish we could have similar activities and dialogues with Palestinians in Australia, but I don't know how to begin.'

Groups in Melbourne that instigate interfaith dialogue, like the Jewish Christian Muslim Association or the Council of Christians and Jews, are usually populated by the elderly or clergy, and while very well-meaning, they fail to attract the younger and more eclectic members of the communities they represent.

Often, people with strong Zionist or pro-Palestinian views shun interfaith organisations. Interfaith groups tend to minimise differences between traditions, instead highlighting commonalities and shared goals, which are anathema to many with more nationalist beliefs in the supremacy of their traditions over others. Opponents of these groups fear that they may have limited freedom of speech in these places, or perhaps they want to avoid being confronted or offended by what others might say about values they hold dear.

Many of these fears can be traced directly back to education. To help combat the gaps in our knowledge when it comes to the narrative of the other, I sometimes suggest to my diaspora friends that before they start a dialogue, they could start a book club.

The two books I recommend they first read and discuss together are *Where the Line Is Drawn* by Raja Shehadeh, published in 2017, and *Zionism: An Emotional State* by Derek Penslar, published in 2023. Each, in their own way, explores the reasons why Jews and Palestinians feel so connected to this land through powerful storytelling and psychology.

Since October 7, the two books I recommend are *The Gates of Gaza: A Story of Betrayal, Survival, and Hope in Israel's Borderlands* by Amir Tibon, and *Daybreak in Gaza* edited by Mahmoud Muna and Matthew Teller. Both were published in 2024. Tibon's book focuses on the horror that befell the tight-knit community of Nahal Oz on October 7, amid the wider story of war, occupation and hostility and the author's enduring hope for peace. *Daybreak in Gaza* is a collection of vignettes about Palestinian people in Gaza. Their stories of love, life, loss and survival humanise them – they are artists, shopkeepers, doctors and teachers, not mere statistics, and the book acts as a mark of resistance to the destruction and a testament to the people of Gaza. As a means of reminding myself of the savagery of war and the resilience of the human spirit, I read parts of both books on Yom Kippur of 2024, a process of moral reckoning that my tradition obliges me to do on that holy day.

Another challenge diaspora supporters of Israel and Palestine need to overcome in order to engage in dialogue is the perception that hearing the story of the other and expressing empathy with their pain is an act of disloyalty or betrayal to one's own nation and people.

Overcoming the ties of loyalty and tribalism that are so often barriers to dialogue is not easy. Yet once this wall is pulled down, the possibilities are endless. I have seen Palestinians visibly moved upon hearing Israeli Jews share stories of their family members who experienced the Holocaust. Acknowledging another's pain can soften even the hardest of hearts.

One such example happened when Palestinian peacemaker Souli Khatib visited Kids4Peace with his Israeli counterpart from Combatants for Peace. Souli had spent time in an Israeli prison from the age of 14. While in prison, he had watched the film *Schindler's List*. He recalled how the film had made him weep, and that it had changed his life forever, making him realise his enemies were actually human beings who were also suffering.[5] As an adult, Khatib has dedicated his life to peacebuilding.

The reverse is also true when Israelis internalise how much Palestinians suffer from the violence, endless bureaucracy and humiliation of the Occupation. Palestinians can feel heard and seen when Jews acknowledge that Palestinian culture is no less rich or vibrant than their own, and this also moves hearts and minds. This is doubly so when Jews learn Arabic, because speaking a language is speaking to the heart.

In 2019, I was facilitating a conversation between a group of 17-year-olds at Kids4Peace. I asked a Palestinian participant how he felt about his Israeli friends from Kids4Peace going to serve in the IDF in the coming year. I expected him to be angry or hurt that his friends would do this. Instead, he surprised me by saying, 'It makes me feel jealous.' He added, 'I know this is something he has to do. It's the law in his country. I can also see the pride many of my Jewish friends have in their uniforms when they serve. As much as I wish the Occupation army didn't exist to oppress me, I also sometimes hope that I too will have a state with a national army that protects and serves my people.'

I also remember facilitating a parents' dialogue in which an Israeli mother shared the great reluctance with which she was sending her son to the army. She explained that in light of her activism and work for peace, she was very concerned about the orders her son might need to follow when in uniform. A Palestinian parent was shocked in response. He said, 'I have never heard an Israeli parent express reluctance about their child joining the army. I used to think you all did this with joy. Now I realise how difficult this is for you.'

On another occasion, a Palestinian parent shared how since Netanyahu came to power, she doesn't wear a hijab in Jewish neighbourhoods. An Israeli parent shared that he feared wearing a kippa in Arab neighbourhoods. Both were quite surprised to learn about the fear of the other, leading them to affirm the safety and welcoming nature of their respective neighbourhoods. To prove the point, one pair of parents even exchanged phone numbers and invited the other to a meal in their homes to show the welcoming character of their faith tradition.

While each of these stories may sound trivial, if you multiply them by a thousand, you can begin to see the humanising impact of dialogue and how quickly it can change the reality of Israeli and Palestinian minds.

Today, most people think there can't be peace because they see polls showing many people taking the most hardline positions possible towards one another. Yet I often think of what would happen in these exact same polls if we felt there was a partner for peace on the other side. What would happen in the polls if Israelis started seeing Palestinian security forces quickly capturing and punishing those who fire rockets into Israel? What if they saw Palestinians returning the Israeli hostages home? Or public opinion shifting decisively against Hamas and other groups who support attacks on civilians?

Consider the impact on Palestinian streets if Israel took swift and decisive action against Israeli civilians involved in 'price-tag' attacks on Palestinians in the West Bank. These extremist settlers often carry out such attacks in retaliation for government actions viewed as antagonistic to settlements or in response to Palestinian violence against Jews. A particularly severe incident occurred in August 2024, when around 100 Jewish Israelis raided the West Bank village of Jit, destroying numerous homes and vehicles, resulting in the death of one Palestinian and injuries to others. IDF Central Commander Major General Avi Bluth described the attack as a 'serious terror incident' aimed at harming Jit residents, acknowledging a failure to protect them in time.[6] Despite the chaos, no one was arrested that night; only four of the participants were detained two weeks later. How might Palestinian perceptions of Israeli security forces change if these rioters faced strong legal repercussions? What if government ministers were held accountable and dismissed from the Knesset for making racist comments against Arabs or justifying price-tag attacks? I believe that, in a short time, the disheartening survey results that currently prevail would begin to shift significantly.

According to philosopher Thomas Hobbes, human beings want to protect their lives and possessions above all else, and their greatest fear is facing violence from others. At the moment, the vast majority of Israelis and Palestinians feel the only way we can preserve our lives is by using extreme violence against our enemies. Therefore, we remain in a constant state of war with each other. This warfare tends to be chronic because there are no strong external forces that can enforce peace on both sides. Our only hope is not to wait for the Americans, the European Union or the United Nations to save us, but rather to work on ourselves to imagine different possibilities and solutions to our age-old problems.

Let's think for a moment what a few small acts of recognition, which don't cost a shekel to either side, could do to public opinion. Consider what would happen if Israeli or Palestinian leaders made moving speeches empathising with the pain of the Holocaust, the Nakba, the terrorism done in the name of freeing Palestine, or the suffering caused by the walls and checkpoints. I have seen this happen many times in dialogue circles, but it rarely happens in politics.

Probably the rare exception was way back in 1977, when Anwar Sadat, the Egyptian prime minister who had been responsible for over 2650 Israeli deaths in the Yom Kippur War just four years previously, boarded a plane to Israel. From the podium of the Knesset in Jerusalem, he said, 'You want to live with us in this part of the world … In all sincerity, I tell you, we welcome you among us, with full security and safety.' Within a year, this moment of humanity and empathy turned into a signed peace agreement that has kept the peace between Israel and Egypt for over 40 years. That's the power of acknowledgment and the magic that can happen when each feels there is a partner for peace on the other side.

CHAPTER 9

Gaza: The quest
for reckoning

The Great Omari Mosque in Gaza's Old City was built 1400 years ago. Before it was a Muslim holy place, it was a Byzantine church, of which one part was an Israelite synagogue, and before that, a Philistine temple. The main hall could hold over 4000 people, who would bow down in prayer to Allah on its majestic blue carpet, which echoed the colours of the Mediterranean Sea.

The mosque was damaged by British bombing in World War I then repaired in 1925 by the Supreme Muslim Council. Destroyed again by an Israeli airstrike on December 7, 2023, it is now in ruins, with only the minaret left standing.

The story of the mosque is the story of Gaza.

As a home for so many by the sea, Gaza has been inhabited for at least 5000 years and ruled by the Philistines, Canaanites, Ancient Egyptians, Romans, Greeks, Crusaders and various Arab and Islamic dynasties.

In the Bible, Gaza is the place where Samson committed a murderous suicide that brought the house down on himself and 3000 Philistines, choosing death over living without honour.

The Gaza region was a popular area for various rulers to conquer because, in addition to being on an important trade route for thousands of years, the land was well suited to agriculture. From the late 18th until the mid-19th century, Gaza was the world's leading producer of barley, which fuelled the British beer industry for almost a hundred years. For 1400 years up until the construction of the Hijaz Railway (which no longer exists) in 1908, pilgrims would stop in Gaza on their way to Mecca and Medina for the annual Hajj.

The borders of the Gaza Strip today were created by the wider Arab–Israeli conflict. During the war of 1948, Israel conquered and forcibly relocated 200,000 Palestinians from the much larger Gaza district and pushed them into what became known as the Gaza Strip. As a result, there are now eight permanent refugee camps in Gaza.

Today, Gaza's ancient history and heritage have been immeasurably ravaged by war. Its towering high-density apartment buildings and seaside restaurants and its many museums and archaeological sites are in ruins. At the time of writing, in 2024, Palestinians who know Gaza as their only home find much of it uninhabitable, with dire food shortages, lack of housing and barely any functioning hospitals. The situation is so devastating that some families have resorted to writing their children's names on their hands and legs to identify them in case they are killed in an Israeli airstrike, while others have shared personal information on Facebook so that, in death, they wouldn't become just another statistic.[1]

In the 2021 Gaza War, Belal Iyad Akel from Gaza posted, 'My name is Belal, I am 23 years old and this is what I look like in my profile picture. I am not an ordinary young man, nor a number. It took me 23 years to become as you see now ... I have a home, friends, a memory and a lot of pain.' At the time, Belal was living in the Nuseirat refugee camp, where shelling was constant and fierce. Belal's moving post reflected an increasing fear that he would die nameless, and only be remembered as a 'number among numbers ... a young man ... martyred along [with] three others in an attack on a civilian house'.[2]

On July 20, 2024, Belal's deepest fears came true. The day before, an Israeli bomb struck the home where he was living with 12 family members, including his father, Iyad, grandfather Zaki, and his beloved nieces and nephews, Razan, Rim, Mohammed and Rana. His father was killed and Belal was badly wounded. Tragically, he died the following day.[3]

The destruction of Gaza: Suffering beyonds words

Of the many horrific things I have heard from Gaza, there was one headline in *Haaretz* newspaper on March 7, 2024 that I had to read three times before I could absorb its shocking reality. It said: 'This International Women's Day, Palestinian women in Gaza are making period products out of tents'. The subheading added, 'The Gazan women cutting off their hair in the face of a water crisis, surviving C-sections without anaesthesia and fashioning period products from scraps are showing strength and ingenuity in impossible circumstances.'[4]

I stared at my screen in shock. How could my people do such a thing to these women? How am I living two hours away from a place where young men of 23 are posting their wills on

Facebook and women are enduring surgeries without something as crucial as anaesthetic? I couldn't help but feel responsible for the horror they were suffering in the pursuit of my security.

As a result of the war, thousands of Palestinians have been killed, with many of the survivors – men, women and children – losing limbs, suffering from burns and carrying infected wounds for a lack of bandages and medicine. Many will suffer from PTSD for the rest of their lives. It's hard to comprehend such immense trauma.

In December 2023, the International Rescue Committee (IRC) reported that the majority of the houses in Gaza had been 'partially or totally destroyed'.[5]

I remember reading this and thinking, 'What does it mean to have a "partially" destroyed house? Does that mean it no longer has interior walls, a roof, windows, running water and electricity? How is that different from a "totally destroyed" house that is now a pile of concrete cinders and rubble – if both are unliveable?'

As Israeli journalist Amira Hass wrote in *Haaretz*, 'The quantification doesn't include the contents of the apartments. Simple or elegant. Gold jewels or private libraries, so dear to the hearts of their owners. Their books were used at a certain point as kindling, in lack of fuel or wood.'

The 'quantification' suggested by the IRC report also didn't include what Hass described as:

longing for the sight of the sea as seen from the window,
the stories and poems that were recorded on a desktop
computer without backup. The paintings. The importance
of home to people who grew up on the formative disaster

of the 1948 war: leaving home and expulsion from it.
Memories of one's daughter's first step. The pride and
joy when slowly accumulated savings added up to an
apartment separate from parents or siblings.[6]

How can one comprehend such loss?

Even aid workers haven't been spared. On April 1, 2024,
Israeli drones targeted a three-car convoy belonging to the
World Central Kitchen (WCK) killing seven aid workers,
including Australian volunteer Lalzawmi 'Zomi' Frankcom.
Her friend Teresa Gray remembered her by writing that 'Zomi
was fierce and loyal and loving and funny. She had this amazing
smile that was ever-present and she was the best hugger I've ever
known.'[7]

The aid workers had been managing the transfer of food
into the northern Gaza Strip, an area severely affected by Israel's
invasion and blockade, which was pushing it towards famine.
Despite coordinating the route and timing with the IDF in
advance, a fact acknowledged by the IDF, the clearly marked
WCK convoy was attacked. An inquiry conducted by Australian
Special Adviser Air Chief Marshal Mark Binskin attributed the
IDF's erroneous strikes to significant failures in adhering to
procedures as well as mistaken identification of a target. The
IDF admitted that the 'incident should not have occurred' and
was a 'grave mistake'.[8]

Days after this tragedy, the *Jerusalem Post* ran an editorial
under the heading, 'Unintentional killings of WCK workers is
tragic, but Hamas is still to blame for war'. Their view reflected
that of many Israelis who were more perturbed by the diplomatic
fallout from the attack than the attack itself. Conversely, José

Andrés, the founder of the WCK, wrote an article that was translated to Hebrew and published in the prominent Israeli newspaper *Yediot*, saying:

> We know Israelis. Israelis, in their heart of hearts, know
> that food is not a weapon of war. Israel is better than the
> way this war is being waged. It is better than blocking
> food and medicine to civilians. It is better than killing aid
> workers who coordinate their movements with the IDF.
> The Israeli government needs to open land routes to food
> and medicine today.

He went on to give some much-needed advice that I wished my people had heard:

> Israel needs to stop killing civilians and aid workers
> today. It needs to start the long journey to peace today.
> In the worst conditions, after the worst terrorist attack
> in its history, it's time for the best of Israel to show up.
> You cannot save the hostages by bombing every building
> in Gaza. You cannot win this war by starving an entire
> population. The probe into the deaths of WCK volunteers
> needs to start from the top, not just the bottom. It is not a
> sign of weakness to feed strangers; it is a sign of strength.
> The people of Israel need to remember, at this darkest
> hour, what strength truly looks like.[9]

His ability to show grace when most would expect anger, to appeal to our better angels and to remind us what true strength means resonated deeply with me.

Moral reckoning

Rabbi Abraham Joshua Heschel, a prolific writer, thinker and civil-rights activist, said in 1973 that, morally speaking, according to his understanding of the Hebrew prophets, 'there is no limit to one's concern for human beings' suffering'. He added that 'indifference to evil is worse than evil itself, [and] in a free society, some are guilty, but all are responsible'.[10] These are words I have carried with me throughout the war.

On day 24 of the Israel–Gaza War, October 31, 2023, I went to an event in Jerusalem that was sponsored by members of Kibbutz Nir Oz. Before the war, this kibbutz, less than three kilometres from the Gaza border, was known for its silicon sealant factory and for being a significant exporter of asparagus. It had 400 residents. On October 7, 72 of its residents were taken hostage in Gaza and 38 were murdered by Hamas. After losing more than a quarter of its population in such a brutal manner, members of the kibbutz came to Jerusalem. In the vast forecourt of the Jerusalem Municipality they set up 110 harrowingly vacant beds. Each had blankets, pillows and even some teddy bears. There were also a few cots with toys in them. Hundreds of people walked around them in silence, trying to absorb the loss suffered by this community.

Towards the end of the event, which included singing, candle-lighting, prayers and several speeches from residents, I saw Naama Lazimi, a member of the Knesset (MK) from the Israeli Labor Party, whom I admired for her outspoken stances favouring workers' rights and the LGBTQIA+ community. Lazimi smiled when she first saw me because I had interviewed her before. But I approached her with trepidation, as I had a question that I was terrified to ask.

'Naama,' I began hesitatingly, 'I feel for all the pain of the people here from Kibbutz Nir Oz and pray that all the hostages should come home soon, but I also feel for the pain of people in Gaza. To this day, eight thousand, five hundred people have been killed there already. Is it possible for you to raise a question in the Knesset about the amount of force the government is using against the people there?'

Lazimi's expression immediately changed from warmth to anger. 'How dare you ask me such a question while I am still burying my extended family members in Kibbutz Be'eri?' she replied, then promptly walked away.

Five months later, on day 145 of the war, February 28, 2024, I was at a conference of the 'faithful left' in Jerusalem when I met Naama Lazimi again. She was one of the speakers at the event, along with many other religious and traditional Jews who came to hear about the value of pidyon shvuyi. Meaning 'redemption of captives', pidyon shvuyi is a religious duty that compels Jews to bring about the release of their brethren captured by robbers and slave dealers or imprisoned unjustly.

At that time, 136 Israelis were still captive in Gaza. After the main event, there were several breakout sessions on topics such as the importance of negotiating with Hamas to release the Israeli hostages, workers' rights in Judaism, peace education in times of war, life in Gaza, testimonies from soldiers who had served in Gaza and were critical of the war, and the outcomes of Israel weapons exports to countries with poor human-rights records.

I attended a session called 'The impact of the war on the political sphere'. The three members of the panel were Lazimi, her fellow Labor party MK Rabbi Gilad Kariv and Moshe

Tur-Paz from the centrist party Yesh Atid. All were in opposition to the Netanyahu coalition at that time.

After listening to more than an hour of conversation, I quietly raised my hand and made eye contact with the panel host, my friend Pnina Pfeuffer, whom I had met in a secular–Haredi dialogue group. With five minutes left before the night's end, I asked a similar question to the one I had posed to Lazimi on day 24 of the war.

I felt anxious about posing my question to the panel and about the reaction of the hundred or so people in the room, not knowing what any of them had experienced during the war. I said:

> I watch the evening news every night. I see the pain of
> the hostages, of the bereaved families, the people from the
> Nova Festival. After that, I also watch foreign media every
> night. I see many hungry families in Gaza. I see bereaved
> families there. I see people performing surgery without
> anaesthesia. That also is very painful for me, as a Jew. You
> spoke, Rabbi Kariv, about a spiritual reckoning. So, after
> the war – I'm not asking for a political perspective, but as
> a question of morality, as a rabbi – do the Jewish people
> need to engage in some sort of spiritual reckoning about
> what happened in Gaza too?

To my surprise and relief, no one on the panel or in the room responded with angry growls or scolded me for asking the question. Lazimi even nodded in sympathy as I described the situation in Gaza. Rabbi Kariv responded with much honesty and openness:

Over the past four months, in Israeli media and Israeli discourse, there has been a phenomenon that we can understand in terms of the dimensions of the horror of the Simchat Torah [October 7] catastrophe. We may understand it, but we also have to confront its harms. Israeli society ignores the dimensions of the destruction and the human cost for the Palestinian community in Gaza.

The result of this is that the cup of vengeance and fury [is not full].

So the cup of vengeance and fury, we all hold that. The fact that they [the media] don't show us what is happening there [in Gaza] means that our cup of vengeance and fury, even after four months, remains unfilled.

At the same time, I think this [war against Hamas] was imperative and correct, for the sake of the two-state solution as well. If anyone thinks that with Hamas remaining the ruling power in Gaza there would be any future for the Palestinian Authority and the peace process with moderate actors, they are misreading the map. A decisive victory over Hamas, as a ruling and military power, is a prerequisite for the two-state solution.

So, my conclusion in this matter is unambiguous: we must begin to confront the scale of the destruction – and the human horror – that is happening in Gaza. I'm sorry, but without this we will not know how to stop ourselves in the process. As I've said, we've already missed the opportunity to do much of what needed to be done over the past two months. We must begin to see what is happening in Gaza.

It took me a few days to process the answer, for several reasons. The reactions from Kariv and Lazimi were very different to the ones from four months earlier. Several people in the room even approached me and thanked me for asking the question, which hadn't been asked in Hebrew by any journalist to any Israeli MK until that point in the war. Yet the hardest part to process was Kariv acknowledging 'the fact that they [Israeli media] don't show us what is happening there means that our cup of vengeance and fury, even after four months, remains unfilled'.

Does every Jewish victim of October 7 have a cup of vengeance? Aren't we, the people who every Passover remove a drop of wine from our glasses as we recite the ten plagues our God inflicted on the Egyptians, taught to eschew vengeance? That was the Judaism I believed in. Yet here was one of the most liberal rabbis in Israel telling me and the public that supports him that without seeing the graphic horror from Gaza, this war will not be able to end, as our need for vengeance will not be satisfied.

A week later, Noah Efron, Allison Kaplan Sommer and Linda Gradstein discussed my question and the answer to it on *The Promised Podcast*, a weekly conversation between three journalists about the politics and culture of this land. I have been listening to this podcast regularly for over a decade. Allison agreed with Rabbi Kariv, saying Israelis can't evaluate the actions of their army in Gaza without squarely looking into the face of what our actions are doing to the civilian population. Noah disagreed, saying that most Israelis know what is happening in Gaza despite it not being on the nightly news because we all have Google and speak to soldiers who were there. He further added that no amount of footage would make Israelis support the war less, because most felt at the time, as did Kariv, that defeating Hamas was essential to reduce the suffering of both Palestinians and Israelis. Unlike me, few could think of any way to achieve this goal other than war.

Linda shared the tragic story of Hind Rajab, a six-year-old Palestinian girl who dreamed of becoming a dentist. Her life ended in the most horrific of ways after her family's car came under gunfire as they were evacuating south from Gaza City on orders from the Israeli army. After her aunt, uncle and four cousins were killed, Hind called a Palestinian Red Crescent dispatcher to send help. The recording of her call was heard around the world. As an ambulance was making its way to her, she stayed on the line for several hours with the dispatcher, and also briefly with her mother, who read the Quran to her and played counting games to distract her from the horror. Yet the ambulance never came. Twelve days later, the two first responders were found dead barely 500 metres from the car that contained the bodies of Hind and her family members.

After describing the way Hind spent the last hours of her life, Linda concluded by saying, 'We are responsible for this, the authors of something horrible.'

The conversation strengthened what I already felt. If we cannot see another's suffering, there is no place for empathy, compassion or any human emotions that we are innately wired to feel when we see another's distress. From a place where we deny another's suffering, our own suffering takes centre stage, and we become consumed by it, allowing dehumanisation to flourish. So much of our decision-making – in negotiations at a political level or even on a battlefield – is impacted as a result.

Spiritual reckoning must be a two-way street. For the same reason, almost every Israeli I know will find it hard to speak to Palestinians who won't unequivocally condemn the atrocities of October 7; many Palestinians will find it hard to speak with Israelis until they say, 'I take responsibility as an Israeli because the atrocities committed by Israel in Gaza were done in my name.'

I truly believe that we can one day share this land without war, but it is essential that citizens in both nations are able to utter these words and then do the spiritual reckoning required to process their meaning. To do this myself, I shared the following words with my community in a Facebook post on March 4, 2024.

What haven't we seen in the past 150 days.

The beautiful Bibas children, two red-headed babies kidnapped from their home in Kibbutz Nir Oz.

Women sexually assaulted and then killed at a dance party celebrating peace and love.

Mass displacement of millions of Gazans and thousands of homes destroyed across the strip.

Thousands of rockets fired by Hamas in the south and Hezbollah in the north that have displaced thousands of Israelis.

Immoral justifications for the crimes of October 7 as a legitimate response to the occupation.

Immoral justifications for the collective punishment of Palestinians because of Hamas.

Every day I wake up and turn on my phone to read another horror story. After October 7, I couldn't stop thinking about Shlomo Ron, whose wife, daughter and grandchildren had spent the Simchat Torah holiday with him in Kibbutz Nachal Oz. When he saw the mass murderers raiding his kibbutz, he told all his family to hide in the safe room, while he sat alone in the living room waiting to be killed, thinking that once the killers took his life, they would leave the house alone. His plan saved the lives of his loved ones, but the mere thought that he was ever put in this situation is something I will never forget.

I still remember January 27 when I turned on my phone to see a 35-year-old man from Khan Younis evacuating his elderly mother down to Rafah in a wheelbarrow. I couldn't stop thinking how humiliating it must have been for this senior citizen to flee her home in such a dishonourable manner as if she was a sack of potatoes rather than a dignified elder who should be honoured like a queen.

It's almost impossible for me to walk more than 100 metres in my Jerusalem neighbourhood without coming across huge red banners calling for the release of Hersh Goldberg-Polin who was kidnapped from the Nova. Even though I never met him, I have now seen so many videos of his life that I feel we could be the best of friends. Seeing his mother, Rachel, each day with the tape on her chest marking the growing number of days her son is in captivity, I honour her resilience and unwavering courage to not give up on his fight for freedom, while always humanising the Palestinian mothers who long for the safety and freedom of their children no less than she does for Hersh.

Today, I woke up to read the story of Rania Abu Anza. 'It took ten years and three rounds of in vitro fertilisation for Rania to become pregnant, and only seconds for her to lose her five-month-old twins, a boy and a girl. An Israeli strike hit the home of her extended family in the southern Gaza city of Rafah late Saturday, killing her children, her husband and 11 other relatives and leaving another nine missing under the rubble. She had woken up at around 10 pm to breastfeed Naeim, the boy, and went back to sleep with him in one arm and Wissam, the girl, in the other. Her husband was sleeping beside them. The explosion came an hour and a half later without warning. The house collapsed.'[11]

As someone who supports the cause of self-determination for Palestinians and Israelis, I despair at the immense public support here for the horrific strategies used to achieve these goals, knowing deep in my heart that negotiations and compromise will always be more powerful at achieving freedom and security than guns and F-15s.

After 150 days, I don't know what words we, the peace-seekers of Israel and Palestine, haven't already used to try and soften the hardened hearts of our leaders. What haven't we said to urge them to end this war, to free the hostages, to give their people the right to hold new elections now so that we can replace them and elect women and men who will take a different path.

How many times have we heard 'there is no partner for peace', as both sides do no moral reckoning about how their maximalist demands have led to so many failed peace negotiation processes, which could have largely ended this horrific conflict.

After 150 days, I beg anyone with the power to end this misery to please remember that ultimately 14 million people now live between the Jordan River and the Mediterranean Sea.

About half are Arab and the other half are Jewish.

Whenever this war is over, the survivors will mourn, the dead will be buried and memorials will be built that will etch in our memories forever the price we pay when we fail to compromise for peace.

As a peace activist in Jerusalem, I will continue to hold the stories, the pain, the hopes and dreams of all my Jewish, Christian and Muslim friends together at this time, letting them wrestle within my heart, finding a place to hear and empathise with them all.

The responses to this Facebook post were both challenging and heartfelt. One Israeli friend responded:

Beautifully written, but immoral as well: there cannot be any moral equivalence between the heinous, fully intentional actions of Hamas against unarmed, peaceful civilians (most of whom had been on the left side of our political map, working for peace for many years) on the one hand, and the horrible but unintentional death of non-combatants in Gaza as a result of the legitimate response of the IDF in defence of Israeli civilians against Hamas, on the other hand.

Another Israeli friend wrote:

I appreciate what you wrote here as I too was moved this
morning by the story of Rania Abu Anza and her twins.
It was the closest I have come in the last 150 days towards
actual sympathy for the Gazans. The most frightening
aspect of this for me is how little sympathy I feel for the
plight of the Gazans. Intellectually I agree with everything
you have written, but I think I feel for the suffering of 'the
other' much like Private Ryan's mother or Anne Frank's
father would have felt for the civilians of Dresden.

Another Jewish friend on the far left responded:

This is really beautiful and eloquent, but through
absolutely no fault of Ittay's, it's too little and about
20 years too late. We needed a majority of worldwide
Jewry to be more or less on this page many years ago,
so that by today, despite the shock and horror of 10/7,
we would be able confidently to go much farther, and
wouldn't be in the shameful place where these words
remain edgy and controversial and require caveats when
sharing even among very liberal Jews. I can't imagine
which words of these liberal Jewish leaders, including
one of my own teachers, would feel unable to join
themselves to. This is all so tame, so axiomatic. Nothing
crazy, nothing edgy, no radioactive buzzwords that echo
antisemitic left-wing talking points. Just the most basic
empathy and the most basic moral truths that would
not be controversial in any sector of k'lal yisrael [or Klal

Yisrael – the collective of the Jewish people] if any of us were remotely in touch with Torah values.

As I always do, I reflected on the critiques of my words from the right and the left. There was probably some truth in both these responses, which is why the post was so hard for me to write.

The resilience of Gazan Palestinians

When most people around the world think of Gaza today, death and destruction are all they can see. Yet before this war, Gaza City was known as one of the world's oldest cities, and once housed the second-largest library in antiquity. It was home to beautiful beaches, rich history and more than two million people.

Gaza is also the place where, more than anywhere else, Palestinians live the concept of sumud, literally translated as 'steadfastness', which means a strong determination to stay in their country, on their land. It is likely that sumud was part of a collective Palestinian consciousness of struggling for and clinging to the land that goes back at least to the British Mandate time.[12]

The olive tree with its deep roots in the land, bearing fruits only after several years of growth, is a widely used metaphorical expression of sumud.

Here are some prominent examples of sumud in Gaza during the current war:

- The fisherman who risks life and limb to find a catch to feed his family.
- The farmer who braves airstrikes to harvest their balah dates, carrots, cucumbers and tomatoes.

- The sanitation worker who goes to work without a pay cheque in order to prevent the further outbreak of a deadly disease.
- The ambulance driver who rushes to a destroyed building to risk their life and dig out people from under the rubble.
- The artist, who now has no income, who spends their days teaching children to paint with very limited supplies, giving children an outlet to process their trauma.
- The nurse who has lost seven relatives in the past month yet still comes to work on time to save lives at the hospital.
- The photojournalist from Beit Hanoun, whose family has been displaced nine times yet remains in the north of Gaza, who keeps documenting the reality of death and life in a manner that people like me find so confronting and shattering while knowing we have a duty not to look away.

CHAPTER 10

Peace journalism: All the news we never print

A huge obstacle to peace is how Israelis and Palestinians produce and consume media. In order to reach a day when Palestinians and Israelis care for the wellbeing of one another's children, a day when we can move away from certainty and righteousness to a place of curiosity and openness, we desperately need a media that helps us imagine this as a possibility.

While I have always known that the media coverage of our reality is a source of deep consternation on both sides, I didn't realise the extent of it until 2018 when I started working as the Jerusalem correspondent for *The Jewish Independent*, a news website dedicated to providing a broader range of perspectives than can be found in most other Australian Jewish news sites.

Every word a journalist chooses to use carries profound meaning. Almost every word has a bias, and no words are neutral. To help explain this dilemma, this table reflects some

166

of the language choices available when writing about war and peace from Jerusalem.

Land and Place	Name of the Conflict	The People
• Israel, Palestine or Israel/Palestine	• Israeli–Palestinian Conflict	• Arab Israelis or Palestinian citizens of Israel
• West Bank or Judea and Samaria (Yesha)	• Jewish–Arab Conflict	• Colonisers or indigenous
• Occupied Territories or Disputed Territories	• War against Hamas terror	• Terrorists or militants
• The Green Line or June 1967 Borders or 1949 Armistice Line	• Genocide / ethnic cleansing of the Palestinian people	• Zionists, Israelis or Jews
• Golan Heights or Occupied Syria	• Struggle against Israeli apartheid	• Palestinians or Arabs
• Eretz Yisrael or Medinat Yisrael	• Intifada for victory	• Israel Defense Force (IDF) or Israel Occupying Forces (IOF)
• Temple Mount or Al-Aqsa	• Resistance against occupation	
	• War on radical Islam	
	• Operation Swords of Iron	
	• Matzav (Situation)	
	• Jihad	
	• Milchama (War)	

To readers who have been following this subject for a long time, the mere presence in an article of the words 'Judea and Samaria' instead of the 'West Bank' will immediately indicate that the writer is coming from an Israeli right-wing perspective. Should one read 'Occupied East Jerusalem', 'Al-Aqsa', or 'resistance' instead of 'Israel's united capital Jerusalem', 'Temple Mount' or 'terrorism', one will know immediately that the writer is coming from a Palestinian perspective.

As a writer for *The Jewish Independent*, I have a little more freedom in my word choices. Yet I know that the wrong word, choice of voice and decision about who I do or don't humanise can lead to a flood of complaints from readers.

Choice of voice

'Voice' refers to the form of a verb that indicates whether a grammatical subject performs the action or is the receiver of the action. When a sentence is written in the active voice, the subject performs the action; in the passive voice, the subject receives the action.

The passive voice is not a grammatical error. It's a style choice. However, most readers prefer the active voice. For example, in a report by the Islamophobia Register Australia entitled *A War of Words: Preliminary Media Analysis of the 2023 Israel-Gaza War*, a concern was raised about the passive voice used in this headline from the *Daily Telegraph*: 'Orange flashes have lit up the night sky over Gaza City as air strikes pounded the region'.

The report noted that 'lit up the night sky' removes and obscures Israel as the source of the attacks. It added further that 'this is particularly notable when contrasted to the voice used in the same story when discussing attacks on Israelis by Hamas ("A terrorist attack by Hamas forces in southern Israel") that stipulate the actor (Hamas).'

The report added:

> The positioning of Israel as the greater and named
> recipient of harm continued, as the number of reported
> deaths and abductions of Israelis on Oct 7 were stated
> in the post, but the reported deaths of Palestinians up to

the date of the post were not stated. This omission again reinforces the narrative that not only are Israelis the main victims in the current war, but they are the only victims in the current war.[1]

Meanwhile, the Zionist website *Honest Reporting* made a similar complaint about this headline on CNN that read: 'Two dead including child as car rams people at Jerusalem bus stop'.

The article was about an incident in February 2023, when a Palestinian attacker later identified as Hossein Karaka, a 31-year-old from East Jerusalem, drove his car into a crowd of civilians waiting at a bus stop in the Ramot neighbourhood of Jerusalem.

Honest Reporting noted:

> CNN appeared to go out of its way to conceal the identity
> of the attacker in its headline above the story about the
> incident. In an example of wording that completely distorts
> what had occurred, the headline suggested a 'car' had
> rammed into the crowd of people, allowing the publication
> to make no reference to the person who was actually
> behind the wheel of the vehicle. Cars do not drive into
> people on their own accord, CNN. Cars are controlled by
> their driver – in this case, a Palestinian terrorist.[2]

First-person narratives

While they don't tell a complete story, live eyewitness videos are very important for understanding one person's experience of a newsworthy event. The abundance of mobile phones has given anyone with a wifi connection the ability to broadcast to millions. Many traditional news organisations break stories by sharing firsthand reports from these individuals well before professional journalists can arrive on the scene – if they are even able to. A famous example of this is the film footage of George Floyd's murder that was captured by 17-year-old Darnella Frazier. Had she not pulled out her phone, the world may not have known what happened. After her ten minutes of footage went viral, over 20 million Americans protested against police brutality. Tim Walz, the governor of Minnesota, thanked Frazier, saying, 'Taking that video – I think many folks know – is maybe the only reason that Derek Chauvin will go to prison.'[3]

These witnesses who have the wherewithal to film in some of the most extreme moments in their lives play an important public service.

During the war that began on October 7, Australians seeking news from Gaza were far more likely to follow young Palestinian journalists on Instagram such as Motaz Azaiza, Plestia Alaqad and Bisan Owda than ABC or Channel 9. Their daily updates, always filmed on their phones with no producers, lighting or make-up, made their reporting feel much more real, intimate and immediate than a traditional news report. Viewers experienced these reports as if they were a personal diary of trauma, every video giving them the feeling that it was personally addressed to them – something that rarely happens in traditional news reporting, which often uses cold, detached and analytical language and tone.

While Israel has some high-profile celebrities promoting their narrative on social media, such as Gal Gadot, Jerry Seinfeld and Debra Messing, their reach was only a fraction of what was achieved by Palestinians on Instagram.

The power of social media algorithms

Many young adults today don't seek news about world events through traditional media. In a mainstream TV news site or broadsheet, an editor chooses all the stories that will appear, giving some more prominence than others, and then sometimes includes an editorial supporting a certain narrative of the said news stories. Every reader or viewer receives the same product at the same time.

On social media, no two users will have the same feed, and each individual will be served a completely different version of events based on their past history of 'likes', 'comments' and 'shares' using a certain app. The algorithm that determines a user's feed will largely exclude all news and opinions that do not fit their worldview, and will prioritise engagement and watch time, often favouring sensational or polarising content. This is in contrast to traditional media, which, at least in theory, strives to uphold journalistic values of balance and integrity.

The *Digital News Report: Australia 2023* by the University of Canberra found that the overall use of social media platforms for news in Australia has risen significantly. The largest growth of news sources was Instagram (26% of users using the platform for news, reflecting an increase of +6%) and YouTube (23%, +4%) followed by TikTok (17%, +4%) and WhatsApp (10%, +4%).[4] Only 30% of Australians now use search engines to find news stories.

There are many accounts run by journalists with integrity, who give a range of opinions to help people understand a variety of perspectives, with *The Daily Aus* being a leader in this field. But unless users of these apps have education in media literacy, it's sometimes very hard to tell the difference between a verified and accurate news source, and an item that is designed to misinform or mislead its readers for a specific propaganda purpose.

Seeing the pain

The media is not just a mirror of society. The TV stations we watch are also the glasses through which we see parts of the world we can't see with our own eyes. During the five wars between Israel and Hamas from 2007 to 2024, the media acted as a powerful lens that distorted and inhibited our ability to see the full picture.

Neither the Israeli nor the Palestinian media reported violence in a manner that encouraged empathy with the other side of the conflict. In effect, our two nations saw completely different wars on their TV screens and social media feeds.

I want you to put this book down for a moment and watch a heart-wrenching interview, which was aired live on Israel's mainstream Channel 13 during the 2009 Gaza war. It is with a grieving father in Gaza who had, minutes before, lost his three precious daughters: Bessan, 21; Mayar, 15; and Aya, 13. You can find it by typing into YouTube: 'Gaza father on phone with Israeli TV as tank shells kill his three daughters.'

It was unusually long for an interview in a live news bulletin. For four minutes, Israeli journalist Shlomi Eldar listens attentively to the pain and tears of his old friend Dr Izzeldin Abuelaish, whose house had been bombed in an IDF strike despite having no affiliation with a terror organisation and being a well-known doctor to many Jewish patients at Tel HaShomer Hospital in Tel Aviv. During the interview, Eldar asks Abuelaish for his exact location to try to get an ambulance there to help the injured. Even when Eldar's co-host suggests they end the call, Eldar stays on the line, trying to do all he can to get a medical team there, clearly showing empathy for Abuelaish's torment.

It was a moment that really shook Israelis to the core. Dr Abuelaish, a Palestinian gynaecologist and fertility specialist, had given regular updates to the media in Hebrew from Gaza during the war. When this interview with Eldar was broadcast, it was not a tragedy happening to a stranger. This was someone the public knew. It suddenly showed Israelis that *these* are the Palestinian people. After the broadcast, some Israelis even called Abuelaish to apologise on behalf of their country.

Rewatching this interview in 2023, I imagined how Israelis would feel about the current war if Gazan residents were given regular spots on Israeli TV to share their stories. There are still some people there that used to work in Israel and who speak Hebrew fluently. Imagine what it would be like to switch on government broadcaster KAN and watch a lead story about a hungry mother in tears over her inability to feed her two young children in northern Gaza, or a bereaved father living in a leaky tent for three months after being displaced four times on orders from the IDF. Imagine how differently Israelis might feel towards the suffering of Palestinians in Jabaliya, Khan Younis and Deir al Balah.

I then imagined how Palestinians would feel if Al Jazeera or Al Mayadeen regularly aired interviews with the Jewish and Arab families from Eilat to Majdal Shams who lost loved ones on October 7 or from Hezbollah rockets, especially those who can't sleep at night as they are filled with fear and trepidation over the fate of family members who are still captive in the dark tunnels of Hamas. Imagine if their reporting sought to affirm the harrowing stories of trauma that so many Israelis experienced on October 7, rather than cast aspersions about their authenticity. If the framing question of more reports sought to humanise the average person living in Kibbutz Be'eri or Sderot, how would that make Palestinians feel towards their Israeli neighbours?

Of all the human emotions, empathy across lines of difference seems to be the one in shortest supply when we fight, but it is ultimately the emotion we need most to end war, for the sake of all our children, who deserve to one day share this land in peace.

For that, our failing TV news media is largely to blame.

Navigating the heartache

In the midst of the ongoing Israeli–Palestinian war, a profound and deeply felt pain reverberates through both communities. This shared anguish, born from generations of conflict and loss, inevitably colours how news is perceived and internalised. In times of distress and uncertainty, it's only natural for people to seek solace in familiar narratives. Both Israelis and Palestinians, carrying the weight of our collective histories, find reassurance in stories that align with our experiences and validate our struggles. This tendency isn't a flaw, but a very human response to trauma and fear.

The horror of the war often makes it difficult for news outlets to provide full context for every event. When faced with threats or losses, it's understandable that individuals might focus on the immediate impact rather than broader historical contexts. The pain of a family losing their home or a community mourning a victim of violence is raw and immediate, making it challenging to consider wider perspectives. For instance, reports of violence against Israelis will not delve into how the Occupation has harmed Palestinians, just as news of Palestinian suffering will not explore Israeli security concerns.

A nightly news ritual: Bereavement, analysis and hope

During the war, the four main Israeli TV news channels have developed a sombre narrative arc for their daily 8 pm slots. The 90-minute news bulletins usually begin by highlighting the heroism of any recently fallen soldiers. Then comes a live security briefing with IDF spokesman Rear Admiral Daniel Hagari, who often outlines Israeli military operations in Gaza or Lebanon, in addition to sharing any important public-security information such as whether schools remain open or a threat level has been escalated. Interspersed between boisterous panel discussions and analysis about strategies to defeat Hamas or Hezbollah are deeply emotive interviews with survivors of October 7, bereaved families, hostages' families, returned hostages and small-business owners from the north and south who have had their livelihoods ruined.

An example of this was in August 2024 on Tu B'Av, a Jewish festival celebrating romantic love. Ziv Abud, whose fiancé Eliya Cohen is a hostage in Gaza, set up a romantic dinner for two at sunset on the Tel Aviv beach promenade, but instead of sitting opposite her partner, she faces an empty chair. In a video captured by Channel 12, Ziv is comforted and embraced by passers-by, many of whom stop to hear her story and are visibly moved. While the purpose of these stories is to keep the hostages in the forefront of public discourse, for many Israelis, the prevalence of these stories also makes every day feel like it is October 7, even a year afterwards.

The nightly show usually concludes with inspirational montages of Israelis demonstrating resilience and spirit through volunteering. Throughout the bulletin, a graphic of an Israeli flag with the words 'B'yachad nenatzeach' – 'Together we will be victorious' – appears in the top left corner of the screen.

Many Jewish people in the diaspora felt an acute absence of these humanising Israeli stories in the foreign press as the war progressed.

To date, Israeli TV news has largely ignored any stories of Palestinian suffering that would humanise the bereaved parents who lost their children in IDF airstrikes. They refrain from critiquing the reports by the IDF spokesperson, accepting the casualty numbers and descriptions of events as presented. Humanising stories of Palestinians that feature heavily in the international press, such as long lines of Gazan children waiting for food, interviews with displaced families in flimsy tents who had been forced to relocate, or images of mass casualties from IDF airstrikes, rarely feature on Israeli TV news.

A notable exception has been the *Haaretz* newspaper, especially journalists such as Amira Hass and Sheren Falah Saab, who have highlighted these civilian tragedies regularly. However, given that *Haaretz* has less than 5% of the total Israeli print-media readership, these articles don't have a significant effect on shaping public opinion.

The impact of these journalistic choices was clearly visible in a poll conducted by the Israel Democracy Institute in December 2023. It found that 81% of Jewish Israelis thought the suffering of the Palestinian population should not be taken into account in the planning of military operations against Hamas. Meanwhile, the same poll found that 83% of Arab Israelis thought the suffering of Palestinians should be considered in the planning of any military operations.[5]

Beyond the obvious national affiliations, a significant factor motivating these poll results is that many Arab Israelis see updates from Hebrew news services but also have cable news networks such as Al Jazeera and Al Mayadeen running in the background of their living rooms most of the day.

On those networks, the most common stories during the war have been images of people running to hospitals carrying the injured with their bare hands amid piles of rubble from damaged schools and hospitals. There are also frightening scenes showing collapsed civilian buildings following massive explosions, which looked far from the 'surgical' precision Netanyahu claimed would be a hallmark of the IDF's response to October 7.

Photos are shown of the children killed in airstrikes, alongside video testimonies from grieving family members. Extracts from their diaries are read out, along with social media posts sharing their unfulfilled dreams to be doctors or firefighters, lamenting the tragedy of innocent lives cut short.

Neither network has interviews with Israelis who have lost loved ones, nor with families of hostages or those living under constant Hamas rocket fire. When misfired Hamas or Palestinian Islamic Jihad (PIJ) rockets cause civilian deaths in Gaza that are initially attributed to Israel, the networks fail to issue corrections. Nor do they report on the daily rocket attacks on northern Israel, which cause civilian injuries and death, damage to homes and farms from rockets and subsequent fires, or share stories of the more than 80,000 evacuated Israelis who haven't returned home since October 7.

Turning-point images

Many people believe a single photo taken by Nick Ut in 1972 changed the course of the Vietnam War. It shows nine-year-old Kim Phúc Phan Thị fleeing her village after being torched by napalm dropped by a South Vietnamese Air Force Skyraider. The *New York Times* editors initially hesitated to consider the photo for publication because of her nudity, but they eventually approved it. A cropped version of the photo was featured on the front page the next day. It was also the subject of an editorial in the *New York Post*, and captioned, 'The picture of the children will never leave anyone who saw it.'[6] It later earned a Pulitzer Prize and was chosen as the World Press Photo of the Year for 1973.

Reflecting on the impact of the photo, which accelerated existing anti-war sentiment in the United States, Nick Ut wrote in 2022 that 'it depicts the absolute horrors of war – defined by a young girl running naked amid devastation and death'. He is proud of the photo and the way it sparked discussions around the world and potentially made a difference in bringing the war to an end, and notes that truth remains essential and that the work of photojournalists today is as crucial now as it ever was.[7]

A decade after Ut photographed 'Napalm Girl', another horrific photo was taken that changed the course of a war. During the 1982 Lebanon War, United States president Ronald Reagan wrote the following in his diary after seeing a particularly graphic picture of an injured infant:

I was angry. I told him [Prime Minister Menachem Begin] it had to stop or our entire future relationship was endangered. I used the word 'holocaust' deliberately and said that the symbol of his war was becoming a picture of a 7-month-old baby with its arms blown off. Twenty minutes later, he called to tell me he'd ordered an end to the barrage and pled for our continued friendship.[8]

In December 2023, *Guardian* journalist Jonathan Freedland asked Israeli journalist Ilana Dayan on the *Unholy: Two Jews on the News* podcast whether a photo like 'Napalm Girl' could ever open a news broadcast on a mainstream station such as N12 where she was a senior reporter. While acknowledging that it's perfectly normal for a country at war to limit the destruction its civilian population sees from the other side, he wondered whether there was a point where Israelis should start watching and hearing the stories of grieving families in Gaza holding the bodies of loved ones pulled out from the rubble of destroyed apartment buildings.

Dayan rejected his suggestion, explaining that in light of the trauma Israelis endured on October 7, it was understandable that a grieving Israel was too broken to have a reservoir of empathy for the other, for the enemy.

Freedland raised the fact that, unlike Israeli Jews who didn't have to see the harrowing images of Gaza every day in their news, every diaspora Jew who watched the BBC or CNN did, which was why so many of them were constantly torn in the space between two very opposing narratives.

For Jewish Israelis, Dayan replied, nothing would change in their approach to the war by seeing pictures from Gaza, because letting 'the monster' (Hamas) live on their doorstep was impossible for their future safety, and therefore, Israelis were willing to pay the high price that entailed bringing it down.

She added that she was also torn between two choices as an Israeli reporter. The first was loyalty to her journalistic ethos to provide the whole story, and the second was the Israeli ethos demanding solidarity during the war, especially in one of the darkest chapters in Jewish history since the Holocaust.[9]

As both a journalist and an Israeli, I found the conversation fascinating. It reminded me of the tough choices I have faced during the war – deciding which stories to share on social media, and, just as importantly, which ones to leave out.

The vast majority of the Israeli media seem to agree with Ilana Dayan.

In May 2024, Israeli Communications Minister Shlomo Karhi went even further to hide the pain of Palestinians and the narrative of Hamas and Hezbollah, banning the broadcasting of Al Jazeera and Al Mayadeen in Israel and blocking access to their websites for all Israelis after security agencies submitted updated position papers, 'which unambiguously determined that the broadcasts of their channels constitute actual harm to state security'.[10]

Furthermore, a September 2024 *Haaretz* editorial observed that Israel's control over the Gaza border crossings prevented any foreign journalist from entering the Strip without state approval. The editorial, published in the dovish Israeli newspaper, criticised the ban on entry without an escort from the IDF Spokesperson's Unit, arguing that it severely hampers independent reporting and undermines the public's right – both in Israel and internationally – to be informed about the situation in Gaza. It also cited data from the Committee to Protect Journalists, noting that at least 111 Palestinian journalists and media workers had been killed during the conflict, though the

Israeli military identified three of them as members of Hamas or PIJ.[11]

A better way

For anyone working on finding a path to end the war, the failure of the media to cover the other side is deeply disappointing.

In this era of profound Israeli–Palestinian separation – with walls, checkpoints and anti-normalisation movements that reject positive contact with the other side – the media provides one of the few lenses through which Israelis and Palestinians could better understand each other.

That's why I believe journalists and editors have a responsibility to platform the minority voices of people who are working to promote a narrative that could end the war. Otherwise, we are left with dehumanising stereotypes, decontextualised violence, and a sense that violence and revenge are unavoidable and inherent to the very identity of the other.

The Center for Global Peace Journalism at Park University in Missouri has advanced the concept of peace journalism, a practice in which 'editors and reporters make choices that improve the prospects for peace'.[12] Those involved in peace journalism portray stories that help people imagine alternatives to the status quo, including creative solutions to conflict, while highlighting potential partners for peace. Their research has found that this exposure to another choice lowers the risk of the next conflict erupting.

Perhaps some will say that peace journalism is no less biased than classic 'pro-Israel' or 'pro-Palestine' journalism in that it too is just advocating an agenda rather than telling the whole story. While I see this criticism as valid, I can also imagine that both Israeli and Palestinian society would look very different today if our media served less as propaganda arms for our governments at war and more as voices that allow us to see the humanity of the other, especially at times when our hearts are least open to doing so.

I know such suggestions fly in the face of the many commercial considerations news broadcasters have when choosing which stories to air, but I also feel that it could only do good for both peoples in the long run. Consuming 'peace media', as I often do from Israel/Palestine, often involves finding all the news stories we never print.

Peace journalism might include a video of a bereaved Israeli mother such as Elana Kaminka expressing her pain with a bereaved Palestinian mother – at the end of a long article about what happened on October 7. Or a poem from Gaza that speaks of the desire to one day share the land with the Jewish people in peace – at the end of a long article about the war that ravaged the Strip.

In times of conflict, finding videos of Israelis and Palestinians promoting messages of empathy for both sides is like finding gold in a river of pebbles. Yet it is precisely these videos and stories that interrupt my newsfeed of horror and misery and give me hope that another way is possible.

Towards healing

In these trying times, there's a growing need for journalism that not only informs but also heals. Journalists who approach their work with compassion and a genuine desire to understand all perspectives can play a crucial role. By gently encouraging readers and interviewees to consider alternative viewpoints, we can help build bridges of understanding without dismissing the very real pain felt by all involved. Journalists like Dahlia Scheindlin, Dina Kraft, Nicholas Kristof, Ezra Klein and Krista Tippett exemplify this approach, pushing readers and interviewees to consider alternative viewpoints and question deeply held beliefs.

As this war rages on, it's vital to remember that behind every headline and statistic are real people, families and communities, all deserving of compassion and understanding.

CHAPTER 11

To the boys in the room: Hearing the missing voices of women

In the ancient Greek play *Lysistrata*, Aristophanes presents one of the earliest literary explorations of women participating in civil resistance and peacebuilding in the face of violent conflict. The main character, Lysistrata, orchestrates a pan-Hellenic sex strike to compel the warring states of Athens and Sparta to negotiate peace, effectively ending the Peloponnesian War. A 2017 report entitled 'Women in nonviolent movements' uses the example of the play to pose this fascinating question: does the inclusion of women in nonviolent strategies for peace influence the chances of a successful outcome?[1]

In 1976, Protestant Betty Williams and Catholic Mairead Corrigan started a peace movement that softened the hearts from people on both sides of the Troubles in Northern Ireland. They began working together in Belfast after a tragic incident on

August 10, 1976, when a car driven by an IRA member crashed into a family, killing three young children who were the niece and nephews of Corrigan. Williams, who witnessed the event, went door-to-door with a petition against violence, and Corrigan led a televised appeal for peace. United, they co-founded the Community of Peace People, a grassroots movement aimed at promoting peace and reconciliation in Northern Ireland. Six months after they launched their joint campaign in response to this tragic incident, the violence in Northern Ireland had declined by 70 per cent. The following year, Williams and Corrigan were awarded the Nobel Peace Prize for their efforts. Alongside the Northern Ireland Women's Coalition, their advocacy for integrated education played an essential role in the peace negotiations that led to the 1998 Good Friday Agreement.

Reading their story in Jerusalem, I wonder how our lives here could be different if the many women who have suffered so much loss were followed by the masses, as they were in Belfast.

The cost of excluding women from hostage and peace negotiations

Understanding the reasons for failed peace processes is essential to creating successful ones in the future. The Oslo Accords of 1993, a pair of interim agreements between Israel and the PLO, marked a significant turning point in the conflict, providing a framework for peace after years of violence. Despite their failure, the Oslo Accords are still used as a benchmark for other negotiations, with major anniversaries prompting numerous analyses. However, many reviews of the process overlook two critical factors: the absence of female political leaders, and the lack of religious leaders in the planning and implementation of the peace roadmap.

The negotiators and architects of the Oslo Accords were Ahmed Qurei, Hassan Asfour, Yasser Arafat and Mahmoud Abbas on the Palestinian side, and Yossi Beilin, Yair Hirschfeld, Shimon Peres, Ron Pundak, Yitzhak Rabin, Uri Savir and Joel Singer on the Israeli side. While I commend these visionaries for taking risks for the wellbeing of their people, it's important to remember that not only were they all male, they were all largely secular in their religious outlook. While it is impossible to definitively state that a more diverse negotiating team would have yielded a more resilient agreement and implementation, extensive research suggests that broader representation could have significantly impacted the outcome.

Studies on conflict resolution show that when women actively participate in resistance campaigns, nonviolent methods are far more commonly adopted and have a better chance of reaching their goals.[2]

A study of 40 peace processes across 35 countries since the 1990s showed that agreement was substantially more likely to be reached when women played a significant role in creating the proposed agreement. Furthermore, involving influential women in the implementation of the agreements also created a more enduring peace.[3]

Despite research supporting women's positive impact on peace efforts, their formal involvement in peace negotiations remains minimal. In UN-led or co-led peace processes in 2022, women made up only 6% of negotiators, down from 23% in 2020. Notably, negotiating teams for conflicts in Ethiopia, Myanmar, the Balkans, Sudan and Yemen completely lacked female representation. Colombia stood out as the sole exception, where women achieved near-equal representation in both government and rebel negotiating teams.[4]

In 2000, the UN Security Council adopted Resolution 1325 to address the underrepresentation of women in peacebuilding and the unique challenges they face during conflicts. This resolution highlights that women and girls are disproportionately affected by violence and emphasises their vital role in peace processes. It asserts that the inclusion of women leads to more sustainable peace, as they contribute significantly to conflict prevention, relief efforts and the rebuilding of communities.

On day 184 of the Israel–Hamas War, April 11, 2024, Rachel Goldberg-Polin shared a poem about how the fate of her son Hersh, then a hostage held by Hamas, and the fate of suffering civilians in Gaza could be different if women were negotiating a deal to end the war. Entitled 'To the Boys in the Room', it was recited with deep emotion at a rally in New York opposite the headquarters of the United Nations.

To the boys in the room,
There are thousands and thousands and thousands and
thousands of innocent civilians suffering terribly in Gaza,
but I only know one of them. He and I share the same
DNA, and we are both left-handed. Oh, now only one of
us is left-handed. And he lived and grew inside of me for
nine months, many moons ago.

To the boys in the room,
Every folk tale begins with the four words 'once upon
a time', and every deal or negotiation that you think of
crafting should begin with one word: 'hostages'.

To the boys in the room,
To motivate and incentivise you, you will now be asked to
hand over one of your family members. Your spouse, your
father, your sister, your son, your brother, your daughter,
your mother, your grandfather. If he has already passed
on to the next world, we will supply you with a shovel.
We will then hold on to your beloved one, and treat them
exactly as our beloved have been treated until you come up
with a plan for how to get these people back. And I reckon
it will take you less than 184 days.

To the boys in the room,
Our Father who art in Heaven, call him by any name you
wish; he will be home soon and, boys, just you wait till
your father gets home.[5]

This searing admonishment of men for failing to think creatively
to end the cycle of violence has been heard many times from
Rachel throughout the war. At the same time, she has always
noted the 'surplus of agony on all sides of the tragic conflict', even
from the main stage of the DNC convention where she spoke
with her husband, Jon, just before Kamala Harris was nominated
as the Democratic candidate for president in August 2024.

Tragically, Hersh Goldberg-Polin was murdered in a Gaza
tunnel by Hamas alongside five other hostages with whom he
was being held captive, just days before the IDF approached to
rescue him. He was buried on September 2, 2024, the same day
a national strike had been called by the Histadrut labour union,
with over 700,000 Israelis protesting their government over
their failure to make a deal that could have brought the hostages

home alive.[6] At his funeral, his parents said of Hersh, 'May his memory be a revolution.'

Together with thousands of people from across the country, I visited the mourning tent of Jon and Rachel in the week after his funeral. As I sat with them in their pain, knowing that our world had just lost an incredible peacemaker and bridgebuilder, I thanked them both for always centring the humanity of their son, all the hostages and all the innocent civilians of Gaza whenever they spoke. Inside that tent, I couldn't help but feel that if Rachel and a mother from Gaza had been leading the negotiations, their children could have come out of this war alive.

The women who are fighting for a seat at the table

Women Wage Peace (WWP) began in 2014, in the aftermath of the 50-day Gaza war that left 2125 Palestinians and 73 Israelis dead. The founders were motivated by the noble desire to prevent further bloodshed and to push for a diplomatic solution to end the Israeli–Palestinian conflict.

In its early days, the movement organised its first significant action – a gathering of a thousand women from all over Israel in Sderot, a city often targeted by rockets from Gaza, to say 'enough!' to the cycle of violence. Since then, WWP has grown into the largest grassroots peace movement in Israel, with over 50,000 members as of 2024, continuing to advocate for peaceful resolutions to the ongoing war.

On October 4, 2023, just days before the tragic events of October 7, WWP and the Palestinian movement Women of the Sun united for the 'Mothers' Call', a joint initiative calling for conflict resolution. The day's activities began at the Bethlehem checkpoint and concluded at the Dead Sea, featuring an exhibition of peace quilts and a symbolic negotiation table. Leaders from both movements spoke about their determination to end the cycle of violence and create a better future for their children.

Three days later, Vivian Silver, a founding member of WWP and a key organiser of the event, was murdered by Hamas in the October 7 attack. Silver, a 74-year-old Canadian– Israeli peace activist, had dedicated her life to fostering Israeli–Palestinian understanding and cooperation, leaving an immeasurable impact on the broader peace movement. In July 2024, a community space and kitchen was opened by a charity supporting Gazans and named in memory of Vivian Silver at the Zomi camp in the al-Mawasi humanitarian zone in southern Gaza. A large banner on the outside of the kitchen includes Vivian's name and a photo of her smiling face. At a time when some IDF soldiers were writing the names of Israelis who had been killed on October 7 on tank shells aimed at Hamas, Vivien's son, Yonatan Zeigen, tweeted a picture of the sign, writing, 'In these heartbreaking circumstances, I would rather know that my beloved mom Vivian's name is helping to feed children in Gaza than see it engraved on a missile that kills them.'[7]

While many peacebuilding groups paused or closed during the war, one that was able to grow was an initiative of those two women's groups, Building Bridges, which included a component on harnessing religion for peace-making. Under the leadership of Peta Jones Pellach from Jerusalem and Raefa Hakroush from Haifa, Israeli religious women from varied backgrounds and faith communities began an intense program to promote peace and understanding.

Each session began and concluded with prayers in both Hebrew and Arabic, creating a sacred atmosphere for the transformative experience. Participants explored deep themes such as 'the stranger', 'kindness', 'justice' and 'truth', examining these ideas through their own religious perspectives. In one of their meetings, the group studied the Book of Ruth, my favourite book in the Bible. This story begins with a Romeo- and-Juliet narrative that takes place in a time of deep historical animosity between the Israelite and Moabite nations. Yet it is far from a romantic tragedy centred on young love. The biblical story is centrally about familial love and loyalty rather than romantic passion. It also has a far more redemptive ending, with the union of Boaz the Israelite and Ruth the Moabite following her conversion to Judaism. Together, they are the great-grandparents of King David, who is remembered in Judaism as the most exalted psalmist, warrior and leader, and the ancestor of the future messiah.

Despite strong resistance from several characters to the union of Boaz and Ruth, the narrative suggests that individuals should be judged by the content of their character rather than the God they were raised to worship. Today, Ruth is a very common Jewish name for women, and her story is studied universally as a symbol of loyalty, faith and compassion.

Although groups like Women Wage Peace from Israel and Women of the Sun from Palestine currently have limited influence in their respective societies, I hope that their leadership might one day play a crucial role in future Israeli–Palestinian peace talks. Based on resolved conflicts, the potential involvement of these women-led organisations in negotiations could potentially lead to more favourable outcomes for everyone who desperately wants to end the war and build peace.

CHAPTER 12

If it be your will:
Faith and peacebuilding

Irish playwright George Bernard Shaw once observed that no man ever believes that the Bible means what it says: he is always convinced that it says what he means. I often think of this observation when it comes to the role of religion in peace-making, because the same sacred text can be used as a source of division or a source of connection.

A significant obstacle to peace is the fundamentalism of religious principles by radical groups, reinterpreted to justify violence and hatred of the other. We see this perpetrated by radical groups such as Hamas, Hezbollah, the Houthis and the Islamic Republic of Iran, as well as Jewish extremists in the messianic settler movement.

Hamas is an acronym for Ḥarakat al-Muqāwamah al-ʾIslāmiyyah – Islamic Resistance Movement. When I watched the shocking GoPro footage of their fighters carrying out the October 7 attack, murdering Israelis in their homes early on a Saturday morning, there were several Arabic cries invoking Allah's name rather than cries for the liberation of Palestine. And when the victims are mentioned – such as in the phone recording from one attacker to his parents bragging about how many people he had just killed – there is no use of the terms 'colonial settlers' or 'Israelis'. They are simply called 'Jews'.

According to Hamas, the first goal of the October 7 attack was to stop the 'Israeli plans to the blessed Al-Aqsa Mosque … as well as the intensification of the Israeli settlers' incursions into the holy mosque'.[1] Hamas spokesperson Bassem Naim said, 'This round of conflict is being waged by the resistance under the name "Al-Aqsa Flood". It is not for the sake of Gaza or the West Bank, but rather for the sake of Jerusalem and Al-Aqsa.'[2]

Palestinian Islamic Jihad Deputy Secretary-General Muhammad Al-Hindi also invoked religious language when he described the recruitment process for fighters against Israel in a September 2024 interview. He explained that their slogans, such as 'Jihad until victory or martyrdom' and 'Our dead are in Paradise and yours in Hell', are powerful motivators that require little additional persuasion. Al-Hindi emphasised that young Palestinians are mobilised through religious texts passed down generationally. He contrasted this with past efforts by secular and Marxist groups, stating that inspiring martyrdom attacks (such as suicide bombings) was nearly impossible for them.

According to Al-Hindi, the current recruitment process is simplified, often requiring only a brief Quranic verse or passage to motivate potential fighters. He specifically mentioned the opening of Surah Al-Isra as an example of a text used to inspire martyrdom operations, saying that after certain people read this text about the prophet Muhammad's night journey from Mecca to Al-Aqsa they don't need encouragement to fight and die to liberate it.[3]

Recognising that Hamas or PIJ claim to act in the name of their religion does not equate to maligning Islam. It's evident that they do not represent the entire faith, which has billions of adherents. However, overlooking the religious justification for their political violence can hinder efforts to find a solution.

Meanwhile in Israel, the aftermath of the October 7 attack saw a significant rise in religious nationalist rhetoric. In January 2024, a Jerusalem conference supporting Israeli resettlement in Gaza drew 5000 participants. Speakers at the event used both security concerns and biblical references to argue for what they described as the 'humane solution' to end the war, advocating for the 'emigration' of Palestinians from Gaza. To justify this extreme policy position, National Security Minister Itamar Ben Gvir referenced Numbers 33:55, which states, 'Drive out all the inhabitants of the land before you … But if you do not drive out the inhabitants, those you allow to remain will become barbs in your eyes and thorns in your sides.'[4]

In a July 2024 meeting with settlers from the Hebron Hills outpost of Givat Hanan, the far-right Minister of Settlements and National Missions Orit Strock expressed her excitement about the 'miracle period' of settlement expansion initiated by the government during the war. Her remarks coincided with Israel's largest land appropriation in the West Bank since the 1993 Oslo Accords and followed the legalisation of five other outposts in the area. She likened the situation to standing at a traffic light waiting for it to turn green and referred to expanding settlements on West Bank land that was once part of Biblical Israel as 'a sacred task'.[5]

Additionally, there has been a noticeable increase in the number of religious Zionists seeking to assert Jewish sovereignty over the Dome of the Rock in Jerusalem, a site that holds significant religious importance for both Jews and Muslims. Yitzchak Reuven, director of the Temple Institute, an Israeli organisation that seeks to build a third Temple in place of the Al-Aqsa mosque, said quite clearly, 'The Muslims correctly understand the historical and religious significance of the Temple Mount for the Jewish people and therefore focus their incitement on the Temple Mount. In effect, the war in Gaza is very much a war over the Temple Mount.'[6]

Recognising that individuals in the Temple Institute or far-right ministers in Israel claim to act in the name of their religion does not equate to maligning Judaism. It's evident that they do not represent the entire faith, which has 16 million adherents. However, overlooking the religious justification for their political rhetoric can hinder efforts to find a solution.

Despite these religiously motivated calls to kill, control and remove the other, there are voices of moderation in both Islam and Judaism who draw on their religious tradition to embrace a different path.

Wasatia: Religious moderation in Islam

Religious leaders and academics advocating for interfaith dialogue, particularly during a time of war, are unfortunately rare in Palestine and Israel today. However, they do exist. Back in 2019, one of the speakers at Kids4Peace was Professor Mohammed Dajani Daoudi, a scholar from East Jerusalem. Dajani, who was a lecturer in Holocaust studies at Al-Quds University, led a delegation of 30 Palestinian students to

Auschwitz–Birkenau, in what was said to be the first organised visit by Palestinian students to a concentration camp. Regrettably, the ensuing controversy led to his resignation.

Dajani is a former Fatah fighter who was banned from Israel for 25 years. Now, he is the founder of the Wasatia movement, which advocates for moderation, reconciliation, dialogue and peace between Palestinians and Israelis. The term 'wasatia', means 'middle path' in Arabic, and it underscores the significance of a moderate Islamic perspective for fostering peaceful relations in the region. It advocates for dialogue and mutual understanding among diverse religious and political groups.

During his address to the youth at Kids4Peace, Dajani recounted a lesson from his school days about an old man planting an olive tree. He explained, 'Our ancestors planted trees and we ate the fruits; so too, we plant trees so that our grandchildren will eat.' This story, which also appears in the Jewish Talmud, resonated with Dajani, who, in his seventies, emphasised the responsibility of the older generation to cultivate peace for the younger generation to inherit.

Inspired by teachings such as this, on October 30, 2023, the Haifa Laboratory for Religious Studies and the Ahmadiyya Muslim Community organised a significant multi-faith gathering at their mosque in Haifa, Israel, amid the ongoing war in Gaza. The event attracted over 600 participants from the local Muslim and Jewish communities, along with representatives from Christian and Buddhist faiths, all united in their call for a ceasefire in Gaza and an end to the killing of civilians in Israel.

The keynote address was delivered by Sheikh Muhammad Sharif Odeh, the leader of the Ahmadiyya Muslim Community in the Holy Land. He passionately conveyed that 'We can't fight ideology with force. We fight ideology with an alternative ideology.' Odeh stressed that the foundation of their community is to counteract the radicalisation stemming from certain political movements within Islam. He articulated that the essence of God's message through prophets was not to establish nations or engage in politics but to promote equality among all citizens. He referenced the historical constitution of Medina, which exemplified the principle of equality between Muslims and Jews.

He also pointed out that the term 'jihad' in the Quran is never associated with warfare, emphasising that even in defensive wars, violence against non-combatants is strictly prohibited. He concluded by reinforcing the idea that all humanity is interconnected and that the most cherished individuals in God's eyes are those who contribute positively to the welfare of others, regardless of their background. The gathering served as a poignant reminder of the potential for coexistence and dialogue in the face of adversity.

Many who left the mosque in Haifa that night did so with a sense of relief, a sense that maybe, just maybe, our religious inheritance might one day be a source of unity instead of enmity.[7]

Religious leaders feeling the pain of the others

Sheikh Muhammad Sharif Odeh visits the homes of Jewish victims affected by terrorism linked to radical Islam. Stabbings or shootings of Jews driving in cars, or standing at bus stops or at entrances to their communities, are common occurrences throughout Israel. In each condolence visit, he emphasises his identity as a Muslim and Arab, stating that following each terror attack, he feels compelled to offer his condolences. From his home in the north of Israel, he has travelled across the country, including visiting homes of bereaved families in West Bank settlements, driven by a sense of accountability before God.

Gadi Gvaryahu is a kippa-wearing Orthodox Jew and the leader of Tag Meir, which organises Jewish groups to express condolences to the families of Muslim and Christian victims of terrorism at the hands of Jewish extremists. He articulates a commitment to view all individuals as equals, asserting that humanity is a singular creation of God. Gvaryahu's motivation for these visits stems from a desire for coexistence, as he believes that by rejecting religious extremism, we can one day live together in peace.

As a member of Tag Meir, I have personally participated in numerous visits after Jewish-settler arson attacks on private homes, olive groves and mosques in the West Bank. One memorable journey was to Huwara the day after a violent rampage by hundreds of settlers seeking vengeance for the tragic shooting of two Israelis in the village. Characterised as a 'pogrom' by a local Israeli commander, the attack left over 100 Palestinians wounded and claimed one life. During the solidarity visit with Tag Meir, I was invited to the home of one of the victims to hear their story. After treading through shattered glass, with the acrid scent of smouldering embers still lingering, I listened as a Palestinian woman recounted her harrowing ordeal of fear and terror. The experience of bearing witness to the aftermath of such brutality and hearing firsthand accounts of the trauma endured was deeply affecting.

On the long bus ride back to Jerusalem, I felt deep despair over the violence I had witnessed but also a glimmer of hope that the empathy being demonstrated by this small group of Jews might one day not only condemn religiously motivated violence but also turn into a movement that can prevent it.

An eye for an eye makes the whole world blind

Between East and West Jerusalem, there have been few victims mourned by both Israelis and Palestinians. One exception was Mohammed Abu Khdeir, a 16-year-old Palestinian teenager who was kidnapped outside his home and burned alive by three Israeli yeshiva students in a 'price tag' attack following the kidnapping and murder of three Israeli yeshiva students in the summer of 2014.

The religious and political motivation for this child's murder was directly condemned by then Israeli president Ruvi Rivlin, who said:

> 'And cursed be he who cries out: Revenge.' So wrote
> Bialik. Cursed be the ruinous destructive revenge that
> inflicts pain for pain's sake and harms the innocent.
> A national struggle does not justify terrorism. Terrorism
> does not justify revenge. Even in the face of anger and
> frustration, violence and pain, there is another way,
> another path must be taken.
>
> Our duty, the duty of the Jewish and Muslim
> leadership, is to stop the incitement campaign.
> We must understand that we have no other way
> apart from living together. The bloodshed will stop
> only when we understand that living together is not
> something we are forced to do, but something we are
> meant to do.

We are in the midst of the month of Ramadan and it
is not long before the Three Weeks of Jewish mourning for
ancient Jerusalem. These should be the days of tolerance
and creation, not days of destruction. I call on each and
every one of us, Arab and Jew, to stop, to opt for the joint
path and to reaffirm our belief in our ability to live here
together, on this land. We have no other option, we have
no other country.[8]

Once Rivlin, as the president, set this example of religious
peacebuilding, the people followed. Several hundred Israelis
visited the Abu Khdeir family home in Shuafat to pay their
respects to the family.

Abu Khdeir's cousin Kefah Abukhdeir noted that
Mohammed was the first child mourned by both sides, and that
his death made visible our common humanity:

After his shroud disappeared into Palestine's belly,
I thought of the anger that compelled us to pick up
stones. But then I turned around to see the crowd that
had gathered in my village. I saw all the nations who
gathered to honour Mohammed. I saw Shuafat extend
from my grandfather's headstones to Palestine and beyond.

I started to listen to the land that honoured
Mohammed in accepting his body. The land asked me why
we only gathered for the dead. The land asked me when
we would honour her with our life.

We are from the same rib of that land between the
river and the sea, and I know you as well as you know me.
Can true lovers of our land cherish freedom and liberty

for all? Must we challenge each other's love for our land? Might we stand together in Palestine, loving Israel, and vice versa?

Perhaps together we can unchain our youth from their shackles of military service. Can we remember the collective us that stands before God?

We all belong to Jerusalem, Al-Quds. Her love waits for us to honour her.[9]

These male and female peacebuilders, politicians and religious leaders – who say these words from their parliaments, pulpits, minbars, places of mourning, schools, yeshivot and madrasas – are the people whose voices need to be amplified across our holy land.

When these voices of moderation hold space for the human spirit to overcome our most base urges of revenge, affirming that all humans are created in the image of God, our world will be better for it.

CHAPTER 13

Inside the classroom: Dominant narratives and untold stories

So far in this book, we have explored a number of areas where change is needed for peace – from understanding our history, to youth movements that keep hope alive, to the stories of other conflicts that have found resolution, such as the one in Northern Ireland. Furthermore, we've explored the challenges of dialogue, the importance of moral reckoning, journalism that promotes solutions, and the role of women leaders and faith-based initiatives. Now we'll turn to the role of narratives born in our education system.

Every person carries within them a unique story, shaped by their experiences, relationships and circumstances. A narrative is more than just a sequence of events; it is the way we make sense of the world and our place in it. It defines how we perceive ourselves and others, and over time, it moulds the choices we make, the values we hold and the person we eventually become. Narratives begin at home and are enhanced by the type of education we receive, and are then cemented by the societal messaging we encounter.

The narratives in our textbooks

In 2023, I conducted an interview about textbooks with Dr Samira Alayan, who is a senior lecturer and a researcher on Palestinian textbooks at the Hebrew University and David Yellin College of Education. She shared with me that, after 1993, some Palestinian Authority textbooks were published in the spirit of Oslo, including maps of the 1967 Green Line demarcating Israel from the Palestinian territories and making reference to peace and coexistence. But after Trump recognised Jerusalem as the capital of Israel in 2018, Palestinian textbooks took a more hardline view, with direct references against soldiers, checkpoints and the Occupation. Today, a student learning from a Palestinian Authority textbook would have little understanding of why Israel is important to Jews, the legacy of the Holocaust on Jewish identity, or the prevalence of antisemitism beyond Israel's borders. Instead, they are exposed to many examples of how the birth of Israel was and continues to be a catastrophe for them.[1]

Israeli textbooks are sadly not much better for seekers of peace. Most completely ignore the Nakba, have no Green Line showing the border between Israel and the Palestinian territories on their maps, and include no stories of Palestinian suffering as a result of the IDF presence in the West Bank or the siege on Gaza. The Zionist narrative inculcated in Israeli schools often describes an eternal battle of the Jews against non-Jewish conquerors, usurpers of the land and persecutors.

A solution to this challenge is the use of dual-narrative textbooks in high schools. One such project was developed for a pilot program by Sami Adwan and Dan Bar-On, the co-founders of the Peace Research Institute in the Middle East (PRIME). The textbook has a dual-narrative history of every controversial event, from the Balfour Declaration to the Oslo Accords, side by side. One teacher, Rachel, summarised the process she went through in the four years of using the textbook in her classroom:

> When I first saw the narrative of their side, I was angry
> and frustrated at how different it is from ours. I felt it was
> not based on facts but on stories and emotions. Later, I
> learned to cognitively accept the difference, but still felt
> our narrative was superior to theirs. Only recently did I
> learn to see the logic behind their narrative and even to
> emotionally feel empathy for what they went through.
> If this took me four years, imagine what it will take the
> pupils and their parents.[2]

Many others in the program shared similar experiences, highlighting both the difficulty of implementing this change and the potential benefits it offers. As a result, only a few schools in Israel and Palestine have adopted this approach, though there are some notable exceptions. These include the Hagar Association, which runs a bilingual school in Be'er Sheva, and the Neve Shalom/Wahat al-Salam School, a bilingual, binational primary school in the mixed Jewish–Arab community of the same name. The largest, however, is the Hand in Hand network, which began with just 50 children in 1998 and now operates six campuses with thousands of students nationwide. Although I can't be certain, I strongly believe that as enrolment in these schools increases, so does the potential for peace.

Arabic and Hebrew

Our narratives are entirely shaped by our language and culture. One of the things we haven't yet sufficiently tried in Israel and Palestine as a means to bridge the divides between us is widescale instruction of one another's languages. In Jerusalem today, very few Jews speak Arabic. In East Jerusalem, more people speak Hebrew out of necessity, but it's usually learned on the job or at a post-high-school Ulpan – the Hebrew language instruction schools often run for Arab and international students.

I believe that if all Jews spoke Arabic and all Palestinians spoke Hebrew, it would further promote the possibility of this land being shared. The reason for this is that language is far more than words. It's culture. It's religion. It's food and it's a way of life.

When I began learning Arabic in 2018, the teacher explained the difference between Fusha (formal Arabic for writing) and Amiye (spoken Arabic). We then learned that there were different dialects. For example, Jerusalem is called 'Al-Quds' by those from the city and 'Al-Uds' by those from the villages. Both words mean 'the Holy'. The Hebrew name for the city is 'Yerushalayim'. It's a combination of the words 'Yeru' and 'Shalem', meaning 'see' and 'whole' or 'peace', articulating the Jewish view that Jerusalem is only whole when it is at peace.

Hebrew and Arabic also have much in common. They are both Semitic languages that share common words, gender inanimate objects and are written from right to left.

What does learning a language have to do with peace? Quite simply, when a time comes that we can not only speak each other's language but also use that language to understand how much this place means to the other through literally every word we speak, it will be very hard for us to continue holding on to the false notion that the other has no place here.

Yet language instruction alone is no solution. Russians and Ukrainians can largely understand one another, and that didn't stop them from going to war in February 2022. Neither did it stop the bloody civil war in Syria, which has taken over half a million lives, despite all armed groups and their supporters speaking Arabic. Beyond a common language, what's needed is to find a better balance between memory and forgetting.

Shedding our memories of persecution and amplifying counternarratives

In May 2024, a three-minute clip called 'Never again is all over again', from the Israeli comedy series *The Jews Are Coming*, went viral. The skit linked the events of October 7 to six unrelated historical attacks on Jews. These included the destruction of the Second Temple by the Romans in 70 CE, the Crusades, the Kishinev Pogrom, Kristallnacht, the Hebron Massacre, and the Farhud, the 1941 pogrom immediately following the British victory in the Anglo–Iraqi War in Baghdad.

It's a powerful, simple piece of drama, but it is fundamentally deceptive. It paints Jewish history as one long chain of antisemitism, ignoring both the context of individual events and the many generations of interfaith harmony in between these crises. Each of these events happened in the context of larger wars conducted by empires that also had millions of non-

Jewish victims. They also ignore golden ages, such as the 1500 years of Jewish flourishing in Babylon, or the 800 years when our greatest rabbinic works were written in Poland.

Jewish history is much more than a series of anti-Jewish pogroms. There have been many cases where Jews were saved by righteous non-Jews, such as that of the mother of the former Knesset Speaker Avraham Burg, whose mother was saved by her Arab neighbours from the Hebron rioters in 1929. Burg reflected, 'I owe my life and my children's lives to the heroes Abu Shaker and Umm Shaker. Righteous among the Nations who risked being killed by their own people, those who had lost the image of God within them and mercilessly slaughtered as many of Hebron's Jewish population as they could lay hands on.'[3]

And then we get to Kfar Azza, the kibbutz which is emblematic of the Hamas massacre on October 7. To paint this massacre – as the 'Never again' clip does – as merely another point in a chain of antisemitism misses the experiences of Bedouin citizens and Thai workers who were also kidnapped or killed on October 7. It also discounts the non-Jews who stood up and saved Jews on October 7. Hamid Abu Arar rescued several Israeli soldiers from Hamas, immediately after Hamas operatives shot and killed his wife. Ismail Alkrenawi from Rahat saved the life of Aya Meydan from Kibbutz Be'eri and the lives of 40 people fleeing from the Nova festival. Suleiman Shalibi formed a group of hundreds of volunteers from the Arab community, who put their lives on the line and, under fire, helped to rescue people they didn't know from certain death. Their stories were all featured in a series of videos produced by the Jewish–Arab partnership organisation Have You Seen the

Horizon Lately, yet their names are largely unknown in the Israeli mainstream.[4]

Importantly, unlike the other historical events, October 7 was an attack on a people with one of the most powerful armies on earth – an army that failed to protect them. The political leaders responsible for this failure are still in power. Yet that is nowhere in this story. All we learn from the 'Never again' clip is that in every place Jews have lived, we have been slaughtered or tortured.

The clip largely misses the lessons we should learn from these six events. What they all have in common, in addition to antisemitism, is xenophobia and racism. Each illustrates the devastating effects of totalitarian regimes, where there are no restrictions on the use of violence to pursue political goals, ultimately destroying the lives of both Jews and non-Jews.

As much as we must remember our history to learn from it, part of our healing from trauma involves distancing ourselves from our collective suffering to move forward.

In order to do this, alongside every dominant historical narrative, we need to make space to acknowledge the non-dominant one. This means remembering not only the non-Jews who saved Jewish lives but also those who were victims themselves on October 7. It also includes recalling the thousands of Israelis who donated food for hundreds of aid trucks to Gaza, organised by the Jewish–Arab solidarity group Standing Together, and those who contributed millions of shekels to GoFundMe campaigns supporting Gazans in need. Their acts of solidarity must be woven into the memory of this war no less than the stories of Palestinian citizens of Israel supporting Jewish evacuees from the north or the Sudanese and Eritrean asylum seekers who volunteered, donated and supported Jewish Israelis in their hour of need.[5]

The path to peace between Israelis and Palestinians is challenging but not impossible. By creating space for one another's narratives, learning one another's languages, taking a wider view of our history and uplifting the often-ignored stories that show there is a partner for peace, a new future becomes possible. Once all these grassroots actions have been taken, the next step is adopting the best political solution.

CHAPTER 14

So, what's your solution for Israel/Palestine?

If I had a star for every time I've been asked this question, I'd have a Milky Way of my own. I'm most frequently asked this question by friends visiting Jerusalem, and even more so on social media or WhatsApp from those in Australia. Especially since October 7, many of the people who asked the question were former students or people who had read my posts on Facebook. Lurking behind the question was often curiosity about whether I had changed my opinion in light of a recent event or would change my opinion in response to a hypothetical event.

There are many ways to answer this question. I'm sharing here the international community's dominant response and a lesser-known solution that I prefer.

The answer of the international community: A two-state solution

The vast majority of nations in the United Nations support the very old idea of partitioning the land into two independent states: Israel and Palestine. Previous attempts have come close to making this a reality. For example, through the negotiations in the 2007–2008 Annapolis process, Israeli prime minister Ehud Olmert offered the Palestinians the creation of a state based on 1967 borders, with 6.3% of West Bank annexed to Israel, while Israel would swap territories with Palestinians on a one-to-one basis. Palestinian President Mahmoud Abbas made a counteroffer that proposed an Israeli annexation of 1.9% only, the sticking point being the inclusion of the Ariel settlement within the areas annexed by Israel – 26 kilometres into the West Bank. Israel rejected this. Reaching an agreement was also hampered by Olmert's complicated legal situation ahead of his corruption trial, Abbas's weakness and the end of George Bush's term in the White House. The United States was the key mediator for these talks.

Olmert tried again in July 2024, in the midst of the war. He and former Palestinian foreign minister Nasser al-Kidwa called on Israel and Palestine to adopt their proposal that called for an immediate ceasefire in Gaza and a full withdrawal of Israeli troops. It also called on Hamas to release all hostages in exchange for a number of Palestinian prisoners released from Israel, and a return to Israel's 1967 borders with the establishment of a corridor linking the Gaza Strip and the West Bank as part of a 4.4% land exchange that would be annexed to the State of Palestine. In October 2024, both former leaders met with the Pope who blessed their initiative. Neither government has addressed the proposal in any official manner, showing how unpopular the two-state solution is to most Israelis and Palestinians.

The political vision I support

I support the vision proposed by the group A Land for All of 'Two States, One Homeland'.[1] Under this model, Palestine and Israel will recognise one another, and their territories will be based on the 1967 borders but there will be no hard border. The two states would form a confederation within a single homeland, allowing citizens from one state to live as permanent residents in the other. There would be freedom of movement for everyone, and Jerusalem would serve as the capital for both states, but each national group would only vote in elections for its own state. Israel and Palestine would be jointly responsible for security and economic matters that affect both populations.

I prefer this model because it draws on ideals of sovereignty and cooperation that are elements of other successful peace processes. This is primarily because, unlike the two-state model that the international community has backed for decades, it rejects complete separation as a condition for peace, based on the high likelihood that under the two-state model, both nations would remain deeply hostile to one another. It also doesn't call for Israelis or Palestinians to extinguish their dream of national self-determination in any part of the land, making all the territory from the river to the sea a land for all.

Living and working in the space between East and West Jerusalem, which is today a culturally divided city for two nationalities under one sovereign, I experience a confederation model regularly. Yet, unlike the reality that now exists in Jerusalem, the confederation model I dream of will be one where all people have full equality in social, economic and political rights.

However, no matter which of the three solutions one supports – one-state, two-state or confederation – one thing is missing that will allow any of them to become a reality. That ingredient is called trust. Former US secretary of state John Kerry summed it up in 2016, following four years of attempts to bridge the divides:

> In the end, I believe the negotiations did not fail because the gaps were too wide, but because the level of trust was too low. Both sides were concerned that any concessions would not be reciprocated and would come at too great a political cost. And the deep public scepticism only made it more difficult for them to be able to take risks.[2]

Without combatting dehumanisation and bolstering the belief in the ability of the other side to enact the policies that are formed through agreements, no political solution will ever be possible.

CHAPTER 15

Challenging dehumanisation and suspending disbelief

Of all the factors that make peace impossible, perhaps the greatest is dehumanisation. This process of depriving individuals or groups of their human qualities is something I see all around me, and it breaks my heart. Dehumanisation often arises from psychological processes categorising others into 'us' versus 'them' groups. When individuals or groups are perceived as different or threatening, it becomes easier for people to justify collective violence against them.

Dehumanisation has been a prevalent factor in almost every act of discrimination, persecution, war and genocide that has ever happened. Dehumanisation can occur when individuals fail to empathise with others or recognise their inherent worth and dignity. This lack of empathy allows people to justify harmful actions or indifference towards those perceived as different or inferior.

Given that Arabs make up 21% of the population in Israel, there aren't any Jewish Israelis who don't know or interact regularly with Arab and Palestinian citizens of the country. Most of these interactions happen in workplaces, shopping centres and hospitals. While there are always underlying tensions, these relations are usually cordial and respectful on both sides. Yet the relationship with Palestinians in Gaza is something else.

Since October 7, the indifference I have observed among so many of my Jewish-Israeli acquaintances to Palestinian civilians suffering in Gaza is something that doesn't surprise me but leaves me saddened. While I understand that it comes from a place of rage after the horrendous Hamas attack, the fact that it has lasted for so long and is so immune to the many harrowing personal stories of loss and grief in Gaza is hard to fathom. It manifests in several ways, from disregard and sometimes even complete denial of the humanitarian situation in Gaza to justifications for the destruction of every home and life in Gaza.

In one particularly extreme case, a 13-year-old Bedouin girl at a secular state school with predominantly Jewish students in Be'er Sheva was suspended for three days after she said in a class discussion approaching the one-year anniversary of October 7 that 'there are hungry children in Gaza, there are children without a home'. After she was suspended 'to protect her from harassment', videos of her classmates went viral with them chanting, 'Am Yisrael Chai' (the nation of Israel lives) and 'May your village burn'.[1]

When I raise this issue of dehumanisation in conversation with friends who express these views, the most common comments I hear in response are:

- Why should I care about them when they don't care about me and celebrate my people's murder and kidnapping with sweets and merriment?
- They are all radical Muslims, the same as ISIS. They hold an ideology that must be afforded no quarter and must be destroyed. You don't negotiate with terrorists. This is an existential war we must win at all costs. I won't tolerate any disrespect towards our brave soldiers.
- They hate us because we are Jewish. Anti-Semites want to see us all dead.
- Let me explain to you, Ittay, we Israelis want peace and have offered solutions to end the conflict many times to the Palestinians, which they have rejected. We do this because we value life. They just want death and to take all our land. The Arabs would rather kill us than live.

When I share that I work with many Palestinians in interfaith dialogue and know many people who just want to live alongside us in peace and worry about normal things like paying taxes and getting a mortgage, the usual response I hear is, 'You live in a bubble and because you didn't grow up here, you don't understand what Arabs want like I do.'

Perhaps some of the people who hold these views are reading this book. If so, I hope this chapter can open their hearts to a different possibility.

The 3000 Hamas men who crossed into Israel on October 7 clearly didn't see as humans the Israeli men, women and children they killed in their homes, at the Nova rave and on army bases.

No matter whether these people had a weapon or not, whether they were asleep or awake, at a dance party or just having breakfast with their family in their homes, all were murdered, many at point-blank range. The UN Office on Sexual Violence in Conflict also found reasonable grounds to believe that sexual violence occurred on October 7 and that captives in Gaza have been subjected to sexual violence too.[2]

Soon after the horrific attack, some Palestinians and their supporters justified and rationalised this violence by reducing all Israelis, and in some extreme cases, all Jews, to proxies of Israeli oppression. Even child hostages received no sympathy, with images of their faces being torn down in many Western capitals.

Their supporters on college campuses across the globe chanted slogans such as:

'Ya Qasam [Hamas's armed wing] make us proud, burn
   Tel Aviv to the ground.'
'There is only one solution: intifada revolution.'
'Go back to Poland, go back to Europe.'
'There is no safe place! Death to the Zionist state!'

When I try to suggest to people who express these views that Jews do feel a deep religious, historical connection to the land and that there are many – myself included – who oppose the violence of the Occupation and believe that the realisation of the Zionist dream need not come at the expense of a free Palestine, I am often told that I represent no one, or that my kind words mean nothing when the government that represents me does horrific things to Palestinians.

Perhaps some of the people who hold these views are reading this book. If so, I hope this chapter can open their hearts to a different possibility.

Selective confirmation bias

Selective confirmation bias is a tendency to process information by interpreting reality in a manner that supports what one already believes while rejecting evidence that supports a different conclusion. Many would say it's something I suffer from in my belief that peace is possible, yet I also see it as a blindness that plagues the majority of Palestinians and Israelis.

As a result of dehumanisation, the vast majority of us believe that the 'other side' not only doesn't want peace but largely wants our side dead. We tend to think that the 'other side' are all liars unless they are proposing views that reflect our deepest fears and stereotypes of them.

Consuming immense amounts of polarising information on social media causes many to suffer from a fundamental attribution error: we assume that our radicals are exceptional, while the other side's radicals are definitive. On the flip side, in the cases where Palestinian and Israeli civilians or leaders express calls for peace or empathy, they are branded as liars or traitors who are not speaking the truth about their national project. Therefore, a key element for change is adopting a new way of thinking.

Suspension of disbelief as a tool for peace-making

Suspension of disbelief happens when we temporarily allow ourselves to believe something that isn't true, usually to enjoy a work of fiction or a fantasy film. Yet this thinking technique is also an essential tool for social-change movements. Take, for example, the case of women's rights.

In the 1910s, the National Association Opposed to Women's Suffrage published a pamphlet arguing against women's right to vote in the United States. Some of their points included that '90% of women either do not want it or do not care', that 'it means competition between women and men instead of cooperation', and that '80% of women eligible to vote are married and can only double or annul their husband's votes'. They also argued that 'it can provide no benefit commensurate with the additional expense involved' and warned that it was 'unwise to risk the good we already have for the potential evil that may occur'.[3]

While many American men and women once believed these arguments, the suffragettes refused to give up. They defied the sceptics who said their movement had no chance of success. While the struggle for gender equality is far from complete today, not only can women vote in almost every country on Earth, but 59 countries have had female heads of state. This exemplifies what happens when 'suspension of disbelief' animates a social movement determined to counter all who say such a social change is impossible.

Beliefs and actions we need for peace

Since October 7, many people have shared versions of a particular meme on social media: 'It's okay to be heartbroken for more than one group of people at the same time.' I didn't ever post it because it felt too simplistic and obvious a statement to share, akin to saying, 'the sky is blue' or 'fire is hot'. Yet the more time I spend thinking and reflecting as I write this book, the more I realise it's not a belief that can be taken for granted.

Most Israelis believe that if they took down walls, checkpoints and other security measures against Palestinians, they would be slaughtered in an instant.

Most Palestinians believe that if their resistance organisations stopped fighting for freedom, Israel would permanently annex all of their land and never support their right to statehood, seeing this capitulation as Israel's long-awaited moment of victory.

As hard as it may be, these are two deeply entrenched beliefs we Israelis and Palestinians hold that need to be suspended for there to ever be peace. For good reason, these two beliefs have become even stronger since the horrors of October 7 and the destruction of almost every home and countless lives in Gaza.

Yet, for us to share this land, we both must believe that when the day comes that we choose to stop inflicting violence, the other will respond by ending their campaigns of violence against us. Nurturing and spreading this belief was the key to ending the troubles in Northern Ireland, and it is a belief we will also need to adopt here.

For Jewish Israelis, this could mean returning to the approach of Rabbi Hillel from the Talmud, who taught: 'What is hateful to you, do not do to your neighbour.' For Palestinian Muslims and Christians, this could involve re-embracing the Hadith of the prophet Muhammad: 'None of you truly believes until you wish for others what you wish for yourself' or the words of Jesus: 'In everything, do unto others as you would have them do unto you.'

It will mean encouraging both traditional and social media companies to abandon polarising reporting and algorithms that spread hate, and replacing it with peace journalism that is both self-critical and capable of building hope for an alternative future.

These words, written in white chalk on a garage door somewhere in the world, became one of the most shared memes by peace activists during the Israel–Gaza War that began in 2023.

It will mean having more women in leadership positions who can bring a wider array of perspectives and creative solutions for conflict to the negotiating table, leading to structural changes that provide security for all.

To stop the violence, we need to believe that there are partners for peace on the other side, by embracing shared learning opportunities and building more social, religious and political institutions based on the principles of justice and equality. Without increasing lived experiences of coexistence, we will always go back to the memories of fear and hatred that have plagued this land for so many years.

One of the best ways to dispel the belief that compromise is a weakness is to take responsibility for the injustices caused in the name of our national struggles. To hold those who commit war crimes accountable in our own courts of Palestine and Israel before the ICC needs to intervene. To believe that our conflict has solutions and that compromise is an act of strength and courage for the wellbeing of future generations. It must also involve acknowledging the massive power imbalance between Israel and Palestine.

To grow these realisations, thousands of grassroots conversations need to be held that move us from sympathy to empathy based on the belief that the purpose of dialogue is not to win, but rather to understand and take responsibility to improve one another's reality. This entails trusting that the enduring security derived from agreements, such as those between Israel, Jordan and Egypt, far surpasses the temporary safety that might be achieved through military actions. It involves recognising each other's humanity, and understanding that the love Palestinian and Israeli parents hold for our children is the same, as is the profound grief we experience when they are taken from us.

It means embracing the notion that injustice anywhere poses a threat to justice everywhere and that security of one side requires security for the other.

It means Palestinians believing that Jews in Israel are not colonisers and that they have a deep historical connection to this land, and that their security fears are real and not just made up in response to the Holocaust. It means Jews believing that Palestinians are a real nation with deep roots in this land between the river and the sea with the undeniable right to self-determination and freedom in their only homeland. It means acknowledging that not only is neither nation going to leave but that the existence of the other on the same land is desirable in building more liberal and tolerant nations that learn and grow through their shared experiences together.

While I may not have the means to convince the majority of people of these truths today, I firmly believe that if we set our sights on making these beliefs mainstream within the next ten years, it will be the most effective way to prevent the next war and eventually share this land with peace and dignity for all.

CHAPTER 16

Letters to Israeli and Palestinian children

This chapter has been one of the most difficult, yet most meaningful, to write. Before composing the two letters on the following pages, I thought of all the Palestinian and Israeli children I have met in Jerusalem. I then contemplated all the people whose lives have been cut short or impacted by loss, tragedy, fear and suffering. Thinking about how to end the violence one day inspired me to write these letters to future generations. While the names are made up, the people who I am addressing are very real: they are the future generations of this land I hold so dear.

Letter to an Israeli teenager

Dear Noa,

You have much to celebrate here in Israel, the country in which you were privileged to be born. When you walk to school each day from your home in Talpiot, down the Tayelet Promenade of Armon Hanatziv, overlooking the majestic vista of the Old City, know that you are walking in the same footsteps our ancestor Abraham trod as he fulfilled God's words to make Eretz Yisrael his home.

For thousands of years, your ancestors could only dream of the life you live today. After your great-grandparents perished in the fires of Auschwitz, you now live in a reality that could only have been imagined in their wildest dreams. Today, your home is in a country where the street signs carry the names of your prophets and national heroes, where your dominant language is the same as the one used to write the Torah and where national holidays are those from the ancient Jewish calendar. Embedded through your flag, national emblem, anthem and Declaration of Independence are the deep Jewish dreams for justice, freedom and peace as envisioned by the prophets of Israel.

Know too that even though you have a house or apartment where you live to enjoy these rights and freedoms, sadly, you are not at home. As one of your most celebrated authors, David Grossman, once explained: a home is a place whose borders are accepted by the whole world. It's a place where you and your friends will feel safe and secure as a place to raise your children.[1]

After 76 years, Israel is many wonderful things. A start-up nation, a land of festivals, an innovation nation; a land filled with the most beautiful hiking trails and natural springs to cool your body and mind in the hot months of summer. Yet it is not a home. All the patriotic speeches dripping with milk and honey can't change that fact.

As a beautiful and hopeful child of Jerusalem, you don't deserve to be burdened with the wars of your forefathers. There is this unwritten rule that our goal in life should be to leave a world for our children that is better than the one we received. I am sorry, Noa, but we have failed at that mission. You were born in a time when our state is far more dangerous and tenuous than when I was born.

You are alive at a time when our people suffered the greatest loss of life in a single day since the Shoah. You are alive at a time when our army has wrought immense destruction and devastation on Gaza, destroying more Palestinian lives, homes and dreams in a single year since the Nakba. You are alive at a time when almost no one believes in peace.

Resolving this complex situation often feels like a challenge harder than parting the Red Sea our ancestors crossed when we left Egypt. Over so many generations, war has taken countless lives and diminished the ability to thrive and flourish for so many of the living. Until this land is a safe and secure home for Palestinians, it will never be a home that is safe and secure for Israelis.

Noa, one day, I hope you will live in peace and safety where people will only be judged by the content of their character and not by their ethnic background, level of religious observance or the colour of their ID card.

When you turn 18, you will need to make a choice about either serving in the army or doing national service, such as in a school or a hospital. I know your sister was drafted into the army, and that she felt trepidation and pride when she first wore the green beret of the Nachal unit. Like you, she felt the tension between keeping our homeland safe and following some of the orders she would be required to obey to make it so. If you follow in her footsteps, please always be guided by your humanity, even in the most challenging of situations. Remember that no matter what orders you are given, it is your obligation to uphold the rules of international law at all times.

Know that, despite all the slogans you heard growing up, from 'their death gave us life' and 'together we will win', there is no victory that can happen on the battlefield without it being accompanied by an agreement around a negotiating table. The greatest victory will come by following a process of truth and reconciliation, which will be more physically and emotionally draining than a thousand Yom Kippur fast days, but also redemptive by the end.

Noa, I know you love your country. You love being outdoors, hiking and camping, and attending dance festivals. You have also told me of the many protests you attend with your friends, using your voice and your banners to raise awareness of things that matter to you. Use your passionate heart to keep making this place better. Consider joining one of the many grassroots organisations that exist throughout this land, from Standing Together and Have You Seen the Horizon Lately to the Parents Circle – Families Forum and Women Wage Peace. I hope you join or even lead one of these groups someday.

As you approach 18 years of age, the choice is in your hands. Speak out against collective punishment of your neighbours in Gaza, the West Bank and East Jerusalem, against revenge and using a 'firm hand to restore deterrence', which only ever seems to cause more violent responses. Flip the script that taught you that it's honourable to die for your country to one that says the greatest honour comes to those who honour others.

I know what I am asking is hard, and I know that it is risky. For so many years, you were taught that only a strong army can bring us security. Yet I am asking you to consider an alternative, one that believes the greatest security comes from peace. It happened with Egypt after four bloody wars between 1948 and 1973, and it can happen with the Palestinians. Once you decide that the path of equality and justice is one you seek, you will find many willing partners in Palestinian peace movements, from Taghyeer and the Gaza Youth Committee to the Sulha Peace Project and Zimam Palestine.

Please remember the words of your great sage Rabbi Hillel and think of how to build your future in this twice-promised land.

אם אין אני לי מי לי וכשאני לעצמי מה אני ואם לא עכשיו אימתי

If I am not for myself, who will be for me?

If I am only for myself, what am I?

And if not now, when?

Go in peace.

Your teacher and friend,

Ittay

Letter to a Palestinian teenager

Dear Hamed,

As you walk through the old cities of Hebron, Nablus and the greatest of them all, Jerusalem, remember this as you raise your eyes to see the glory of Al-Aqsa.

Your connection to Palestine is deeply rooted in the land itself. Palestine's lush landscapes are adorned with apricot and almond orchards and sprawling olive groves. These natural treasures are not just a source of sustenance but a representation of the resilience and endurance of the Palestinian people. These orchards and groves have been passed down through generations, embodying your steadfast attachment to the land.

Ancient cisterns, with their historical importance and architectural significance, are a testament to your deep connection to Palestine's past. These cisterns were built by your ancestors to capture and store precious rainwater in a land where water is scarce. They stand as a testament of the enduring spirit of your people who have, for centuries, found ways to thrive in your parched land.

As the famous poet Mahmoud Darwish once said:

We Palestinians suffer from an incurable disease called 'hope'.

Hope for liberation and independence.

Hope for a normal life where we shall be neither heroes nor victims.

Hope to see our children go to school without danger.

Hope for a pregnant woman to give birth to a living baby, in a hospital, and not to a dead child in front of a military control post.

Hope that our poets will see the beauty of the colour red in roses, rather than in blood.

Hope that this land will recover its original name: 'Land of hope and peace.'[2]

No matter how bad your mobile reception may be in the West Bank, or how long you need to wait for your WhatsApp to send, I know how much you love to post pictures of sunsets over the green hills surrounding the villages of Raba and Al-Zababdeh and the beautiful waters of Buhaira Tabariya.

Hamed, I know how much you dream of the day when you will be able to drive the beautiful road from Jenin to Nablus without encountering IDF soldiers, or the Mu'arrajjat road from East of Ramallah to the oasis of Jericho without roadblocks.

I know you dream of the perfect day where you will have breakfast in Yafa, midday prayers in Quds, lunch in Beirut and dinner in Damascus, with the countries of the Middle East existing without hard borders and walls, where Palestine will be an organic part of the Arab world.

From Ras Al-Naqoura to Umm Al-Rashrash, your people continue to both plant new roots and choose life, while your enemy continues to destroy and erase so much of what you hold dear, bearing truth to the words of Darwish: 'If the olive trees knew the hands that planted them, their oil would become tears.'[3]

If there were justice, the many signs along all the roads and highways would again bear the names of your prophets and heroes.

If there was justice, the immense time you waste at checkpoints and worrying for your friends in jail would be spent building your home on land you own, knowing that it would never be demolished by an occupying power.

If there were justice, parents in Gaza would never have to write their children's names on their hands so that they could be identified if a bomb destroys their house.

If there were justice, the hungry hearts at the Qalandia checkpoint and outside the Damascus Gate would no longer need to beg for sustenance.

Today, your Palestinian friend's Instagram feed blends images of them celebrating a graduation or Dabkeh dancing alongside desperate heartfelt stories crying out for the world not to stand idly by the destruction of your people.

At the same time, your Jewish counterpart posts images from parties or holidays while fearing kidnap, rocket attacks and bombings. Do you feel their pain as well? I know it's hard because the dead on your side are so many more, but think for a moment how your world would be if your relationship with Jews was based on the principle that every human must love their neighbour as themselves.

In his 1979 book *The Question of Palestine*, Edward Said reflected honestly on the path he chose in his struggle for liberation:

> Speaking only as one Palestinian, I have been horrified
> at the hijacking of planes, the suicide missions, the
> assassinations, the bombing of schools and hotels.
> Horrified both at the terror visited upon its victims and
> horrified by the terror in Palestinian men and women who
> were driven to do such things.

While not denying the extreme measures taken by some individuals, Said's horror at the loss of life and community on both sides of the conflict shows us that the Palestinian people are more and greater than the sum of their extremists' actions.

I can hear you asking, why should I respect or care for the Israelis and their pain, when they are my occupiers? How can I be friends with a Jewish child who will one day grow to be a soldier, who may one day stop and harass me at a checkpoint, or demolish my home or push the button from an F-16 that destroys an entire neighbourhood or a university in Gaza?

To this question, I would say that believing in peace with your Jewish friends doesn't make you a traitor; it makes you a human. The greatest danger for us all is the loss of humanity. The loss of the ability to see that there are innocents in two places. There will be no freedom for Palestine anywhere between the river and the sea without some process of truth and reconciliation, which will be more overwhelming and draining than a thousand Ramadans but hopefully redemptive by its end.

Yasser Arafat famously said in front of the assembled member nations of the UN in 1974, using words written by Darwish, 'Today I have come bearing an olive branch and a freedom fighter's gun. Do not let the olive branch fall from my hand. I repeat: do not let the olive branch fall from my hand.'

Arafat bravely chose the path of peace by signing the Oslo Accords. Yet later, he chose the gun over the olive branch, as have many Palestinian leaders in Gaza. Living in a country that is liberated through violence against innocents will leave deep trauma in those who carry it out, and produce vengeful neighbours. Even though this strategy may lead to a 'Free Palestine' at some point in the future, don't choose that option.

Use the power of international law, grassroots coalition building and political negotiations on your journey to freedom. Wherever possible, take this path.

For there to be justice, you need to acknowledge that even though you may see the Jews as colonisers, they are never going back to Europe or Iraq. They are here to stay in this land, and you must find a way to share it with them, together.

Until you are liberated, may your people find protection and safety in Palestine. May Allah ease your pain and suffering and help those who are in need and fortify their hearts and calm them like He granted Yousef's heart peace in the well. May Allah continue to be the Opener of Doors, granting you the victory of peace, and may your Palestinian Christian neighbours also be blessed with protection and freedom.

يعطيك العافية

May God give you health and wellness.
Your teacher and friend,
Ittay

Australian Ambassador Paul Griffiths and Turkish Defence Attaché Captain Yusuf Gorkem in front of the cenotaph at the Commonwealth War Cemetery in Jerusalem, 2022.

CHAPTER 17

When there is peace

At dawn on April 25, 2022, I found myself among a sea of graves at the Commonwealth War Cemetery in Jerusalem, a place where the whispers of history echo in solemn reverence. Together with hundreds of other Australians, we stood united to honour the valiant spirits of Australian and New Zealander troops who met their fate on the shores of Gallipoli, a campaign that began under a sombre sky on April 25, 1915. Wreaths – symbols of remembrance and reconciliation – were tenderly placed by dignitaries of Australia and Türkiye, two nations once locked in the tumult of war across the Middle East.

I was inspired seeing their presence side by side amid a vast resting place where so many youthful dreams lay eternally still. Over the eight-month mission to capture that beach, 8700 young Australians died in the labyrinthine spurs and ravines between the Dardanelles and the Aegean Sea, while 87,000 Turkish and Arab soldiers fell defending Gallipoli. Over the course of World War I, an unfathomable 40 million people were killed or injured. How does one grasp such immense loss?

As the memorial drew to a close, I approached the Australian ambassador, Paul Griffiths, and Turkish defence attaché, Captain Yusuf Gorkem, to request a photograph of them shaking hands before the cenotaph. After they kindly obliged, they asked why this photo was important to me.

I told them that seeing them together and knowing that Türkiye and Australia no longer seek to invade or destroy one another was remarkably inspiring. I wondered how all the 'Johnnies' and the 'Mehmets' who fell in World War I would feel seeing this image. What would they say to us, looking down on this moment?

I shared the picture on the *Jewish Independent*'s Twitter account, where it garnered just two likes and one retweet – my own. Perhaps this was a sign that such a poignant moment, in which representatives of two former adversaries were shaking hands, was not seen as exceptional. It was simply taken for granted. The annual Jerusalem Anzac memorial, a testament to reconciliation, passed without protest or condemnation, reflecting the enduring peace and warm diplomatic relations these two nations have enjoyed for decades.

I think about this moment often when I imagine peace between Israelis and Palestinians.

A joint memorial for Israelis and Palestinians

A week later, on May 3, 2022, a joint memorial was held for the 17th consecutive year for Palestinian and Israeli families who had lost loved ones killed in war. The ceremony, hosted by Combatants for Peace and the Parents Circle, is conducted in Hebrew and Arabic with simultaneous translation. Usually, equal time is given to testimonies from bereaved Jewish and Palestinian family members to share their pain and loss, interspersed with moving musical items, poems and videos highlighting the futility of revenge and the importance of justice and equality for a shared future.

I attend the memorial every year on what Israelis call Yom HaZikaron (Remembrance Day for Fallen Soldiers and Victims of Terrorism). The 18th memorial in 2023 was the largest ever, attended by over 150,000 people in Tel Aviv's Ganei Yehoshua Park, with around 95% of the attendees being Jewish Israelis. A further 200,000 people watched the event online and in various viewing locations in the West Bank and Washington, DC.

The May 2024 memorial was constrained by wartime restrictions preventing Palestinians from the West Bank and Gaza from visiting Israel amid heightened security concerns. The memorial was pre-recorded via Zoom a few days prior and streamed online.

Among the Israeli speakers were Yonatan Zeigen, son of Canadian–Israeli peace activist Vivian Silver, who was tragically murdered on October 7 near the Gaza border, and Michal Halev, mother of Laor Abramov, a DJ from New Jersey who was killed at the Nova music festival. Michal joined the Parents Circle after sitting amid the flickering candles of shiva in her Pardes Hannah home. She struggled with calls for vengeance and the cries to flatten Gaza, rejecting such notions in her name and especially in Laor's, who was murdered in a public bomb shelter near Kibbutz Re'im after escaping the nearby party.

The Palestinian speakers included Ahmed Helou, who lost 60 members of his extended family in Gaza. Another participant named Najlaa joined the joint Parents Circle – Families Forum after October 7. She left Gaza in her twenties to move to Hebron, an ancient West Bank city where she lives to this day. In December 2023, her young nephew Abed al-Rahman was killed by an IDF bomb near Khan Younis. He was 28, had been married for two years and was the father of 18-month-old twin boys. 'He spoke with me every day, asked how me and my children were,' she said in an interview with *Haaretz*. 'He was very sensitive, with a wide and generous heart.'

When asked why she joined the Parents Circle – Families Forum, she said that despite the situation being complicated, she wanted to be in a group that also included Jews during this ongoing war.

> I explained to my family that it's important for me to have my voice heard, to talk about my pain. Bereaved Israeli mothers strongly identified with my pain when I shared it with them. Some of them really cried. I don't want to lose anyone else; enough already. We're tired of the war, we're tired of the loss.[1]

In contrast to the Anzac dawn service in Jerusalem, which commemorates Gallipoli and World War I, the joint memorial for Palestinian and Israeli families is frequently met with strong opposition from the majority within both Palestinian and Israeli communities.

After the 2023 event, Palestinian journalist Hanin Majdali expressed concerns due to the symmetry it presents between Palestinians killed and the fallen IDF soldiers who may have killed them. This, she argued, overlooks the reality of the occupier and the occupied. She was troubled by the notion that both sides were presented as victims of circumstance, seeing this as the depoliticisation of the Palestinian struggle for freedom. Majdali criticised the ceremony for allowing Israelis to mourn their fallen IDF soldiers while Palestinians are excluded from mourning those who engaged in violent resistance, which Israelis deem as terrorism. This, she believes, creates a narrative where Israelis can be seen as victims even as soldiers, but Palestinians are not afforded the same recognition.[2]

On the Israeli side, before the 2015 event, more than 100 bereaved families wrote a letter to the defence minister, Moshe Yaalon, calling on him to revoke entry permits for any Palestinians wanting to attend the event. Their letter stated, 'We are shocked by the fact that the Israeli government allows a joint memorial ceremony for our enemies who took part in murdering and harming our children ... and for our children living in Israel, killed simply for being Jewish.' This was an untrue statement, as bereaved families of Palestinians killed after committing acts of terror against Jews are not permitted to speak at this ceremony. The letter added: 'There are various ways of expressing bereavement and coping with it; but identifying with the enemy on one of the holiest days of the year, while tens of thousands of families remember their loved ones, that's impossible. It's like having a ceremony for Nazi war criminal Adolph Eichmann on Holocaust Memorial Day.'[3]

Acknowledging these objections from both the mainstream Israeli and Palestinian viewpoints, I still attend the joint memorial, knowing that despite the discomfort it causes many today, it is, for me, a taste of the future, an experience of reconciliation, a moment of peace.

A different future is possible

There are many reasons why I need to believe that peace is possible. If it is a choice between holding on to this distant dream or accepting that our fate is an endless war, as most in Israel do, I believe the Jewish story propels us to choose and believe in the good option, the option that affirms life and the best in humanity. If we choose the other option, peace will definitely elude us.

In the tapestry of human history, the struggle between Israel and Palestine seems never-ending, yet even the most entrenched and intractable conflicts have found a resolution. In addition to Northern Ireland, which I have already discussed in depth, consider these examples.

Israel–Egypt conflict: The longstanding conflict between Israel and Egypt involved wars in 1948, 1956 and 1967. The Yom Kippur War of October 1973 took the lives of 2600 Israelis and 9000 Egyptians. The wars between these two countries ended with the signing of the Camp David Accords in 1978. This agreement involved mutual recognition and the return of the Sinai Peninsula to Egypt. Its resolution highlighted the role of third-party mediation and the willingness of leaders to make significant concessions for peace.

Bosnia and Herzegovina: The Dayton Peace Agreement, signed in November 1995, ended the Bosnian War, one of Europe's deadliest conflicts since World War II. The war caused over 100,000 deaths, including the horrific Srebrenica genocide, and displaced more than two million people. Sarajevo endured the longest siege in modern warfare, lasting for 1425 days. It is estimated that between 20,000 to 50,000 women were raped during the war in Bosnia, as part of a strategy of ethnic cleansing.

Thirty years later, Bosnia and Herzegovina still face many challenges. The country has high levels of political corruption and institutionalised ethnic divisions, leading to fierce disagreements about history and governance. Some war criminals are still celebrated, making reconciliation difficult.

Yet despite the challenges, today Bosnia has a three-member presidency representing Bosniaks, Serbs and Croats. The Federation consists of two main areas: the Federation of Bosnia and Herzegovina and Republika Srpska, plus the Brčko District. In 2021, the High Representative for Bosnia and Herzegovina decreed amendments to its criminal code, banning the denial of the 1995 Srebrenica genocide. In 2024, convicted war criminals are banned from standing in elections.

With the support of the Peace Implementation Council, the country is working towards becoming a liberal democracy. A United Nations Peacebuilding Fund helps promote community ties and reconciliation; these are important for Bosnia's goal of joining the European Union, which many feel is the key to making their temporary peace permanent.

Salvadoran Civil War: During the civil war in El Salvador from 1979 to 1992, the country faced immense violence involving the military, rebel groups and paramilitary 'death squads'. The conflict led to more than 75,000 deaths, mostly among civilians. After three years of talks, the government and the largest rebel group, known as the Farabundo Martí National Liberation Front, signed the Chapultepec Peace

Accords in 1992. This agreement ended the war and brought important changes to the country's political and social systems. The United Nations helped mediate the peace talks, acting as a neutral party providing support and oversight to ensure the agreement was followed. The success of the negotiations relied on strong leaders from both sides who were willing to make real commitments to peace. There was also pressure from within the country and from outside forces that made it harder for either side to walk away from the talks. Additionally, a truth commission was set up, made up of foreign experts accepted by both sides, to address human-rights abuses and help with reconciliation.

Apartheid in South Africa: Many thought South Africa's racial segregation, which began in 1948, was insurmountable. Yet, on April 27, 1994, Nelson Mandela cast his first vote for a democratic South Africa at a small school in Inanda established by the founding president of the African National Congress, a liberation movement that had fought for generations to realise this goal.

Rwandan genocide: In just 100 days in 1994, more than 800,000 people were brutally killed in Rwanda during a genocide primarily targeting the Tutsi ethnic group, along with moderate Hutus and Twa people. This horrific time saw many victims murdered in their own communities, often by their neighbours. Hutu militias armed with machetes and rifles actively hunted down people hiding in places such as churches and schools. Sexual violence was rampant, with an estimated 250,000 to 500,000 women raped during this period. The violence only stopped when the Rwandan Patriotic Front, a rebel group composed mainly of Tutsis, took control of the country.

After the genocide, Rwanda focused on peace and reconciliation through various methods. The National Unity and Reconciliation Commission was established, and local community Gacaca courts were used to promote restorative justice. These efforts aimed to rebuild social unity, deliver justice and support sustainable development, showing how combining traditional and modern approaches could help heal deep societal wounds.

European borders: In the shadow of World War II, which took 75 million lives, European borders bristled with walls, guards and barbed wire, separating families, ethnic communities and many indigenous peoples from their lands. Yet less than five decades later, the European Union was born, a beacon of hope that would weave together the frayed threads of the continent. Thanks to the Schengen Agreement, internal border controls and checkpoints have largely been abolished by 29 European nations. Today, it's possible to travel from Rome to Stockholm by train or bus, using one currency to pay fares the whole way while encountering few border controls. Such a feat, which we take for granted, would have been unimaginable to those who perished in World War II.

While these examples are quite different, they make the same point: even the most horrific conflicts can end when those affected decide that they can resolve their differences and achieve their political aims through better means.

Why I am hopeful

Many would say that the struggle between Palestine and Israel is not like any of these examples. Unlike the Catholics and Protestants of Northern Ireland, we don't speak the same language. The Bosnian War lasted about three years, while the Israeli–Palestinian conflict has been ongoing for decades. We are far less forgiving than the Black South Africans, and the strict laws imposed in Rwanda that suppressed racial identities after the genocide are not something that could ever be applied here, as historical memory is so central to national identity formation. Unlike Europe, we haven't endured two world wars killing millions of people, and unlike El Salvador, there is little faith in the United Nations or any third-party mediator that has the trust of both sides. We also largely belong to two very different religions, Judaism and Islam. Despite some golden ages in Spain and Iraq, these faiths have a long history of enmity, especially today with the re-emergence of radical Islam and messianic Judaism into the political mainstream.

For Palestinians, there is a sense that unlike other conflicts where countries which violate international law, such as Russia or North Korea, are boycotted and sanctioned, Israel operates with complete impunity for its crimes against their people. For them, this latest war in Gaza has been a unique, never-ending torment that evokes a deep sense of betrayal at the world's indifference to their suffering.

Add to that a strong desire for revenge on both sides, nationalist pride, poor political systems that punish moderation, the multitude of holy places in this land, chief among them Al-Aqsa/Temple Mount, and many would say that this is indeed the most intractable conflict on earth. While all of this is true,

I don't think it means we can't learn from how other conflicts ended, or that we are destined to fight forever.

I know that more than our desire for land, honour and holy places, Israelis and Palestinians are two people who love life and who have a will to live and survive the most extraordinary of circumstances. I know that from Ramallah to Tel Aviv, we raise our children in a way that makes them much more independent, innovative, resilient and willing to laugh and express emotions than kids from many other nations. I know that despite the horror that has been unleashed in Gaza and Israel since October 7, we will one day overcome the voices that call on us to fight and resist forever and to always eschew compromise.

My reasons for this belief are that it has happened before between Israel and Egypt, which, as we know, fought several wars that took thousands of lives until they decided to engage in a land-for-peace process.

I have spent years meeting and working with Palestinian and Israeli peacemakers who not only say this is possible but who live these values every day. People like Amira Mohammed and Ibrahim Abu Ahmad from the *Unapologetic: The Third Narrative* podcast, authors such as David Grossman and Yuval Noah Harari, and joint movements like Standing Together, Women Wage Peace and Women of the Sun. And then there are bereaved family members such as Aziz Abu Sarah and Moaz Inon, who have lost so much yet continue to advocate for the wellbeing of the other as the greatest investment in their own wellbeing from the streets of New York City to the Vatican in Rome, calling for an end to war, creating hope.

The existence of even one Israeli or Palestinian who believes in coexistence after they have lost a parent, partner or child is exceptional. The existence of organisations such as the Parents Circle and Combatants for Peace, which bring together thousands of people who have all the reason in the world to support revenge and retribution for the injustices done to them yet still believe this land can be shared, is nothing short of miraculous.

Because of these people and movements, because of our love of life, because I know we are better than everything you have seen us do to each other, I know that one day, we will share this land in peace.

When there is peace

In times when I feel most deflated and hopeless, I dream of peace between Palestine and Israel and what it might look like.

When there is peace, the Israeli prime minister will tenderly place a wreath for the victims of the 1948 Nakba at the Muqata in Ramallah and at the memorial that will likely be built from the ruins of Gaza City in what was once the largest Palestinian city in the world. At the ceremony, she will read from the same book of Ecclesiastes that Yitzhak Rabin did when the Oslo Accords were signed, affirming the time for peace.

When there is peace, the Palestinian prime minister will honour the fallen soldiers and victims of terror at the memorials on Har Herzl and the October 7 Nova massacre site, laying wreaths with solemn grace. He will read the thirty-second verse of the fifth Sura of the Quran, a retelling of the Biblical story of Cain and Abel: 'For this reason we have ordained for the Children of Israel that whoever kills a person, unless it be for manslaughter or [as a punishment] for spreading disorder on the earth, it is as though he had killed all men. And whoever saves a life, it is as though he had saved the lives of all men.'

These acts of recognition and empathy, once fraught with controversy, will become as normal as the ones I attend each year on Anzac Day in Jerusalem. People will perceive the events marked by these memorials not as chains binding their identities or animating revenge but as commemorating pivotal moments that have shaped their nations. Events they will never forget, events that must never be repeated.

When there is peace, Israelis and Palestinians will see the borders of their states clearly defined, with mutual recognition and acceptance of each other's sovereignty. Israeli and Palestinian flags will fly side by side above the confederation parliament, where the government will sit to pass laws that create a land for all. The Israeli ambassador to Palestine will host an iftar meal in his Ramallah villa, while the Palestinian ambassador to Israel will invite dignitaries and friends to an annual Chanukah candle-lighting event at her Herzliya residence.

When there is peace, Jerusalem will stand as a shared capital, a city of coexistence where both people can celebrate their cultural and religious heritage side by side. The air-conditioned buses, presently filled with people coming for conflict and occupation tours layered with stories of hardship and misery, will be replaced by visitors coming to the city to learn about the power of Abrahamic religions to foster mutual coexistence.

When there is peace, Palestinian refugees will find a resolution to their longstanding plight, with mechanisms for compensation and the option to return to a liberated Palestinian state, fostering a sense of justice and closure. The keys hanging on their walls will finally have doors to open. The walls and checkpoints that prevent them from moving freely will finally become the doors, gates and windows of a free Palestine.

When there is peace, Israelis will no longer fear stabbings, shootings, rocket attacks or suicide bombers. Instead of responding to threats from Iran or Hamas, the speeches their leaders give at the United Nations will be about Israel's innovation to tackle climate change and progress in medical technology that is improving the lives of millions.

When there is peace, Israeli and Palestinian parents will raise their children in a world where education fosters understanding and mutual respect. Places of learning like the bilingual Hand in Hand school, which already brings Jewish and Arab children together, will be more common, teaching a curriculum that celebrates both cultures and histories.

When there is peace, children will participate in joint activities such as sports and arts programs similar to those organised by Kids4Peace, the Jerusalem Youth Chorus, Kulna and the YMCA, where they can build friendships and learn teamwork beyond cultural divides.

When there is peace, the narratives taught at home and in schools will shift from 'us versus them' to stories of shared humanity, of seeing the presence of the other in this land as a blessing, as do many other successful multicultural nations.

When there is peace, Israelis will speak and understand the beauty and poetry of Arabic no less than Palestinians will know the rich biblical language reborn that is modern Hebrew.

When there is peace, there will be no hostages or prisoners, military service will be optional and limited, with most young men and women spending the most vibrant years of their lives far away from army bases, checkpoints and refugee camps. Instead, they will experience these glorious years of youth working in a professional field they love, studying to expand their horizons, travelling and exploring themselves and the world around them with the vigour and passion that only free people can.

While this may all read like a fantasy, building a road to any destination is impossible without a vision. This is my destination, and I hope this book has helped you begin dreaming of yours. Perhaps you have read or heard my words on a plane or in a car, in your bed or on the couch, or in between a river and a sea. Yet no matter where you engaged with them, as you read this final page know that where and how the next chapter will unfold is in your hands.

You can use this book to begin your process of imagining shared futures in this land. You can use this book as an invitation for new voices and ideas around the table where you break bread with those you love most. You can use this book to write, act and advocate for peace in a manner that is needed now more than ever before, and you can use this book as a block to elevate your laptop to prevent pain in the neck.

Whatever you choose, remember that the quest for peace has often been marked by both the holy and the broken. The holy represents the shared aspirations for a harmonious coexistence rooted in the land's rich cultural and spiritual heritage. The broken signifies the devastation and destruction that have torn apart so many lives.

Yet within this dichotomy, hope can be found.

By embracing the lessons of the past, listening, hearing and believing another way is possible, there is potential to mend what is broken and build a future that honours the holy aspirations of all who call this land home.

Ittay looking at a mural of Srulik and Handala on the wall of the art studio at Givat Haviva, which was the location of the Kids4Peace summer camp in 2019. Credit: Monique Lustig

Those who made me

This book began with the story of my father and the Yom Kippur War that broke out on October 6, 1973, and my experience 50 years and one day later on October 7, 2023. As a journalist, one of my favourite questions for interview subjects is: 'How did you come to view the world the way you do, especially when others around you don't share that perspective?' In these pages, I will share the stories of three individuals who have significantly influenced my outlook on life, forming the basis for how I see the world today.

My father, my country

My father, Reuven Flescher, was born on May 16, 1948, four days after the Israeli Declaration of Independence. He was among the first children born in the State of Israel. Even though I know my father can never read this book, I must include his story because so much of the way I see the world today is thanks to him.

Throughout his life, family celebrations for Yom Ha'atzmaut (Israeli Independence Day) and his birthday were often indistinguishable. Had cancer not taken his life at a young age, in 2023 he would have celebrated his 75th birthday, together with the State of Israel, a country he fought three wars to defend and the place where he found love and brought two children into this world.

Reuven Flescher's mother, Chava Albeck, was one of five children born into the Gur Hasidic sect in Poland. Her own parents had wanted to move to Palestine, but they were forbidden to do so by her ultra-orthodox grandfather, who was against Zionism and forbade it. Instead, they moved to Germany for a better life in the Weimar Republic. One of her brothers was a communist who left the family to participate in the Russian Revolution and later lived in the Jewish Autonomous Oblast of Birobidzhan. Another of her brothers fought and died in the Spanish Civil War. Chava, along with her two other teenaged siblings, joined a hachshara (practical training program) with the Blau Weiss movement, and in 1931 all three boarded a boat to Palestine without their parents, sensing the winds of change that would afflict their German homeland.

After arriving in the sweltering hot valley of Eretz Yisrael to realise her socialist ideals, Chava was one of the founders of Kibbutz Hamadia in 1939. There she met my grandfather Menachem Mendel Flescher, married and gave birth to two children – my uncle Meir and my father, Reuven.

I often imagine what advice my father would give the people of this country today. The words that most frequently come to my mind are those he said to me during my first practical driving lesson. I was 16 then and had just finished my theory exam, which emphasised all the punishments one would receive in Australia for not following the road rules. After driving around for a bit, it was time to try my first right-hand turn. I slowly nudged into the intersection, then hit the brakes hard as the lights turned red, forcing the car behind me to also brake hard and almost causing an accident. My father asked me why I didn't just drive through the intersection.

I said, 'It was a red light. Driving through a red light is a three-hundred-dollar fine.'

He replied, 'Getting killed or killing someone else is much worse.' He then gave me a piece of advice I remember to this day. 'On the road, don't be right, be smart.'

I would learn later in life that this is quite a common Hebrew expression and even a song lyric, but when I heard it from my father back then, I understood that he was sharing something from his own life experience – advice that went far beyond road regulations.

My father was well liked by almost all who knew him. Like me, he always tried to avoid confrontations and sought to find the middle path.

In what became a significant life-changing event for my mother, brother and me, he died at only 51 years of age. I was 21 when he passed away at home, surrounded by close family and friends. Within the next five years, my uncle Meir also passed away, followed by their younger half-brother Eli, a cancer researcher who did much to help my dad throughout his illness.

All three brothers died from pancreatic cancer before the age of 64. This period of my life is one I liken to the tenth plague we commemorate each Passover seder night, but with no culminating exodus or freedom to give any meaning to the great suffering.

While losing a father at such a young age isn't something I would wish upon anyone, there were two incredible gifts that came with his journey from life to death. Firstly, the doctors were able to tell us quite accurately when he was going to die, which gave my mother, brother and me an opportunity to record and cherish ordinary moments in his last months of life that we might have otherwise taken for granted.

Secondly, following his death I experienced the seven-day Jewish mourning ritual, shiva, where I heard so many stories about the kindness and humility of my father that I would never have otherwise known.

About a month before my father passed away, I recorded a conversation with him about a book that had come out in 1999 called *I Wanted to Ask You, Professor Leibowitz*. We chose this book to read and learn together, because his brother Meir was a keen disciple of the Israeli prize-winning scientist and philosopher and had recommended it to us. The author, Yeshayahu Leibowitz, was well known to my father's family because he used to give a regular class about the weekly Torah reading in a cousin's house.

Of all the ideas he wrote, the one he is best known for today is this prophecy written in 1968, just one year after Israel conquered Gaza and the West Bank in the Six-Day War. At a time when the overwhelming mood in Israel was one of euphoria and victory, he warned that if Israel did not choose to exchange these territories for peace instead of becoming the permanent governor of these regions, it would inevitably develop into a police state. He foresaw that Jews would serve as administrators

Reuven and his older brother, Meir, with their grandparents in 1951.

Reuven polishing diamonds at the age of 15 in Petach Tikva.

and enforcers, while Arabs would be reduced to a subjugated workforce. This shift would lead to corruption, suppression of free speech and the degradation of democratic values. He also feared that the IDF would no longer be a people's army, but would instead become an occupying force, tasked with controlling and quelling Arab resistance.[1]

Looking at our reality today, I reflect on what Leibowitz and my father would think if they could walk the streets of Israel and see what this country has become in its 75th year.

During the recurring protests against the planned judicial overhaul in 2023, I remember seeing a lone female democracy protestor in Jerusalem wearing a T-shirt that said, 'Leibowitz was right'. I wondered if my father would approve.

I know my father supported the Oslo Accords, and the only time I saw him cry was when he heard the news in 1995 of Rabin's assassination. He had served under Rabin in 1967 when Rabin was chief of staff. It's hard to know what my father would say about the IDF today and its treatment of Palestinians. Yet I know that many of Leibowitz's ideas resonated with him. I also know that when he was a soldier in 1967 during the Six-Day War, he once didn't obey what he felt was a manifestly illegal order.

The situation occurred when he was the commander of a tank, after the air force had blitzed the Egyptian forces in the Sinai, and many Arab soldiers were waving white flags of surrender. His unit took all the Egyptians as captives but didn't know what to do with them. They had no place to keep their captives because there was no prison in the Sinai. If the captives were let go, they could again attack Israeli positions as the war continued. An order was given to my father by his commander to kill the captured Egyptian soldiers. He was only 18 at the time. My father refused, instead giving the bound and blindfolded Egyptians water from his own bottle (a very scarce resource in the desert) and telling his officer, 'There is no way I am doing that, and if it means I will be court-martialled, so be it.'

I think that decision typifies so much about what my father taught me in our first driving lesson, meaning wisdom is about much more than just following every law or order set from above. When asked to choose between your nation and your personal values, don't be right, be smart.

From my father, I learned that when I seek to develop an opinion on any matter, I should begin by allowing my intuition to shape my initial perspective. It's then essential to explore opposing viewpoints to understand potential flaws and embrace a spirit of creative doubt to uncover information that may challenge my beliefs. Finally, I allow my intuition to guide me in crafting a revised view that sees the humanity of the other.

When do you most need a father?

For most people, this is a question never asked. You need a father your whole life, and if the course of nature is correct, it should also be the child who buries the parent, and never the reverse.

I sometimes think, what would be better? To only have a father from birth to the age of 21, as I did, or to only have him from age 21 to 40? In which years does one most need the guidance of a parent?

Of course, as a child, one needs all the help one can get to learn to walk, speak, write and make sense of the world. The help and support one needs after the age of 20 is different, and can be supplied by so many people who are not one's parents, from rabbis to educators, friends and Wikipedia. Yet all of these sources have biases. My father had biases too, but there is something about hearing wisdom or advice from the person who gave you life that is unmatched by any other source.

I sometimes wonder what he would say if he could read this book, written by an immigrant child whose second language is English. A book about war, peace and humanising the other. Would he agree with my conclusions? Probably not, but would he be proud of the person I have become? I hope that the answer to that would be yes.

When my father turned 50, we celebrated at the Kimberley Gardens Hotel with many close family friends, and he shared a humorous anecdote in his birthday speech. He said of my family, including himself, my Iraqi mother, my Haredi rabbi brother and me:

> My four-member family has within it Ashkenazim,
> Mizrachim, secular and religious. Putting together this
> birthday event, from the food choice to the seating
> arrangement and date we chose for the celebration,
> required much negotiation. Yet, through several specific
> accommodations, here we are, all together. At this time in
> Israel, there is also a great dispute between the four groups,
> and perhaps the reconciliation and understanding we see
> here at this table can be a model for them too in how to
> resolve their differences peacefully.

My father was the king of compromise. He rarely spoke a bad word about anyone and often tried to find the good in others who were different from him. In a world where so many people can struggle to see the glass half full in their own communities, his wisdom, humility and ability to see the good in others is what made him so special to me.

From the rivers of Babylon to Israel

My mother, Carmella, was born on the banks of the Tigris in Baghdad in 1950. She is the youngest of eight children of the Chebazzah (Halahmy) family, who all spoke Arabic at home, calling their mother Ma'ma and their father Ba'ba.

The Halahmy family lived in the Jewish quarter of Baghdad behind the Shorja market, in an alley where doors set in high stone walls opened straight onto the street. Their home had a courtyard open to the sky, with benches placed under palm trees. Surrounding the courtyard were the three floors of their house. Each floor had shady verandas and large windows standing open. In summer, when it was too hot to sleep in the house, beds were set up on the roof and all the family would sleep under the stars.

Every Friday in Iraq, Carmella's Ma'ma, Salimah, took a whole chicken, stuffed it with savoury rice and spices, and baked it on a bed of rice, surrounded by eggs still in their shells. The meal was left simmering on the stove all night. The eggs turned a smooth brown colour and were eaten for breakfast with pita bread and eggplant slices, which had been fried the day before. The chicken was served, still hot, for lunch. But the most prized bit was the thick, crunchy baked crust of rice, which sat at the bottom of the huge family-size pan.

In Baghdad, they also ate mazgouf, the huge red snapper fish that the fishermen caught in the river and grilled for them over great charcoal fires.

This dream coexistence between Jews and Muslims came to an abrupt end when a pro-Nazi government came to power during World War II. In 1941, the Farhud pogrom killed more than 180 Baghdadi Jews during the Jewish festival of Shavuot. By 1950, the Iraqi government announced that if Jews didn't leave within a year, they would be locked into the country forever. At the time, a third of the residents of the Iraqi capital were Jewish – more than 150,000 people. By the end of 1952, there were almost none, their heartbreaking exodus ending a 2500-year presence in the land.

The departing Jews were also forbidden from taking any of their money and were only allowed one suitcase each for personal belongings. How does one fit an entire life of memories into one small bag? Just before leaving Iraq, Carmella's Ba'ba Salach, an established goldsmith, fashioned strips of gold into the heels of the shoes worn by his entire family. It was his ingenious way of taking out some of the wealth they had earned in Baghdad. Fortunately, airports didn't have metal detectors in those days.

As her father locked the door of their beautiful home for the last time, their Muslim neighbour tearfully cried out, 'Abu Haskel! Why are you going? Please don't leave!'

Salach replied, 'It is the government that wants us to leave, not you, our neighbours.'

My grandfather led his family away from his homeland, the place where Abraham was born, where our Talmud was written, and from which our greatest prophets emerged, literally walking with gold in the soles of his shoes. When I picture this image today, I can't think of a more fitting way to close what was truly a golden age in the history of my people.

My mother's arrival in Israel as a three-month-old changed her life forever. The men from the Jewish Agency who encouraged the family to move there promised a land flowing with milk and honey. In reality, her family's first experience after their feet hit the tarmac at Ben Gurion Airport was being sprayed by the poisonous insecticide DDT to prevent the spread of malaria. As the cloud enveloped their family, my grandfather's hair, moustache and eyebrows turned white from the pesticide coating.

The silk tie he was wearing, the buttoned-up shirt and his elegant suit instantly became nothing more than dusty rags. Later, the authorities encouraged the family to Hebraicise the children's names. Abed became Oded. Amira became Tikva, Samir became Avraham, and the family name Chebazzah became Halahmy. They were on their way to 'integration', a process that gave their new lives meaning but would also break the heart of Salach, who always spoke Arabic better than Hebrew and never truly felt at home as an Israeli.

Growing up in a tiny two-bedroom apartment in Ramat Gan with ten people filled my mother's childhood with immense challenges. Due to the colour of her skin and the fact that her parents were of Mizrachi heritage, Carmella faced a great deal of discrimination at a time when the Ashkenazi hegemony didn't see those who came from countries such as Morocco, Yemen or Iraq as equal to them in culture or education. When they were in the huge tent city established for refugees called the Ma'abara, representatives of the Jewish Agency tried to take my mother and her twin brother Rafy away from their family, promising their parents that they would have a better life in a middle-class kibbutz if they agreed. Thankfully, Salima and Salach refused.

Like many of her friends, Carmella finished school when she was just 14, as her parents couldn't afford to pay for her to study in high school, which wasn't free at the time.

My mother was blessed with a beautiful voice. Despite her father's objections, just after the 1967 Six-Day War, Carmella joined the Hanoar Ha'oved Ve'Halomed band. Carmella's father Salach felt that singing wasn't a fitting profession for a respectable woman, but Carmella knew to follow her voice. When Israel played Uruguay in a friendly football match, my mother sang 'Hachayal Sheli' as a soloist just before the game. The crowd of 20,000 at the Ramat Gan Stadium that night included prime minister Golda Meir. After the performance, they shook hands and Golda told Carmella that she would have a bright future as a singer.

A few months later, Carmella, aged just 21, had just spent a long afternoon rehearsing with the Hanoar Ha'oved band in Tel Aviv. My father, Reuven, had spent the afternoon at the American school learning English to fulfil his dream of being a flight attendant and travelling the world. As fate would have it, at the end of their respective days, they both entered the same sherut taxi and sat in silence as they waited for it to fill up to seven people. As the taxi became full and the driver began to move, my father was sitting next to the driver with my mother behind him. Carmella noticed Reuven's height, red hair and alluring appearance; she stared at him the whole ride but never said a word.

Just as the taxi was about to arrive at her stop in Ramat Gan, her life flashed before her eyes and her mother's voice came into her head. Salima would always say, 'When you find a catch, don't hesitate.'

Carmella quickly grabbed a scrap of paper and wrote: 'Dear anonymous redhead, please call me.' She added her name and phone number, and dropped the note on his lap just before leaving the cab. Later she told her parents, 'I met a man in a cab tonight, he's going to be my husband.' An hour later, Reuven called Carmella at home and they spoke for the first time. A year later, they were married.

A new life in Melbourne

Reuven and Carmella moved to Melbourne in 1981, along with my brother, Royi, and me. Reuven would later become the first teacher of diamond sorting and evaluation at the Gemmology School of Australia and worked for many years as the director of Crown Diamonds.

In their early years together, Carmella was incredibly homesick as Reuven worked long hours to establish the business. With very little English and no family in Australia, Carmella overcame many struggles to eventually open a successful costume jewellery business whose products were sold in David Jones and featured on some of Australia's most famous TV Shows, from *Chances* to *Neighbours* and *Home and Away*.

After my father died, my brother and I were in deep mourning, wondering if life would ever be the same again. My mother had to stand on her own two feet. It was like a rebirth – she became much stronger emotionally, and her English improved dramatically as she moved into a new career as a healer. She also delved deeply into the study of Qi Gong.

In 2004, my mother travelled to China to become a Qi Gong master. Now in her seventies, she still teaches this movement-body practice at the University of the Third Age

My father, Reuven (back row, in white), and my mother, Carmella (front row, in black), together with all their siblings and partners in Israel, 1979.

(U3A), providing comfort and healing to many people from all walks of life.

Today, despite our different religious beliefs and political outlooks, the conversations I have with her challenge me to reflect on my biases and justify why I hold the beliefs that I do. Just as my father taught me the value of compromise for the sake of peace, my mother taught me the value of asking questions to build new understandings.

To them both, I am eternally grateful for giving me life.

To the teacher who taught me the meaning of seeing 'both sides now'

After my parents, I think the person who most shaped my worldview about Judaism, Israel and the meaning of life was Mark Raphael Baker, to whom this book is dedicated. Mark was an acclaimed Jewish-Australian author, academic and historian. A deeply reflective individual, his life and work revolved around the exploration of personal and collective trauma, particularly through the lens of his parents' Holocaust experiences and his own journey of love and loss.

I first met Mark as a teenager when I used to pray at Hamakom and later Shira Hadasha in Melbourne. With his acclaimed book *The Fiftieth Gate* being in the VCE/HSC reading list, Mark was to me like a celebrity author. Exceptionally poetic, wise and blessed with the brilliant skill of knowing exactly the right words for every occasion, Mark was truly one-of-a-kind in my community.

What do you say to someone who greatly influenced your life when you see them for the last time? During a month-long visit to Australia in September 2022, I met Mark for what I knew would be the final time. He had terminal cancer. He chose the location, which was the busy Galleon Cafe by Acland Street in Melbourne. We sat outside on that sunny spring morning with a fresh breeze from Port Phillip Bay filling the air in between the two sweet bowls of porridge we'd ordered.

Our conversation began with him asking me questions about my impressions of the Melbourne Jewish community, its synagogues, rabbis and communal politics, and my peace work in Jerusalem. It's a conversation we had had many times, and I was surprised that this was what he asked about. Yet it also attested to his care and concern for the wellbeing of our community and our people.

We spoke at length about Jewish schools because he was in the process of choosing one for his then baby daughter Melila. He asked me what I thought about the social and political orientation of each, and where I would send my children if I still lived in Melbourne. Our conversation then moved on to cancer, and he described the lengthy medical process that led to the confirmation a year prior that his stomach pain was pancreatic cancer. I shared with him that my father and both his brothers lost their lives to pancreatic cancer, and we spoke about the process of storing memories through books, articles and videos, reflecting on how our children and grandchildren might want to remember their predecessors whose lives were cut short.

As our conversation was ending, I told him the reason it was so important for me to see him that first morning after Yom Kippur.

When I was in my twenties in Melbourne, you made an incredible impact on my life. When you first invited me into your home to teach guitar to your children and then later to you, I was in awe of the love between you, Kerryn and your beautiful children, and the incredible art and library in your home.

What you did for our community, being so instrumental in establishing Shira, the New Israel Fund Australia and the community education program of Monash University's Australian Centre for Jewish Civilisation, greatly shaped who I am today. You showed me that it was possible to be both religious and atheist, both Zionist and supportive of Palestinian rights and freedoms.

At a time when I had few other role models showing me that an Orthodox shul could be feminist, LGBTQI+-inclusive and committed to halacha, or that caring about the wellbeing of our people in Israel didn't have to come at the expense of caring for people under Israel's occupation, you never let go of fighting for what seemed like contradictory ideologies in the same breath.

Much of what I believe today, the way I see the world, and my work and writing, are inspired by you. So, thank you for everything.

In his humble manner, Mark immediately responded by saying that all my appreciation should be directed towards others, listing all their names, saying they were also a part of creating these progressive spaces in Melbourne. He was right and I am grateful to all of them too.

As we stood up to leave, he explained how he was responding better to the cancer treatments and hoped to visit Israel soon, and that we may meet again. The last words I said to him with a broad smile were 'Le'shana haba'a b'Yerushalayim – Next year, in Jerusalem'.

May his memory be a blessing

On the morning of May 4, 2023, a Facebook post announced 'No words can capture our grief and love. Marky Baker: an incredible husband, father, son, uncle and friend. We will love you and miss you always.'

Below these words was a moving photo slide show that captured key moments of his life. It was set to the music of 'Both Sides, Now' by Joni Mitchell, a song written in 1969, when Mark was just ten.

The lyrics are a poignant reflection on the complexities of life, love and human perception. The song explores how our understanding of things changes as we gain experience, yet paradoxically leaves us feeling like we know less than we did before.

Exploring clouds, love and life, Mitchell contrasts an idealistic, innocent view of each with a more cynical, experienced perspective. However, rather than simply embracing the 'wiser' viewpoint, the song suggests that true wisdom lies in acknowledging both sides. It was really the perfect song for Mark.

Mark's funeral took place at 11 am on Friday, May 5. My wife, Carm, and I woke up at 2 am to watch it live in Jerusalem from the Chevra Kadisha website, as we both felt like it was a moment we needed to experience together with the hundreds gathered to honour his memory across the ocean in Melbourne.

In her eulogy for her husband, Michelle Lesh shared that his ability to connect and teach manifested itself in different ways with his adult children Gabe, Sarah and Rachel. 'Proud of them beyond measure, he was always fascinated by their lives and interests. No matter how far their endeavours strayed from his own comfort zone and Jewish and political inclinations, his aliveness to them and to the world made him yearn to understand and appreciate them.'[2]

Reading these words, I looked to Carm and hoped that for as long as we live, we will also be able to do the same for each other and our children.

For those who made me

This book would never have been written without my mother, father and Mark Baker. Reuven imbued me with a love of Israel, skills for mediating hard conversations and a desire to see the good in every person. Carmella taught me about patience and honour, especially for one's parents. Mark taught me how to love God while being an atheist, to love Israel while opposing its government, and how to stand in progressive places throughout Australia and Israel as a proud Jew and a human of the world, always striving to balance the obligations that come with both.

I am deeply appreciative for all they taught me.

I am also deeply grateful to all the students I have encountered throughout my life, from Adass and Bialik College, to the King David School, Mount Scopus Memorial College, Florence Melton Mini School, Limmud, Kids4Peace and all the gap-year and college students I have taught in Jerusalem from across the world. All of them have asked hard questions, challenged my beliefs and guided me into the thinking process that helped birth this book.

I wish too that you – and all the readers of this book – may be guided by good people on your life journey. Ultimately, my aim in writing this book was to comfort the troubled and trouble the comfortable.

If you feel either comforted or troubled by anything you have read over the course of this book, then I have achieved my goal.

If you have experienced moments of holiness and brokenness in the many stories shared here, that too was my purpose.

Whether you are at this moment holding this physical book, or reading on a tablet or phone, take a moment to feel grateful for all that is holy in your life, and then commit to fixing all that is broken, because nothing would honour Reuven, Carmella, Mark and me more than that.

TIMELINES

There is no such thing as a neutral timeline on this subject. Reflecting on the fact that knowing each other's history is a key part of peacebuilding, I hope these final pages will serve as a useful resource for understanding the key points of how the conflict began and the agreements that may be the blueprint for how it can end. Every date, word and description chosen or omitted reveals a bias. Standard timelines used by proponents of Zionism and Palestinian nationalism can often promote 'blood and soil' nationalism, the idea that ties a specific group of people to a land, excludes the connections of others to that land and gives them the right to exclusive sovereignty.

In the three timelines on the following pages, I have made a concerted effort to be fair in sharing my understanding of what an outsider should know to understand our history as Israelis and Palestinians. I acknowledge that no single timeline can fully capture the complexity of our history, but I strive to present a balanced perspective that respects multiple viewpoints.

Important events in Palestine and Israel

1047–930 BCE: According to the Hebrew Bible, the Israelites form a united kingdom under Kings Saul, David and Solomon. During this period, the First Temple is built in Jerusalem. This Temple is a permanent home for the Ark of the Covenant, which held the stone tablets of the law Moses received on Mount Sinai. As a result, many Jews feel a religious connection to the land.

430 BCE: The term 'Palestine' first appears in written form, when the ancient Greek historian Herodotus writes in 'The Histories' of a 'district of Syria, called Palaistinê' (Παλαιστίνη in Greek) between Phoenicia and Egypt.

70 CE: The destruction of the Second Jewish Temple by Titus Vespasianus in the Roman Province of Judaea, followed by the dissolution of Jewish sovereignty in 132 CE, launches the second dispersion of the diaspora, the first being the Babylonian exile of 586 BCE. The destruction of these two Temples that once stood in Jerusalem are still mourned by Jews every year on the fast day of Tisha Be'Av.

621: According to the Quran and Hadith, the Prophet Muhammad went on the Isra (a night-time journey) from Mecca to Al-Aqsa (the Noble Sanctuary in Jerusalem) on a horse named Buraq. There, he led other prophets, such as Ibrahim (Abraham), Musa (Moses) and Issa (Jesus), in prayer before ascending to heaven (called Mira'j). As a result, many Muslims feel a religious connection to the land.

1730–1775: The rule of Daher al-Omar in Palestine, the first local leader of a Palestinian Sheikdom within the Ottoman Empire. At the peak of his power, he governs all the land from Gaza to Beirut. He is known for his tolerance, and after he fortifies Acre in 1750, the city becomes the centre of the cotton trade between Palestine and Europe, leading many Jews, Christians and Muslims to settle in the area.

1834: The Peasants' Revolt against Egyptian conscription and taxation policies in Palestine is a collective reaction to Egypt's gradual elimination of the unofficial rights and privileges previously enjoyed by the various classes of society in the Levant under Ottoman rule. The revolt is a formative event for the Palestinian sense of nationhood, bringing together disparate groups against a common enemy.

1858: The Ottoman Land Law of 1858 aims to increase the tax base but lead to significant changes in land ownership patterns. Many local Palestinian peasants, or fellahin, are illiterate and suspicious of the government's intentions, fearing higher taxes and conscription. Consequently, village lands are often registered collectively under the names of local leaders or mukhtars, who later claim ownership and sell these lands to Jewish immigrants. This shift in land ownership facilitates Jewish immigration and settlement, particularly during the first Aliyah (1882–1903), and lays the groundwork for future demographic and political changes in the region.

1878: Mulabbis is the first Arab village whose lands are acquired by Jews for settlement purposes. In its place the Jewish agricultural settlement Petah Tikva is founded by religious Orthodox Jews (known as the 'Old Yishuv'). Malaria and crop failure drive them from the location. In 1883, immigrants from Russia arrive in Petah Tikvah with the financial support of banker Baron Edmond de Rothschild. The group are part of the Bilu movement, who believe in agricultural settlement in the Land of Israel. Their first accomplishment is to drain the swamps, which are a breeding ground for mosquitoes carrying malaria. Citrus groves are planted, and their success stimulates the local economy, drawing more immigrants to reside there.

1881: Many pogroms (mass violence against a minority group, organised or ignored by authorities), previously rare events, sweep the southwestern provinces of the Russian Empire aimed at Jews. Russian authorities make no attempt to stop them. As a result, over two million Jews move to the USA, 113,000 to Argentina and 55,000 to Ottoman Palestine by 1914. The wave of pogroms also leads some Jewish writers, such as Peretz Smolenskin, to call for a physical return to the Jewish homeland as an answer to antisemitism, laying the foundation for the Zionist movement.

1882: First Aliyah. Between 25,000 and 35,000 people, mainly Russian and Eastern European Jews, immigrate to Palestine. Baron Edmond de Rothschild supports their enterprise by donating a series of generous subsidies to the Zionist Yishuv (settlement).

1897: In August, the first Zionist Congress, led by Theodor Herzl, takes place in Basel, Switzerland. This congress marks the formal establishment of the Zionist movement and the World Zionist Organization, emerging as a response to growing antisemitism in Europe and the broader context of nationalist movements of the time. Calling for 'a publicly and legally assured home in Palestine' for the Jewish people, the congress is a pivotal moment in Zionist history.

Throughout its development, Zionism draws on longstanding Jewish connections to the land of Israel, reinterpreting traditional religious and cultural ties through a modern, nationalist framework. The movement faces initial controversy among many Jews but gains wider support, particularly in the aftermath of the Holocaust.

On October 7, the General Jewish Labour Bund in Russia and Poland is founded in Vilna. The Bund aims to unite Jewish workers within the Russian Empire into a worker's party and to forge an alliance with the larger Russian social democratic movement, with the goal of establishing a democratic and socialist Russia.

1901–1920: The Christian-Arab Sursock family sells large areas of land in Haifa Bay, the Galilee and the Jezreel Valley to Jewish buyers, who require it to be available for settlement by Jewish immigrants. Consequently, Palestinian-Arab tenant farmers are evicted, with compensation. These sales account for 22% of all land purchased by Jews in Palestine up until 1948, enabling sizeable Jewish settlement in the north.

1916: European powers conclude the secret Sykes–Picot Agreement, dividing future spheres of influence in Ottoman Empire territories.

1917: Britain's foreign secretary, Lord Arthur Balfour, expresses his government's support for 'the establishment in Palestine of a national home for the Jewish people' in a letter to Baron Walter de Rothschild, a British banker and later president of the Board of Deputies of British Jews.

To Israelis today, the Balfour Declaration marks the first formal utterance from a great power of the state's right to exist; to Palestinians, it is an early sign of their dispossession. The declaration also notes that it is 'clearly understood that nothing shall be done which may prejudice the civil and religious rights of existing non-Jewish communities in Palestine', acknowledging the overwhelming majority Arab population in the region at the time.

1919: King of Iraq, Emir Feisal I, presents a memorandum to the Paris Peace Conference following the end of World War I, outlining the case for the independence of Arab countries.

1922: The League of Nations grants a mandate over the former Ottoman territory of Palestine to the UK. Provisions include terms of the Balfour Declaration, including a 'Jewish national home'.

1929: Riots start on August 23 in response to a flag-waving demonstration at the Western Wall on Tisha Be'Av held by a few hundred Jerusalem schoolchildren from the Betar Zionist youth movement that concluded with the singing of 'Hatikva' (a song that became the Israeli national anthem). False rumours spread that Jews are planning to take control of what Muslims call the Al-Buraq Wall in Jerusalem and threaten Muslim holy sites. During the riots, 133 Jews are killed in Jerusalem and Hebron by Arab attackers. British police kill 116 Arabs while trying to control the violence.

Palestinians refer to the events as the 'Al-Buraq Uprising', while Israelis call it the 'Hebron Massacre'.

Many Palestinians view the events as a reaction to increasing Jewish immigration and land purchases in Palestine, which in turn threaten Palestinian political aspirations and economic future. The brutal attacks on Jews leads to growing unity among a previously divided community of Zionists, non-Zionists, Ashkenazi and Mizrahi Jews, creating a stronger sense of national identity against a serious threat from Arab groups.

1936–1939: The Great Revolt. Palestinians engage in a full-fledged rebellion to dislodge the British Empire and stop Jewish immigration to Palestine, which increased dramatically after Hitler's rise to power in Germany. The revolt is also fuelled by economic hardships, such as debt and dispossession among rural Palestinians, exacerbated by British policies and Zionist land purchases.

While ultimately unsuccessful, and resulting in over 8000 Palestinian deaths, the revolt represents a pivotal point in the history of the Palestinian national movement. It leads to the Palestinian leadership's exile, imprisonment and fragmentation, weakening their political position. It also sets a precedent for future Palestinian resistance against colonial and Zionist policies, highlighting the complexities of the Palestinian struggle, including internal divisions and the challenges of forming a unified front.

1937: The UK's Peel Commission Report publicly recognises the conflict's irreconcilable terms and recommends the partition of Palestine into two states, one Jewish and one Arab.

1939: The UK issues the White Paper limiting Jewish immigration to Palestine.

1939–1945: During World War II, Nazi Germany and its collaborators systematically murder six million Jews across German-occupied Europe. The Holocaust kills around two-thirds of Europe's Jewish population. Many survivors of the war play pivotal roles in the establishment of Israel three years later.

1947: On November 29, the UN General Assembly adopts Resolution 181 by 33 to 13 votes with ten abstentions. The resolution calls for the partition of Palestine into an Arab state and a Jewish state, with the city of Jerusalem as a separate entity to be governed by a special international regime. Immediately after the vote, the Arab states' delegations declare that they will not be bound by the decision and walk out, accompanied by the Indian and Pakistani delegates. The passing of the vote is a moment of great celebration for the Zionist movement.

May 14, 1948: After the UK terminates the Mandate over Palestine, David Ben-Gurion declares the restoration of Jewish sovereignty in Tel Aviv, with some referring to the new state as the 'third Jewish Commonwealth' following the destruction of the First and Second Temples that stood in Jerusalem thousands of years before. This day is celebrated in Israel as Yom Ha'atzmaut, Independence Day.

May 15, 1948: Members of the Arab League – Iraq, Syria, Egypt, Transjordan, the Arab Liberation Army and the Holy War Army led by Abd al-Qadir al-Husayni – invade what had the previous day ceased to be the British Mandate for Palestine and was now Israel.

May 15, 1948: This day is marked in Palestine as Nakba Day, meaning a day of catastrophe. It commemorates the forced displacement by Zionist militias of 750,000 Palestinians that preceded and followed Israel's establishment.

December 1948: UN General Assembly passes Resolution 194, calling for Palestinian refugees to be allowed to return to Israel and for Jerusalem to be under an international regime.

1964: The Palestine Liberation Organisation (PLO) is founded in Cairo.

1967: In a pre-emptive strike against mounting Arab military pressure, Israel launches the Six-Day War, capturing the West Bank, East Jerusalem, Gaza Strip, Sinai Peninsula and Golan Heights. In November, the UN Security Council unanimously adopts Resolution 242 calling for the withdrawal of Israeli armed forces from territories occupied, while also affirming the right of every state in the area to live in peace within secure and recognised boundaries.

1973: Egypt and Syria launch a surprise attack on Israel during Yom Kippur. After initial setbacks, Israel recovers and pushes back the invading forces.

1982: The Lebanon War, initiated by Israel in response to hundreds of Palestinian militant attacks from the north into Israel, results in the PLO's withdrawal to neighbouring countries and the emergence of Hezbollah as a resistance force against Israeli occupation. The conflict also leads to significant political shifts in Lebanon, including the assassination of President Bachir Gemayel and the ongoing Israeli occupation of southern Lebanon until 2000.

1982: Phalangist militias allied with Israel massacre thousands of Palestinian civilians in the Sabra and Shatila refugee camps in Lebanon.

1987: First Intifada begins in the Jabaliya refugee camp in the Gaza Strip.

1988: In July, Jordan renounces claims to the West Bank and recognises the PLO as 'the sole legitimate representative of the Palestinian people'.

In November, in Algiers, the Palestinian National Council adopts the Declaration of Independence of the State of Palestine.

In December, in an address to the UN in Geneva, PLO Chair Yasser Arafat announces that the Palestine National Council accepts UN Security Council Resolutions 242 and 338. Both resolutions emphasise the need for a negotiated settlement to achieve a lasting peace in the Middle East. Resolution 242 specifically outlines the 'Land for Peace' principle, calling for Israeli withdrawal from territories occupied in 1967 in exchange for peaceful recognition by Arab states.

1995: Yitzhak Rabin, the first and only Israeli prime minister to sign a peace agreement with a Palestinian leader, is assassinated at the conclusion of a peace rally in Tel Aviv. The assassin is a right-wing Jew opposed to the Oslo peace process.

1996: For the first time, the prime minister of Israel is elected on a separate ballot from the remaining members of the Knesset. The elections result in a surprise victory for Likud's Benjamin Netanyahu over Labor's Shimon Peres by a margin of 29,457 votes, less than 1% of the total. At 46 years old, Netanyahu becomes Israel's youngest prime minister and the first to be born after the state was founded in 1948. The Likud party leader goes on to become the longest-serving prime minister in Israel's history.

Israel–Gaza wars

1949–1956: The Israeli army (Israel Defense Forces, or IDF) forces thousands of Palestinians to Asqalān/Ashkelon who are eventually deported to Gaza in 1950 and 1951. Tens of thousands of Palestinian refugees in Gaza attempt to return to Israel, overwhelmingly to harvest their crops and collect their belongings. The Israeli army kills upwards of 5000 Palestinians during this time period, deeming them infiltrators. About 400 Israelis are killed by attacks from Gaza led by fedayeen (Palestinian guerilla fighters).

1951: Israel establishes Kibbutz Nahal Oz a mere 800 metres from Gaza to maintain a defensive presence and monitor activity along the sensitive frontier while contributing to agricultural development in the north-western Negev desert. The kibbutz serves as both a military outpost and a symbol of early nation-building efforts in Israel.

1956–1957: France, Britain and Israel attack Egypt. Israel is motivated by a desire to punish Egypt for raids committed against the Jewish population living near the Gaza border, while Britain and France are worried about the threat to international shipping by the nationalisation of the Suez Canal Company, which has been a joint British–French enterprise up to this point.

During the four-month occupation, Israel kills thousands of Gazans, including in documented field executions in Khan

Younis and Rafah. One of them is the uncle of nine-year-old Abdel Aziz al-Rantisi. The trauma of seeing his uncle shot stays with him his whole life and he later becomes the co-founder of Hamas.

1967: In response to Palestinian positions in Gaza opening fire on Israeli settlements, IDF Chief of Staff Yitzhak Rabin overrides Defence Minister Moshe Dayan's instructions to leave Gaza alone, and orders Israeli forces to enter and occupy the Gaza Strip on the second day of the Six-Day War.

August 2005: Israel withdraws 8000 Jewish settlers from the Gush Katif settlement area and other regions of Gaza and the West Bank. On August 15, Israeli Prime Minister Ariel Sharon says in a live television address, 'Gaza cannot be held on to forever. Over one million Palestinians live there, and they double their numbers with every generation. They live in incredibly cramped refugee camps, in poverty and squalor, in hotbeds of ever-increasing hatred, with no hope whatsoever on the horizon. The world is waiting for the Palestinian response [to our leaving] – a hand stretched out to peace or the fire of terror. To an outstretched hand we will respond with an olive branch.'

2006: In January, Hamas wins the Palestinian legislative elections in Gaza and forms the Palestinian Authority government.

In June, Hamas captures Israeli soldier Gilad Shalit in a cross-border raid from Gaza, prompting Israeli air raids and incursions. He is released five years later in exchange for 1027 Palestinian prisoners, one of whom is Yahya Sinwar, the mastermind behind the October 7, 2023 Hamas attack.

In July, Israel goes to war with Hezbollah in Lebanon in response to a cross-border ambush killing three Israeli soldiers and capturing two others.

2007: Israel imposes a blockade on Gaza following Hamas's violent coup over Fatah, citing security concerns and aiming to prevent weapons smuggling and rocket attacks. The blockade restricts a wide range of items, including construction materials, certain foods, agricultural supplies and household goods, which has a significant humanitarian and economic impact on Gaza's population.

December 2008: Hamas continues to fire rockets at the southern border towns in Israel. In response, Israel launches a 22-day military offensive; 1417 Palestinians and 13 Israelis are killed before a ceasefire is agreed on.

November 2012: Israel kills Hamas's military Chief of Staff, Ahmad Jabari, and follows this with eight days of air raids on Gaza in response to thousands of rockets launched from Gaza directed at civilian targets in Israel. Operation Pillar of Defence ends in a ceasefire, with both sides claiming victory.

June–August 2014: Three Israeli teenagers are kidnapped and murdered by Hamas. There is a frantic search over several weeks until their bodies are found. In July, a Palestinian teenager is killed in a revenge attack. A seven-week war ensues in which more than 2100 Palestinians and 73 Israelis are killed in Gaza and southern Israel.

March 2018: A significant wave of protests, known as the 'Great March of Return', begins in Gaza. These demonstrations are organised by Palestinian activists demanding the right of return for Palestinian refugees and protesting against the Israeli blockade of Gaza, which has been in place since 2007. More than 170 Palestinians are killed over several months of protests.

May 2021: After weeks of rising tensions surrounding the potential eviction of East Jerusalem Palestinians from their homes in Sheikh Jarrah during Ramadan, hundreds of Palestinians are injured in clashes with Israeli security forces at the Al-Aqsa Mosque in Jerusalem. In response, Hamas issues an ultimatum to Israel, demanding the withdrawal of forces from Al-Aqsa and Sheikh Jarrah. Following the rejection of their demands, Hamas launches rockets, prompting Israel to respond with extensive airstrikes on the Gaza Strip.

March–August 2022: Between March and May, Israeli Arabs and Palestinians kill 17 Israelis, most of them civilians, and two Ukrainians. In response, the IDF escalates its operations against armed Palestinian groups across the West Bank. By July, at least 30 Palestinians have been killed, including journalist Shireen Abu Akleh who had no role in any fighting, and three perpetrators of the attacks in Israel.

On August 1, Israeli forces arrest Bassam al-Saadi, a senior leader of the Palestinian Islamic Jihad (PIJ), in the West Bank. Tensions escalate, and on August 5, Israel launches Operation Breaking Dawn with airstrikes on Gaza. The initial strike kills Tayseer al-Jabari, another senior PIJ commander. PIJ responds by firing rockets into Israel, leading to three days of fighting.

The conflict ends on August 7 with an Egypt-brokered ceasefire. Notably, this is the first Gaza conflict in which Hamas, the governing authority in Gaza, does not actively participate.

October 2, 2023: Israeli National Security Council chief Tzachi Hanegbi says in a radio interview, 'Since the Operation Guardians of the Wall in May two years ago, the Hamas leadership has taken a decision to exercise unprecedented restraint.' With great confidence, he admits, *'For more than two years, Hamas has not fired a single missile from Gaza. It is restraining itself and knows the repercussions of another provocation. Hamas has been very deterred for at least fifteen years. It is not heading towards escalation.'*

October 7, 2023: Hamas launches a lethal assault on Israel by land, sea and air. Gunmen breach the fence on the Gaza border and use speedboats to access Israel's coastline. They attack military posts, kibbutzim and a music festival, resulting in the deaths of 1195 people, including 815 civilians; 251 men, women and children are taken as hostages to Gaza. UN investigators later find it reasonable to believe that sexual assault occurred.

October 8, 2023: Israel declares war on Hamas.

Hezbollah launches rockets from Lebanon into Israel, which responds with drone strikes and artillery fire targeting Hezbollah positions near the Lebanon–Golan Heights border. Between October 8, 2023 and September 20, 2024, 28 people die in Israel as a result of 1623 Hezbollah attacks, while in Lebanon 798 people die from 8099 Israeli strikes. Hundreds of thousands of people are displaced from their homes on both sides of the border.

October 9, 2023: Israel declares a 'complete siege' of Gaza. Israeli Defence Minister Yoav Gallant says 'no electricity, no food, no fuel' will be allowed to enter.

October 27, 2023: Israel launches a ground invasion of the Gaza Strip with the stated goal of eliminating Hamas and freeing the Israeli hostages.

April 13–14, 2024: In response to Israeli bombing of the Iranian embassy in Damascus, the Iranian military's Islamic Revolutionary Guards Corps, along with Hezbollah, the Islamic Resistance in Iraq and Yemeni Houthis, launch an attack on Israel. It is Iran's first direct attack on Israel since their proxy conflict began. Iran fires about 170 drones, 30 cruise missiles and 120 ballistic missiles. Israeli, American, British, French and Jordanian forces intercept 99% of them, mostly before they enter Israeli airspace. This attack is the largest attempted drone strike in history. In response, Israel carries out limited strikes on Iran on April 18, 2024.

September 2, 2024: Israel's largest trade union, the Histadrut, initiates a general strike after the killing of six Israeli hostages by Hamas in a Rafah tunnel. This is the first anti-government strike since October 7. Over 700,000 Israelis participate in nationwide protests against Netanyahu that day, believing he is preventing a hostage deal for personal political reasons to preserve his seat in office, with the largest demonstrations blocking major highways in Tel Aviv.

September 17, 2024: Gaza's health ministry releases a list identifying 34,344 Palestinians killed by Israeli strikes in the region since October 7. An additional 7613 individuals, included in the total death toll of 41,000 at the time, remained unidentified, though their bodies had been received by hospitals and morgues. The list does not distinguish between Hamas fighters and civilians.

Among the identified are 169 infants born after the Hamas attacks on 7 October, and a man born in 1922 who had lived through more than a century of war and unrest. The victims also include 11,355 children, 2955 individuals aged 60 or older and 6297 women. Hunger, lack of shelter and medication, the rapid spread of infectious diseases and the collapse of the healthcare system have claimed many additional lives.

October 1, 2024: Israel launches an invasion of Lebanon to enforce UN Security Council Resolution 1701, aiming to push Hezbollah forces north of the Litani River. Hezbollah has stated they will continue rocket and drone attacks until Israel ceases military operations in Gaza and Lebanon. In response, Netanyahu has said, 'No country can tolerate [rocket] fire at its residents. The State of Israel cannot tolerate it either. We will do whatever it takes to restore security.'

Agreements, negotiations and peace proposals

1979: The Israel–Egypt Peace Treaty marks a historic turning point in Middle Eastern relations, ending decades of hostility between the two nations. The treaty's key terms include mutual recognition, Israeli withdrawal from the Sinai Peninsula, security arrangements, freedom of navigation through the Suez Canal and Gulf of Aqaba and steps towards normalising relations. The treaty is based on the Camp David Accords that called for Palestinian self-government in the West Bank and Gaza Strip, envisioning a transitional period, free elections and negotiations to determine the final status of these territories. However, these provisions remain largely aspirational and are not fully implemented.

1993 Oslo Accords: The PLO recognises the State of Israel on 78% of what Palestinians consider to be their 'historic homeland', where Arab Palestinians were the majority population until 1948. Israel recognises the PLO as 'the representative of the Palestinian people'. Despite the Oslo Accords stipulating that 'neither side shall initiate or take any step that will change the status of the West Bank and the Gaza Strip pending the outcome of the permanent status negotiations', Israeli settlement expansion continues during the Oslo period, as do Palestinian suicide bombings and Israeli retaliations.

1994: Yitzhak Rabin and King Hussein sign the 'Treaty of Peace Between the State of Israel and the Hashemite Kingdom of

Jordan', formally ending the state of war between the two nations and establishing diplomatic relations. This historic agreement addresses key issues such as borders, security and water rights, making Jordan the second Arab country to recognise Israel.

2000 Camp David Summit: Israeli Prime Minister Ehud Barak offers to create a Palestinian state if Israel can annex 11% of the West Bank, with Abu Dis as the capital of Palestine and two east–west corridors under full Israeli control, cutting the West Bank into three cantons. President of the Palestinian National Authority Yasser Arafat rejects this offer because it does not give Palestinians sovereignty over the Al-Aqsa Mosque. He does not make a counterproposal.

2001 Taba Talks: Ehud Barak offers the creation of a Palestinian state based on 1967 borders with 6% of the West Bank annexed to Israel. Yasser Arafat makes a counteroffer that proposes an Israeli annexation of only 3.1%.

2002 Beirut Declaration: 57 Arab and Muslim countries agree to peace with Israel in exchange for:
- (a) complete withdrawal from the Arab territories occupied in 1967
- b) a just solution to the problem of Palestinian refugees to be agreed upon in accordance with the UN General Assembly Resolution 194
- (c) the establishment of an independent and sovereign Palestinian state on the Palestinian territories occupied since June 4, 1967.

Israel does not respond to the offer.

2003 Geneva Initiative: Israeli politician Yossi Beilin and Palestinian politician Yasser Abed Rabbo come to an agreement for a two-state solution whereby the Palestinians allow Israel to annex 3% of the West Bank, including the Jewish Quarter of the Old City, Gush Etzion, Ma'aleh Adumim, Giv'at Ze'ev, Modi'in settlements to the north of Jerusalem along the Green Line, Alfei Menashe and a few other settlements to the south of Qalqiliya, but not Ariel and Efrat. It also includes a roadway between the West Bank and Gaza, to connect the two territories designated for the State of Palestine.

Israeli Prime Minister Ariel Sharon rejects this offer. Yasser Arafat describes it as promising, but also rejects the initiative.

2007–2008 Annapolis process: Israeli Prime Minister Ehud Olmert offers the Palestinians the creation of a state based on 1967 borders with 6.3% of the West Bank annexed to Israel, and a swap of Israeli territories with Palestinian territories on a one-to-one basis.

Palestinian President Mahmoud Abbas makes a counteroffer that proposes an Israeli annexation of 1.9% only. His primary concern is the inclusion of Ariel – 26 kilometres into the West Bank – within the areas annexed by Israel. Israel rejects this offer.

2020: In January, Donald Trump proposes 'Peace to Prosperity: A Vision to Improve the Lives of the Palestinian and Israeli People'. While it is endorsed by Netanyahu, it is rejected by both the West Bank settlers' Yesha Council and the Palestinian leadership – the former because it envisages a Palestinian state and the latter because it is perceived to be too biased in favour of Israel.

In June, Palestinian Prime Minister Mohammad Shtayyeh presents a counteroffer to the Trump plan that states the willingness of Palestinians to accept a demilitarised state with minor border adjustments. There is no response from Israel.

2020 Abraham Accords: Signed in September, the Abraham Accords normalise relations between Israel, the United Arab Emirates (UAE) and Bahrain. Both countries recognise Israel's sovereignty and establish full diplomatic ties.

Following the initial agreements, Sudan and Morocco also agree to normalise relations with Israel. The US plays a significant role by making concessions, such as removing Sudan from the list of state sponsors of terrorism and recognising Moroccan sovereignty over Western Sahara.

November 2023: A week-long ceasefire between Israel and Hamas leads to 105 civilians being released from Hamas captivity in Gaza: 81 Israelis, 23 Thai nationals and one Filipino. Israel releases 210 Palestinian prisoners from jail in exchange, all of them women or minors.

July 2024: Former Israeli prime minister Ehud Olmert and former Palestinian foreign minister Nasser al-Kidwa sign an agreement to promote peace based on the two-state solution with 1967 borders. The agreement involves a 4.4% annexation of the West Bank by Israel, with land swaps and a corridor linking Gaza and the West Bank. Their agreement supports President Biden's plan for a Council of Commissioners to govern Gaza and prepare for elections, along with a temporary Arab Security Presence. Jerusalem would be divided, with Israel keeping

West Jerusalem and post-1967 Jewish neighbourhoods, while Arab areas join Palestinian Jerusalem. The Old City would be managed by an international trusteeship.

There is no response from Israel, the Palestinian Authority or Hamas to the agreement, and none say it could serve as a basis for negotiations.

ACKNOWLEDGMENTS

The story of how *The Holy and the Broken* came to be in your hands at a time when so many authors struggle to find publishers embodies a remarkable encounter that epitomises the message of this book about interfaith cooperation. Tess Woods is an Australian fiction author in Perth who has been published by both HarperCollins and Penguin. She's Egyptian-born and raised, with the blood of her Palestinian ancestors running through her veins. After Jessica Bowker introduced her to my podcast with Hannah in late 2023, Tess sent us a beautiful email sharing how the conversations we recorded were a beacon for her in a dark time. I responded with much gratitude, and after mentioning that I was writing a book, she offered to read the first chapter. Tess was so moved by it that she connected me to Mary Rennie from HarperCollins, who believed in this book and brought it forward to the acquisitions committee.

The fact that this book, written by a Jewish author, only came to publication through the help of an Arab author on the other side of the world is not something I take for granted at this time. Perhaps our friendship that has emerged as a result of this book can serve as a model to others seeking hope and connection between people of different nationalities who share common dreams.

HarperCollins publisher Mary Rennie's guidance on how to structure the book and tell my story in the most accessible way was invaluable. We exchanged hundreds of emails in the process, on everything from the cover design to marketing and publicity.

Later I worked with copy editor Abigail Nathan and proofreader Alaina Gougoulis who improved this work immensely. Publicist Taylah Massingham also did a wonderful job since the book's publication in helping its message reach the widest possible audience.

The book's main editor, Madeleine James, transformed my meandering, emotional, therapy-processing, post-October-7 writing into a logical and coherent book. I deeply appreciate her time over our many Zoom conversations and emails, and her patience for my late-night draft submissions before deadlines, which led to this book looking the way it does in your hands today.

Finally, Joshua Shanes, a professor of Jewish studies and director of the Arnold Center for Israel Studies at the College of Charleston, proofread the entire manuscript making important timeline corrections and improving the accuracy of descriptions of historic events.

HarperCollins has been incredible throughout the editing, marketing and publication process. I can't thank them enough for believing in me as a first-time author and backing this work.

*

There are so many people whose invaluable advice, friendship and support played a huge part in the writing of *The Holy and the Broken*.

Acclaimed Melbourne author Bram Presser, who wrote the moving Holocaust novel *The Book of Dirt*, was an immense source of support throughout the book's journey, from its inception and writing to the publishing phase. So much of his advice guided how this book appears today.

Author and documentary filmmaker Danny Ben-Moshe, who has also worked with HarperCollins, was very helpful in this regard.

The first of many readers who gave me feedback on various chapters was Ashlea Gild. A former student of mine at Mount Scopus Memorial College, she spent a year in Jerusalem learning at the Pardes Institute for Jewish Studies. Given her recent experience working in Jewish schools specialising in informal education, her feedback on the chapters that dealt with the Melbourne Jewish community was much appreciated.

The next reader was Doodie Ringelblum, a dear friend whom I have come to view as a mentor since the passing of my dad. We have known each other for many years and share a similar outlook on the world, and he not only proofread all the chapters but also spent many hours talking with me after he had read each chapter to unpack all the ideas in depth as if each chapter of the book were a page of Talmud.

Frances Prince, a former teaching colleague and a kind friend, provided invaluable feedback about my writing. A true 'teacher of teachers' as an author and an expert in both Jewish and Holocaust education, her guidance on so many aspects of this book were incredibly appreciated. Living in both Melbourne and Jerusalem at the time the book was written, her insights into both cities, especially highlighting the fears, hopes and dreams of people who live there in ways I may not have seen, helped make the book more balanced and representative.

Julie Faulkner was my lecturer at RMIT when I studied for a diploma of education back in 2002. After October 7, Julie very thoughtfully reached out to me and we reconnected. She shared that she had been doing a masters in professional writing and offered to read the book. Her professional writing skills and keen eye for detail were a true gift.

The chapters about female peacebuilders and role of religion were proofread by Rabbi Elhanan Miller from People of the Book, Peta Jones Pellach from Women Wage Peace and Lindsey Levy, a writing associate at the New Israel Fund. Given all of their expertise on both women's activism and religious peacebuilding, I was grateful to receive their suggestions on how to tell this part of the story.

My uncle Rafy Halahmy and his wife, Miriam Halahmy, both helped me gain a deeper understanding of the Iraqi Jewish Exodus to Israel in the 1950s. Miriam's acclaimed children's book *The Boy from Baghdad*, which is loosely based on my family's story, was also a precious resource.

My mother, Carmella Flescher, also read the coda about my parents, which sparked many hours of conversation between us about how we remember and tell the story of our family. I am deeply grateful to her for all the wisdom she has imparted to me over the years.

Melbourne Law School academic Michelle Lesh helped with feedback on the chapter regarding her late husband Mark Baker, to whom this book is dedicated.

Awad Halabi is a professor in the departments of history and religion at Wright State University in Ohio. The author of the book *Palestinian Rituals of Identity: The Prophet Moses Festival in Jerusalem, 1850-1948*, he reached out to me in late 2023 after hearing my podcast *From the Yarra River to the Mediterranean Sea*. We have spoken a number of times during the war, and I have learned a great deal from him about Palestinian history and identity. He also provided me with important insight into how I wrote letters to Palestinian and Israeli children.

Paul Forgasz, who is a masterful teacher of teachers and a historian, gave me important insight on Chapter 4 about the history of the conflict.

Henry Ralph Carse, the founder of Kids4Peace Jerusalem, gave me useful context I never knew before about our how peace organisation was born. As a result of this book, we met in person for the first time in October 2024. His compassionate nature and faith in children to create a better reality are inspiring.

A post I read from Sydney Educator Adina Roth regarding her experience at the City2Surf of 2024, describing her experience seeing various signs along the fun-run route that made her uncomfortable and what they could say in an ideal future, partly inspired me to write the chapter 'When there is peace'. Her feedback on this chapter, and her own writing about what the future can be in both Jerusalem and Sydney, were much appreciated in helping me formulate my ideas.

Mahmoud Muna, the owner of the Educational Book Shop in East Jerusalem, gave me important feedback on the chapter that featured letters to Israeli and Palestinian children, as did Eliana Pearlman and Lour Dahleh, Jewish and Palestinian graduates of the Kids4Peace program, and Ilana Nelson, a parent of a former participant at Kids4Peace.

Hannah Baker was my co-host on the podcast *From the Yarra River to the Mediterranean Sea*, which was recorded during the first six months of the war, at the same time much of this book was written. I'm grateful for our conversations, which helped inform some of my ideas in this book, especially regarding dehumanisation and the importance of countering this dangerous phenomenon wherever it appears.

Chris Whitman-Abdelkarim is the representative for Medico International in Palestine/Israel. We first met in 2018, and since that time I don't think there is another person in the world to whom I send and receive more WhatsApp messages each day. Jokingly sometimes calling himself 'the Mayor of Kufr Aqab' he obtained his MA from Hebrew University in Islamic and Middle Eastern studies and has worked at a number of Palestinian and Israeli NGOs since 2011 on issues such as labour rights, the Jordan Valley, settlements and human rights. As the representative for Medico International in Palestine/Israel, Chris travelled regularly to Gaza before October 7, and gave me much direct feedback about the Gaza and history chapters. His friendship, sense of humour, and ability to laugh at the darkest and most bizarre moments of our lives here in Jerusalem are all things I admire about him deeply.

I am so appreciative of all the readers who took the time to help me shape this book. None of these readers are responsible for any of this work's errors or shortcomings, for which I take sole responsibility.

*

The team at Kids4Peace Jerusalem, Suma Qawasmi and Angham Hussein, both read parts of this book and supported me in telling our story. I am grateful to both of them for their friendship and resilience in holding our organisation together through so many difficult times. As part of the larger Seeds of Peace movement, I am also grateful to our CEO, Eva Armour, who has done an incredible job raising support for our work from donors across the world who believe in the importance of sustaining our mission. On a personal level, I very much appreciate her tireless support and encouragement for us to succeed.

I will always be grateful to the first editor of *Plus61J Media*, Michael Visontay, for believing in my ability as a writer by offering me the position of Israel correspondent shortly before I moved to Jerusalem in 2018, despite my having no formal training as a journalist. Now called *The Jewish Independent*, with Deborah Stone as editor-in-chief, the whole team, which includes publisher Uri Windt OAM, Shahar Burla, Ilona Lee, Alexandra Senter, Sharon Offenberger and Ruby Kraner-Tucci, are just a pleasure to work with. Their events and partnerships manager, Sharon Berger, was also a highly efficient organiser in her management of the book launch events in Sydney and Melbourne. To them all I am deeply grateful.

The stories they commission, edit and produce each week are a gift to our Jewish community and to all people looking for independent and progressive commentary on Australian Jewish life and Israel.

I'd like to especially acknowledge *The Jewish Independent* executive director Dashiel Lawrence, who provided me with much helpful advice on book publishing and particularly on the chapters about Melbourne.

*

I met my wife, Carm, when we were both 19. Yes, she has the same name as my mother, but that's not the first thing I noticed about her.

Her enormous smile and giant heart that cares so much for everyone and everything around her is what immediately attracted her to me first. When we married at age 25, I sang the songs 'Brown Eyed Girl' and 'Can't Take My Eyes Off You' at our wedding. These are two songs I could still sing to her today, and the lyrics of both still say so much about why I love her.

Over our years as a married couple raising our two wonderful kids, Nava and Eitan, she has always had her feet firmly planted on the ground while my head is often in the clouds dreaming of big ideas.

Nava is an enthusiastic book reader, devouring more novels each week than the average person would have warm dinners. My favourite adventure with Nava was a week we spent together in London in 2023, where we went on various *Harry Potter*-themed tours and saw shows, museums and incredible Edwardian bookstores such as Daunt Books. She is a deeply curious individual who enjoys learning all she can.

Eitan is full of life and loves to laugh and to make others laugh alike. Like me, his favourite colour is yellow, which he wears almost all the time. A playful soul, he has a special place in his heart for the wellbeing of every stray cat in Jerusalem. We enjoy playing chess together, and he often beats me. Eitan loves computer games, solving problems and exploring tech gadgets. I'm sure one day he will create one of his own.

Carm is both an incredible parent and partner. While my enthusiasm for politics can be very focused, perhaps to my detriment, Carm, thankfully, has wider interests, and is very grounded in reality, culture, family life and fun. I love the way we laugh a lot together, both at and with each other, as if we were still teenagers.

Whether it be running part of a marathon on a rainy day to bring a banana to a struggling athlete, or making sure a stranger knows they have left their car lights on, Carm is always thinking, 'How would I want the world to react if this happened to me?' and then doing just that.

She also proofread every chapter of this book multiple times and was both my harshest critic and most ardent supporter.

I don't know what I did in my life to deserve someone like her, so all I can say to you, Carm, is thank you, for everything you are and all we have done together. May we continue to do good for each other and the world around us for many years to come.

*

Thank you for reading *The Holy and the Broken*. For more information go to: www.ittay.au

NOTES

Chapter 1: 50 years and one day: How October 7 changed everything

1   Roger Cohen, 'Slaughter at a festival of peace and love leaves Israel transformed', *New York Times*, October 15, 2023.

2   '"They shot children, babies, old people": kibbutz survivors describe Hamas' deadly assault', *Euronews*, October 10, 2023.

3   Ibid.

4   Elana Sztokman, 'How am I doing really? I feel everything slipping away', The Roar Substack, October 15, 2023.

5   Anita Lester, 'The disturbing silence of creative communities over Hamas's massacre', *Jewish Independent*, October 16, 2023 (updated March 5, 2024).

6   Etan Nechin, 'How can left-wingers hail Hamas atrocities against Israelis as "Palestinian resistance"?', *Haaretz*, October 11, 2023.

7   Vimal Patel and Anemona Hartocollis, 'NYU law student sends anti-Israel message and loses a job offer', *New York Times*, October 11, 2023.

8   Beith Harpaz, 'Leading Israeli leftists rebuke progressives elsewhere for failing to condemn Hamas', *Forward*, November 6, 2023.

9   Yehuda Shohat, 'Undivided: Jerusalem by the numbers', *Ynet*, August 8, 2016.

10 Carl von Clausewitz, *On War*, trans. and eds. Michael Howard and Peter Paret, Princeton University Press, 1976, p.101.

11 'Hamas official says group "well aware" of consequences of attack on Israel, Palestinian liberation comes with "sacrifices"', *Arab News*, October 20, 2023.

12 Yair Kraus and Smadar Perry, 'We've been on tenterhooks, and no one knows when it will end', *Ynet News*, January 4, 2024.

13 Rashid Khalidi, *The Hundred Years' War on Palestine: A history of settler colonialism and resistance, 1917–2017*, Metropolitan Books, 2020, p.245.

14 Gidi Weitz, 'Another concept implodes: Israel can't be managed by a criminal defendant', *Haaretz*, October 9, 2023.

15 Amir Lupovici, 'Israeli deterrence and the October 7 attack', Institute of National Security Studies, July 2024.

16 Chemi Shalev, 'Moshe Dayan's enduring Gaza eulogy: This is the fate of our generation', *Haaretz*, July 20, 2014.

17 Vladimir Ze'ev Jabotinsky, 'The Iron Wall', 1923.

Chapter 2: Holocaust, Hashem and Israel: Reflections on my school education

1 Karen Teshuva, 'Caring for older survivors of genocide and mass trauma', Australian Institute for Primary Care & Ageing, La Trobe University, 2010.

2 'Two leading experts on Jew hatred agree: A lack of unity is our biggest problem to date', *Israel National News*, June 6, 2023.

3 Nino Bucci, 'Jewish creatives allegedly threatened after WhatsApp doxing consider suing *New York Times*', *The Guardian*, August 22, 2024.

4 Andrew Markus, Nicky Jacobs and Tanya Aronov, 'Report Series on the Gen08 Survey: Preliminary Findings: Melbourne & Sydney', Australian Centre for Jewish Civilisation, Monash University, August 2009.

5 John A Krug, 'The Last Jew', National Conference of Synagogue Youth.

Chapter 3: Where it all began: Two nations, one homeland

1 Nur Masalha, *Palestine: A Four Thousand Year History*, Bloomsbury Publishing PLC, 2020, p.221.

2 Ian Black, 'Unseen question? Zionism and the Palestinians under the British Mandate', Balfour Project, October 2020.

3 Joel Beinin and Lisa Hajjar, 'Palestine, Israel and the Arab-Israeli conflict: a primer', Middle East Research and Information Project, 2014.

4 Alan Dowty, *Israel/Palestine*, Polity Press, 2005, p.13.

5 Ghada Karmi, *In Search of Fatima: A Palestinian story*, 2nd ed., Verso, 2009, pp.86–91.

6 Marina Parisinou, 'Semiramis Revisited', My Palestinian Story, August 13, 2021, mypalestinianstory.com.

7 Lawrence Joffe, 'Obituary: Israel Amir', *The Guardian*, December 13, 2022; Larry Collins and Dominique Lapierre, *O Jerusalem!*, Simon & Schuster, 1971.

8 Martin Buber, *A Land of Two Peoples*, University of Chicago Press, 2005, p.61.

Chapter 4: The first Palestinian–Zionist dialogue

1 Rashid Khalidi, 'The erasure of Palestinians from Trump's Mideast "peace plan" has a hundred-year history', *Intercept*, February 1, 2020.

2 Shoshana Solomon, 'Amid COVID, Israel enters top 20 club of nations with highest GDP per capita', *Times of Israel*, April 26, 2021.

Chapter 5: Indigenous Australians, Jews and Palestinians

1   Rachel Perkins and Marcia Langton (eds), *The First Australians: An Illustrated History*, Miegunyah Press, 2008, p.xxii.

2   Luke Pearson, '6 in 10 white Australians claim they have never met an Indigenous person … But so what?', NITV, SBS, November 20, 2016.

3   Ron Castan at the Indigenous–Jewish Forum, Monash University, November 1998, cited in 'Obituary by Mick Dodson and David Allen', *Indigenous Law Bulletin*, October 1999, volume 4, issue 24.

4   Mark Leibler, 'A Voice for the First Australians', *Australian Jewish News*, April 5, 2023.

5   Indigenous Voice Referendum Results 2023 – Electorate of Macnamara, Victoria.

6   Kim Bullimore, 'Aboriginal solidarity with Palestine', *Redflag*, January 17, 2022.

7   Noura Mansour, 'Indigenous-Palestinian solidarity networks challenging settler colonialism in Australia', Near East Policy Forum, October 12, 2023.

8   Vic Alhadeff, 'Nova Peris: "I'm saddened to see our sacred flag misappropriated by anti-Israel groups"', *Jewish Independent*, March 27, 2024.

9   Joshua Shanes, 'Why the Jewish Right is foolish to celebrate the empty Palestinian history "book"', *Haaretz*, June 25, 2017.

10 'The Palestine/Israel Pulse, a Joint Poll', Palestinian Center for Policy and Survey Research, September 12, 2024.

Chapter 6: Keeping hope alive: Inside Jerusalem's youth movement for peace

1   Neil Postman, *The Disappearance of Childhood*, Vintage, 1982, p.xi.

2   Nir Hasson, 'Just 5 percent of E. Jerusalem Palestinians have received Israeli citizenship since 1967', *Haaretz*, May 29, 2022.

3   Lior Detal, 'A threat on the economy? Only 41% of students in Israel are in the secular stream', *Marker*, September 16, 2019.

4   Avi Meyerstein, 'In a tense Jerusalem, an inside look at the city's youth movement for peace', *Times of Israel*, October 16, 2022.

Chapter 7: 'Peace is possible': Lessons from Belfast

1   Irish Foreign Ministry, X, April 7, 2023.

2   'How an international fund helped make peace in Northern Ireland: Lessons from a conflict solved', Alliance for Middle East Peace.

3   'Excerpt from PM Netanyahu's remarks at the state memorial ceremony for Ze'ev Jabotinsky', Prime Minister's Office, July 18, 2023.

Chapter 8: Daring to dialogue: How supporters of Palestine and Israel can talk to one another

1   Mo Husseini, Threads, November 2, 2023.
2   Joel Greenberg, 'Kariel Gardosh, 79, who created Israeli icon', *New York Times*, March 3, 2020.
3   Chen Malul, 'The Book of Srulik', National Library of Israel, January 1, 2018.
4   'British police reopen investigation into 1987 murder of Palestinian cartoonist in London', *Haaretz*, August 29, 2017.
5   Sulaiman Khatib, American Friends of Combatants for Peace. www.afcfp. org/sulaiman-khatib
6   Yonah Jeremy Bob, 'IDF: Extremists attack on Jit was worst Jewish terror event ever', *Jerusalem Post*, August 28, 2024.

Chapter 9: Gaza: The quest for reckoning

1   Abeer Salman, Kareem Khadder, Kareem El Damanhoury, Rhea Mogul and Lauren Said-Moorhouse, 'Names written on children's bodies speak to the fears of Gazan parents amid the Israel-Hamas war', CNN, October 23, 2023.
2   Sheren Falah Saab, '"Remember our names": Fearing oblivion, young Gazans recorded last wills before dying', *Haaretz*, August 15, 2024.
3   Ibid.
4   Nagham Zbeedat, 'This Women's Day, Palestinian women in Gaza are making period products out of tents', *Haaretz*, March 7, 2024.
5   'Gaza: The IRC warns of humanitarian tragedy as conflict resumes, calls for sustained ceasefire', International Rescue Committee, December 5, 2023.
6   Amira Hass, 'Numbers that stagger the imagination: There's no way to quantify the suffering in Gaza', *Haaretz*, April 10, 2024.
7   Teresa Gray, 'Opinion: My dear friend was killed in Gaza. This is what I want people to know about her', CNN, April 6, 2024.
8   Penny Wong, 'Special Adviser report on Israel's response to the IDF strikes against World Central Kitchen', Australian government, August 2, 2024.
9   José Andrés, 'The probe into death of WCK volunteers needs to start from the top', *Ynet News*, April 3, 2024.
10 Abraham Joshua Heschel, 'The Reasons for my involvement in the peace movement (1973)', *Moral Grandeur and Spiritual Audacity*, Farrar, Straus and Giroux, 1996.
11 Wafaa Shurafa and Samy Magdy, 'After 10 years of trying, a Palestinian woman had twins. An Israeli strike killed them both', *AP News*, March 4, 2024.
12 Alexandra Rijke and Toine Van Teeffelen, 'To exist is to resist: sumud, heroism, and the everyday', *Jerusalem Quarterly*, issue 59, Summer 2014.

Chapter 10: Peace journalism: All the news we never print

1 Susan Carland, 'A war of words: Preliminary media analysis of the 2023 Israel-Gaza war', Islamophobia Register Australia, December 2023.

2 Rachel O'Donoghue, 'Jerusalem car-ramming terror attack: The most offensive & misleading headline fails', *Honest Reporting*, February 12, 2023.

3 Jason Hanna and Omar Jimenez, 'Darnella Frazier says she's "a girl trying to heal" a year after recording George Floyd's last moments', CNN, May 26, 2021.

4 'Digital news report Australia 2023: One in five Australians are now paying for online news, trust is slightly up but women lose interest', University of Canberra, June 14, 2023.

5 Tamar Hermann and Or Anabi, 'Even on the right, Israelis want elections immediately after the war', *War in Gaza Survey 7*, Israel Democracy Institute, December 19, 2023.

6 W Joseph Campbell, '50 years after "Napalm Girl", myths distort the reality behind a horrific photo of the Vietnam War and exaggerate its impact', *The Conversation*, June 2, 2022.

7 Nick Ut, 'Opinion: A single photo can change the world. I know, because I took one that did', *Washington Post*, June 2, 2022.

8 'The US and Israel's "special relationship" – Part 1 – Transcript', CBC, July 25, 2024.

9 'Showdown - with Ilana Dayan', episode 99, *Unholy: Two Jews on the News*, March 24, 2023.

10 Jeremy Sharon, 'Communications minister extends order banning Al Jazeera in Israel for 45 more days', *Times of Israel*, June 9, 2024.

11 'Why is Israel afraid to allow foreign journalists in Gaza? What's it hiding?', *Haaretz*, September 11, 2024.

12 'The Center for Peace Media Education', Making Peace Visible. www.makingpeacevisible.org/education

Chapter 11: To the boys in the room: Hearing the missing voices of women

1 Marie A Principe, 'Women in nonviolent movements', Special Report 399, United States Institute of Peace, January 2017.

2 Victor Asal, Richard Legault, Ora Szekely and Jonathan Wilkenfeld, 'Gender ideologies and forms of contentious mobilization in the Middle East', *Journal of Peace Research*, volume 50, issue 3, May 16, 2013; Marie A Principe, 'Women in nonviolent movements', Special Report 399, United States Institute of Peace, January 2017.

3   Marie O'Reilly, Andrea Ó Súilleabháin and Thania Paffenholz, 'Reimagining peacemaking: Women's roles in peace processes', International Peace Institute, June 2015.

4   'Women's participation in peace processes', Council on Foreign Relations. www.cfr.org/womens-participation-in-peace-processes

5   Judith Falk, 'UN rally demands release of hostages', *Jewish Link*, April 11, 2024.

6   Sam Sokol, 'Histadrut labor union announces nationwide strike, over failure to release hostages', *Times of Israel*, September 1, 2024.

7   Yonatan Zeigen, X, July 18, 2024.

Chapter 12: If it be your will: Faith and peacebuilding

1   Kobi Michael, 'The Hamas document of January 21, 2024 – its aspects and meanings', *INSS Insight*, no 1821, Institute for National Security Studies, February 1, 2024.

2   Matthew Tostevin, 'Holy war: Red cows, Gaza and the end of the world', *Newsweek*, April 5, 2024.

3   'Deputy Sec-Gen. of Palestinian Islamic Jihad (PIJ) Muhammad Al-Hindi: Members of Fatah and Palestinian Authority's security forces will ultimately join the resistance; recruiting fighters is easy when they know they will go to paradise if martyred', MEMRI, September 5, 2024.

4   'Conference for "Israel's Victory" | Settlement Brings Security | Speech by the Minister of National Security Itamar Ben-Gvir', YouTube, January 28, 2024.

5   Sam Sokol, 'Far-right minister extols "miracle period" of settlement expansion', *Times of Israel*, July 7, 2004.

6   Matthew Tostevin, 'Holy war: Red cows, Gaza and the end of the world', *Newsweek*, April 5, 2024.

7   '600 Jews and Muslims just met at a mosque in Israel to call for peace. Here's what they said', *Analyst News*, November 6, 2023; Imaduddin Al Masri, 'Paragons of peace amidst horrors of war', *Review of Religions*, November 5, 2023.

8   Reuven Rivlin, Facebook, July 7, 2014.

9   Kefah Abukhdeir, 'My cousin Mohammed Abukhdeir's murder – and the Jews who mourned him – changed me forever', *The Forward*, December 5, 2019.

Chapter 13: Inside the classroom: Dominant narratives and untold stories

1   Deborah Stone, 'Reading between the lines of Palestinian textbooks', *Jewish Independent*, June 27, 2023.

2   Sami Adwan, Dan Bar-On and Eyal Naveh (eds), *Side by Side: Parallel histories of Israel-Palestine*, The New Press, 2012.

3   Avraham Burg, 'How Shoafat 2014 killed Hebron 1929's legacy of hope and gratitude', *Haaretz*, July 10, 2014.

4   Judy Maltz, '"We're in this together": Viral videos spotlight Arab–Israeli heroes of October 7 Hamas attack', *Haaretz*, November 29, 2023.

5   Ben Lynfield, 'Israelis "stand together" to alleviate starvation in Gaza', *Jewish Independent*, August 27, 2024; Gianluca Pacchiani, 'Poll finds high support among Arab Israelis for volunteering during war', *Times of Israel*, December 26, 2023; Sue Sirkes, 'With memories of atrocities in Africa still vivid, asylum seekers are helping Israel', *Times of Israel*, October 26, 2023.

Chapter 14: So, what's your solution for Israel/Palestine?

1   A Land for All – Two States One Homeland. www.alandforall.org/english

2   Sarah Begley, 'John Kerry's full speech on Israeli settlements and a two-state solution', *TIME*, December 28, 2016.

Chapter 15: Challenging dehumanisation and suspending disbelief

1   TOI staff, 'Beersheba girl suspended from school after voicing concern for Gazan kids', *Times of Israel*, September 23, 2024.

2   Ellen Ioanes, 'What the UN report on October 7 sexual violence does – and doesn't – say', Vox, March 8, 2024.

3   'How to find your suffragist/suffragette ancestors: Were they anti-suffragists?', New York Public Library.

Chapter 16: Letters to Israeli and Palestinian children

1   '"Israel is a Fortress, but not yet a home": David Grossman's Memorial Day speech to bereaved Israelis and Palestinians', *Haaretz*, April 18, 2018.

2   Mahmoud Darwish, Speech, 2002, when visited in Palestine by a delegation from the International Parliament of Writers, which included Breyton Breytenbach and Nobel laureates Jose Saramago and Wole Soyinka, quoted in Omid Safi, 'Love in a time of refugees', On Being, September 24, 2015.

3   Mahmoud Darwish, 'On Resiliency', *Awraq al-Zaytun* [Leaves of Olive Trees], Dar al-'Awdah, 1964.

Chapter 17: When there is peace

1   www.instagram.com/theparentscircle/reel/C7i3EN2MDwZ/?locale=ko&hl=am-et; Ran Shimoni and Sheren Falah Saab, 'Michal lost her son on Oct. 7, Najlaa buried her brother in Gaza. Together, they seek a different future', *Haaretz*, May 12, 2024.

2   Hanin Majadli, 'Something bothers me about the Israeli-Palestinian memorial ceremony', *Haaretz*, April 28, 2023.
3   Elhanan Miller, '100 bereaved families try to prevent Israel-Palestinian memorial event', *Times of Israel*, April 20, 2015.

Coda: Those who made me

1   Yeshayahu Leibowitz, *Judaism, Human Values, and the Jewish State*, Harvard University Press, 1992, pp.225 and 226.
2   Michelle Lesh, 'Remembering Mark Raphael Baker (1959–2023): Historian, teacher, writer, father, husband', ABC, June 19, 2023.

Sources for timelines

Sammy Westfall, Brian Murphy, Adam Taylor, Bryan Pietsch and Andrea Salcedo, 'The Israeli-Palestinian conflict: A chronology', *Washington Post*, November 6, 2023.

United Nations, 'The Question of Palestine'. www.un.org/unispal/timeline

John Klier, 'Pogroms', YIVO Encyclopedia of Jews in Eastern Europe.

'Israel's attacks on Gaza since 2005', *Al Jazeera*, August 7, 2022.

Efraim Karsh, 'Why the Oslo Process doomed peace', *Middle East Quarterly*, Fall 2016.

'Prime Minister Ariel Sharon addresses the nation on the day of the implementation of the Disengagement Plan', Ministry of Foreign Affairs, Israel, August 15, 2005.

'Reasonable grounds to believe conflict-related sexual violence occurred in Israel during 7 October attacks, senior UN official tells Security Council', United Nations, March 1, 2024.

Lazar Berman and Emanuel Fabian, 'Netanyahu says Hezbollah "will get the message" after strikes it "never imagined"', *Times of Israel*, September 22, 2024.

Emma Graham-Harrison, 'Gaza publishes identities of 34,344 Palestinians killed in war with Israel', *The Guardian*, September 18, 2024.